Testimonials fo

"As editor for *Bowhunter* magazine, I read thousands of manuscripts, and above all I loved discovering a nugget among the dozens of new writers who submitted manuscripts. Eyad Yehyawi was one of those. From the beginning, he wrote well and exuded enthusiasm for bowhunting.

In his book, *Crimson Arrows: A Bowhunting Odyssey,* Yehyawi details his beginnings and growth as a bowhunter. He starts with whitetails and turkeys in his home state of Iowa and progresses to black bears, pronghorns, mule deer, elk, caribou, musk oxen, bison, and other species. All hunters can relate to his progression as a bowhunter and will find his stories compelling and fun to read."

-Dwight Schuh, former editor, *Bowhunter* magazine
and member of the Bowhunters Hall of Fame

"As a magazine editor, I appreciate quality writing skills and Eyad's "got game" when it comes to expressing himself with the written word. His writing serves as a clear window into the mindset of a bowhunter who treasures every exhilarating aspect of the pursuit of big game with a bow and arrow, right down to the smallest detail. Whether you're looking for escape, adventure, or simply a richer understanding of what we do and why, *Crimson Arrows* is definitely worth your time."

-Curt Wells, editor, *Bowhunter* magazine

"Eyad 'killed' it in this very personal, and very thoughtfully written book that every bowhunter should own. He describes 'perfectly' the essence of bowhunting through a series of hunting experiences and some close calls. I loved this book!"

- Pat Lefemine, founder, Bowsite.com

"Men have been telling hunting stories ever since we lived in caves. I thoroughly enjoyed this new book, full of one person's love of adventure with a bow and arrow in hand. It proved to be very entertaining reading! I felt like I was right there with the author. I hope you enjoy it as much as I have."

- Gene Wensel, author of *Buckskin and Bone*
and co-founder, Brothers of the Bow

"*Crimson Arrows* represents the spirit of bowhunting. It was meant to take you to one place, right into the heart of a bowhunter."

-Joe Bell, author of *Technical Bowhunting*
and former editor, *Bow & Arrow Hunting* magazine

"*Crimson Arrows* provides an engaging account of the author's progress from the beginning to the accomplished stages of his bowhunting career. While the book appropriately devotes plenty of space to the "backyard" species around his Midwestern home (whitetails, turkeys), it also transports the reader to the Far North in search of moose, musk ox, and mountain goat and even to Africa for a plains game hunt. People and places are portrayed as sharply as the game and the hunting, making *Crimson Arrows* an engrossing read throughout."

-E. Donnall Thomas Jr., author of *The Double Helix*
and co-editor, *Traditional Bowhunter* magazine

"This is one of those rare honest books about the essence of the hunt. It is not about the glorification of the author, but rather an ethical examination of everything to do with one of the most natural and misunderstood pursuits we humans can and should do. This is especially true now that so many are interested in the green, natural, locavore movement. *Crimson Arrows* cuts right to the heart of the hunt. A great book, worthy of residing beside the greatest bowhunting works."

-Lou Phillippe, Outdoor writer

"The first thing one notices about Yehyawi's writing is the sincerity; each story hums with personal touches and genuine emotion. He is able to dig through his memories, some from decades in the past, and pluck out striking moments of authenticity. It is one thing to recall and connect seminal events in one's life, it is quite another to find wisdom in those experiences. Yehyawi writes with an original voice all his own that is both poetic and confident. The stories are not only a study in the skills required to be a truly great hunter, but also an homage to America, and the great wilderness that still exists here.

There is a long and proud tradition in this country for hunting, and wilderness bowhunting requires an even greater level of dedication and reverence. The author captures that energy and spirit beautifully in these pages. This book may be a portrait of the author through a specific lens, but hunting has clearly provided a formative code for his life. The guidelines forged through daunting trials and ecstatic successes extend far beyond the chapters of this book, or the boundaries of the forest. Whether Yehyawi was intending it to be or not, this collection is an impressive celebration of living well in all ways – and staying wild.

The writing is polished and clearly well-edited, and the stories flow at a good pace. The author is a man dedicated to his craft – both as a writer and a bowhunter – and both of those qualities come across powerfully in this collection. An emotive collection of adventure and personal exploration, *Crimson Arrows* may focus on becoming an expert in a particular sport, but it is also refreshing for an author to take such an unabashed look at their achievements and failings, and spill that truth so gracefully on the page."

-Self-Publishing Review ★★★★½

"Yehyawi's attention to detail engages readers, and his writing skills elevate the narrative. Bowhunters especially will enjoy the stories in *Crimson Arrows*—and lessons in life as well."

-BlueInk Review

"Whether walking through southern forests or the frigid Arctic tundra, the elemental role of hunter and hunted within the human existence weaves throughout *Crimson Arrows: A Bowhunting Odyssey*. Yehyawi's stories reveal his desire to preserve these wildernesses and the respect for the people-and animals-that populate the wilds. The writing is lyrical and deftly captures the majesty of mountains, the solemnness of misty creek beds and the awe-inspiring vastness of the African wilderness. *Crimson Arrows* can be enjoyed as adventure tales, a heartfelt poem about the sacredness of the hunt or a 30-year journey about one man's passion. Regardless of how readers take in the tales, they are sure to be satisfied."

-IndieReader ★★★★

"*Crimson Arrows* is a meditative but rousing reflection on a life devoted to hunting that will surely appeal to those with similar enthusiasms. The author communicates his adoration of bowhunting and the wilderness with an effusive, infectious love that can be moving. But the central theme of the book remains the pursuit of a fiery lodestar, a clarion call that provides a lifetime of excitement. Especially for outdoors fans, this is a thoughtful and affecting collection of reminiscences."

-Kirkus Reviews

"The stories in *Crimson Arrows* are fantastic...a bible in the bowhunting realm."

-Feathered Quill Book Reviews

"*Crimson Arrows* is one of the most well-written and interesting books I have edited during my career. The vivid narrative engages all your senses, making you feel as if you are right there with Yehyawi as he is bowhunting. I personally had a visceral reaction to both the emotions and the physical conditions the author shares in his 32 captivating stories. This book has potential for wide appeal—it's not just a story about bowhunting but about nature, animal behavior, and physical and psychological challenges. Really super book."

-L. Wilhelm, editor, Writing Works, LLC

"To be honest, the closest I've ever come to bowhunting is watching Katniss Everdeen in The Hunger Games. However, after reading Crimson Arrows, I think I'm a convert. In this compelling and excellently written memoir, the author, Eyad H. Yehyawi, works hard to put across the excitement and exhilaration of hunting big game with a bow and arrow. Although many people are opposed to any sort of blood sports, I think most readers will still find this not only educational but will also be impressed by the enthusiasm the writer has for this activity.

I was also very impressed by the author's writing style. I often find with 'sports' books, the writing can be a little dull and clumsy. But that's not the case here. The author is a capable writer, delivering to the reader a bounty of information on how, why, where and when he hunts big game. After reading it, like me, you will come away understanding the mindset of this man and why he enjoys hunting in this way so very much.

So, can I recommend this book? Totally. Who to? Well, I think if you enjoy a good adventure yourself, you'll very much appreciate this man's journey. The book is, at the end of the day, a gripping read. And, even if the author's way of life is not for you, I still think most people will appreciate the author's energy and determination in putting over his story. Reading this book is like sitting around a campfire and listening to a hunting story. It's a 'back to basics' sort of thing, and I, for one, loved it!"

-A Wishing Shelf Review

"Crimson Arrows is a beautiful work of storytelling that will appeal to anyone who has a personal connection to hunting with a bow and arrow."

-Midwest Book Awards

Literary Awards for *Crimson Arrows*

WINNER 2020
Pinnacle Book Achievement Awards

WINNER 2020
Book Excellence Awards

FINALIST 2020
Wishing Shelf Book Awards

FINALIST 2020
Midwest Book Awards

Crimson Arrows

A Bowhunting Odyssey

Eyad H. Yehyawi

For information about this title or to order other books and/or electronic media, contact the publisher:

iowaarrows@gmail.com
www.crimsonarrowsmedia.com

ISBN: 978-1-7352073-2-2 (jacketed hardcover)
       978-1-7352073-8-4 (hardcover)
       978-1-7352073-7-7 (paperback)
       978-1-7352073-6-0 (ebook)

Book Design: In collaboration with Van-garde Imagery, Inc.
Cover Art: Deer Skull and Arrow courtesy of Kathy Marlin
Cover Art: Arrowheads courtesy of Dallen Lambson
Cover Design: In collaboration with Julss Designs
Page 24, 88: Photos courtesy of Nabeel Yehyawi
Page 106: Photo courtesy of Corey Jarvis
Page 178, 187: Photos courtesy of Byron Stewart
Page 204: Artwork courtesy of Larry Zach
Pages 282, 286-287, 308, 316 (archer), 317, back cover: Photos courtesy of North Bend Studios
Page 295: Artwork courtesy of Dallen Lambson

Printed in the United States of America

For ZJ and CW

Foreword

If there is one thing I admire in this world—it's passion. I often describe this attribute as motivation and desire that comes from the heart. Applied, it's a force that is larger than life. It echoes the sentiment, "If there's a will, there's a way."

Another noteworthy trait about passion is that it's difficult to imitate. You can sense someone's enthusiasm and love for something...and see that telltale sparkle in their eye! I know this phenomenon well, I believe. It's what has carried me as an archer and bowhunter. I'm not the most talented person, but with passion, I'm able to enter deeper realms of mastery in these admirable disciplines. I believe it's what gives me grit when the going gets tough, so I don't give up. I value this trait more than words can say.

So, it's only natural that I would recognize and admire this same quality in others. One person that exudes this trait is my friend Eyad Yehyawi.

As a bowhunting magazine editor for nearly two decades, I've come across various types of enthusiasts. Although I appreciate anyone with a strong interest in bowhunting, some just seem to be in it for all the right reasons and carry an intense fervor for the pursuit of archery-hunting excellence.

Eyad hits the mark exactly here, because he's intelligent, creative, and detail-oriented. He pens his manuscripts like he approaches the archery discipline—in a methodical, precise, and all-encompassing way. He strives for perfection, and this is what I admire in him the most. He's a bundle of bowhunting talent and enthusiasm. In many ways, I believe we are kindred spirits. We think alike and savor technical proficiency, a fair-chase hunt, and a memorable bowhunting journey. We place extreme value on the bowhunting *experience*...certainly more than the result itself. This is where the real satisfaction lies. Eyad knows this, and it's evidenced throughout the pages of this book.

Crimson Arrows: A Bowhunting Odyssey is a reflection of this man's heart, and it captures his spirit, humbleness, and ability in a profound way. Chapter by chapter oozes of a die-hard bowhunter relishing in the craft...mystified by the art of the chase and harvest. Fulfillment and a deep sense of gratitude is detected in every facet of each experience.

There are three strong qualities that this book delivers: emotion, excitement, and lots of detail. All of it will keep you eager to turn the page, almost as if you are there, reliving the moments of this bowhunting voyage.

Here are some short passages that highlight these elements.

Emotionally Powerful

Eyad tells us about a terrible accident his brother was in, and he was full of remorse for thinking about leaving on his planned Alberta mule deer hunt. Yet his brother, now recovering from a serious injury, told him to go, to enjoy the journey. Eyad begrudgingly obeyed.

"Surrounded by some of the most beautiful country I've ever seen, I took it all in, so grateful for life's blessings," Eyad describes, sharing with us his spirit for the experience. *"Whenever I think back on that fateful summer, or see prairie grass blowing in the wind, I'm reminded of many things. The power of faith, the importance of family, and the harsh reality of life all come to mind."*

Incredibly Exciting

Excitement is why we hunt, and Eyad tells of a thrilling moment during an Alaskan moose hunt.

"...As if by a cruel twist of fate, a strong gust of wind blew my arrow off the rest like a feather," he writes. *"...I grabbed my arrow and placed it back on the rest, noticing the calm demeanor I had exuded before was nowhere to be found. With shaking hands, I attempted to attach my release to the D-loop, but the harder I tried the more difficult it became. Finally, the jaws of the caliper swallowed the*

loop, but I feared my efforts were in vain. Looking up as my eyes strained to re-focus, I watched as the giant walked toward a thicket, taking with him the little hope I had left. Then I heard a noise from behind me."

Packed with Detail

Today's bowhunters, including me, appreciate specifics and attention to detail, as well as a strong technical flair regarding shooting gear and technique. Eyad delivers this, particularly in the story "Glacier Ghosts." As he closes in on a trophy Rocky Mountain goat, he prepares for the shot...a once-in-a-lifetime moment.

"I leaned over the windswept ledge, the sheer force of the elements wreaking havoc on my balance, and came to full draw. The snow and sleet continued to bite my face like miniscule shards of glass, adding to the treachery of the storm. Steadfast while settling my pin, I added tension to the release and my arrow was gone. The broadhead arced through the air, twisting through an ocean of ice and wind, striking the billy...."

Perhaps most importantly, *Crimson Arrows* represents the spirit of bowhunting. It's a compilation of bowhunting adventures, lessons learned, and a series of trials and victories. It's a journey that symbolizes one man's love for shooting a bow and spending time in the great outdoors pursuing God's wonderful creatures, which are worthy of all our respect and most deliberate use of ethics. It's a personal mission fueled by love and passion. By reading this book, you'll value where desire can take a person, and what it can help to accomplish. It's in this you'll glean the real beauty of what this book represents and means. It was meant to take you to one place, right into the heart of a bowhunter.

Joe Bell, author of *Technical Bowhunting* and former editor, *Bow & Arrow Hunting* magazine

"There are some who can live without wild things, and some who cannot."

-Aldo Leopold

Table of Contents

Acknowledgments

I was born and raised in Keokuk, Iowa, a small town on the Mississippi River. The oldest son among five siblings, I was drawn to the outdoors at an early age. Where this passion originated remains a mystery, as neither of my parents had any experience in the field. Still, they pushed me to chase my dreams, and I owe them more than words can say. Whether it was exploring local woodlots or fishing in farm ponds, my mom and dad were always there to take me. In time, my grandfather caught wind of my outdoor interests and began writing me letters. Each envelope was like a treasure chest, filled with tales of giant walleyes, deer hunting, and upland game. I cherish the time we spent together, and I hope he would have been proud of this book.

I also extend a special thanks to those who took me under their wing as a youngster and allowed me to experience so much in the outdoors. Now a father of two, I realize how important those years were to my future endeavors and how excited I was to tag along. The artwork on the cover is courtesy of Kathy Marlin and Dallen Lambson, whose artistic talents never cease to amaze me. Thank you for your friendship. My family and friends were also instrumental in seeing this book through. I can't thank them enough for their honesty and input. Finally, I want to thank Joe Bell and Dwight Schuh who gave me the opportunity to share my stories in print and pushed me to keep writing. I wouldn't have pursued this venture without their influence and want to thank them for giving me a chance.

Preface

It's late here in Iowa, with a north wind blowing against the window with increasing force. No stranger to December, this Midwest storm promises to drape the landscape in a blanket of snow. The lights are turned down in the kitchen as I stare back at a blank sheet of paper. I have one more page to write after years of working on this manuscript, and yet, these last words are the most difficult. I've sat here for the longest time, trying to give credence to the work, to lay out exactly why anyone would want to read this book. These pages include 30 years of bowhunting adventures—from Florida to the Arctic Circle and Alaska to Africa. Compiled from notes, old pictures, and memories, they may have remained as such until in recent years when I found myself reading to my kids late at night. From *The Berenstain Bears* to *Bambi*, we covered it all, and sometimes more than once. When the last page was finished and the lights were turned off, my oldest would ask me to tell him a story. Most often the stories encompassed baseball or superhero tales. But as he grew older, he asked about my bowhunting adventures. "Tell me about the bear in the swamp…about the moose on the mountain…or the explosion where you almost died." I did my best to narrate the stories but could never convey the emotions or details in full. As I revisited these adventures with pen and paper, they brought back memories and mishaps from many years ago. For each success, there were multiple failures, with some close calls and frightening moments along the way. The stories wrote themselves. They are transparent and honest, with each one offering its own lessons. I hope you enjoy reading this book as much as I did writing it. And to my boys—who always asked me for one more story—here they are.

Eyad Yehyawi
Iowa

CHAPTER 1

Embers of October

W e drove along the banks of the mighty Mississippi, following Highway 61's serpentine course. It was the fall of 1991, my freshman year in high school, and my dad and I were on our way to Iowa's Hunter Education Program. My parents weren't surprised when I expressed an interest in hunting, but were hesitant at first, having no experience in the field themselves. Still, they understood my passion for the outdoors and gave me the green light, provided I received the proper training and tutelage. Iowa requires the completion of a Hunter Education Program before you can purchase a license, and I thought it would be a good place to start.

There I first met Andy and Roger, two individuals who would profoundly change my life. Andy was Roger's youngest son, and although he was a few years my junior, we seemed to share the same passion for the outdoors. At the end of the afternoon session, Roger offered to take me squirrel hunting with Andy that fall. I couldn't say yes fast enough, and a few short weeks later we were doing just that. After one such venture chasing bushytails on a warm October afternoon, Roger and Andy put their .22 rifles away and pulled two bows from their car trunk. They practiced in the fading light, flinging arrow after arrow downrange. I can still see those fletching flying through the autumn air, piling into an old Pizza Hut box propped against a hay bale. To say I was in awe is an understatement, and I knew in that moment I wanted to be a bowhunter.

For Christmas that year I received my first compound bow and a dozen aluminum arrows. Looking back now, the draw length was much too long and the arrows close to the same, but I knew no different and could not have cared less. With more naivety than knowledge, I began practicing in the front yard, and let's just say Robin Hood's job wasn't in jeopardy. In the weeks and months that followed, I slowly improved, shooting hours upon hours

Andy and Eyad—First Day Bowhunting
October 1992

at bottle caps, tennis balls, and a three-dimensional deer target placed below our tree house. I would shoot nearly every day, often until the sunset closed the door on my practice sessions. After watching Andy and me improve throughout the spring and summer, Roger felt that we were ready to bowhunt whitetails that fall.

My learning curve was steep, and that first autumn was filled with more trials and tribulations than I can count. Although I tried to keep my glass half full, it wasn't always easy, and I learned some painful lessons along the way. In late November of that '92 season, I made a poor shot on a giant buck, hitting him high in the shoulder at last light. Despite an extensive search the next day, we never found a trace of him or the arrow. To add insult to injury, it was a whitetail the landowner had been pursuing all season. That was a tough pill to swallow, but unfortunately, the autumn of 1993 was no better. I failed to recover two does that I drew blood on, hitting them too far back and trailing them much too soon. Lying awake at night with regret at the mistakes I'd made almost made me quit. Some of my peers advised me to take up other forms of hunting, salting a wound that wouldn't heal. The harsh reality of bowhunting was beginning to take its toll.

As the fall of 1994 drew closer, my third season with the stick and string, I focused on the positives rather than the negatives. Although I had made mistakes my first two years, I'd also learned a great deal along the way. My goal that summer was to find a farm closer to home, so I could hunt more during the week. I eventually gained access to a property I would come to cherish, owned by a farmer to whom I will always be indebted. A stone's throw away from my parents' house, its proximity meant that I could hunt after school, which would allow more time in a treestand. Soon, the dog days of summer relinquished their bind, and yet another whitetail season began to unfold.

On October 26, 1994, nestled in an oak tree on the new farm, I finally harvested my first whitetail. Based on fresh sign and easy access, I had hung a stand at the base of a ridge, returning a few days later on a perfect fall morning. Not long after daybreak, I noticed five does working their way toward my stand where they milled around eating acorns. I released what appeared to be an accurate arrow and watched with trepidation as the white-tails bounded down the ridge and out of sight, much like the first two I had lost the previous fall. There was something different this time, though. I thought I'd seen a flash of white and heard a subtle crash at the base of the ridge. I wanted to appease my curiosity, but because of my previous missteps, I elected to back out and get help before pursuing the trail. I called my best friend, Ryan, and we were back in the timber within an hour. Unable to locate any sign initially, we spread out, hoping to gain insight into the severity of the hit. We were moving down the oak-laden hillside at a snail's pace when Ryan suddenly called out ahead. The doe was lying at the base of the ridge, her form obscured by the leaves through which she had tumbled. It was my first animal with a bow and arrow, and as we dragged the doe from the timber that day, I felt a sense of pride that is difficult to describe.

As my fourth season rolled around, the autumn of 1995, I set forth with a new goal in mind. I could not have cared less about score, size, or maturity; I simply wanted to wrap my hands around the antlers of an Iowa whitetail. I scouted through the heat and humidity, shot more arrows than my shoulder appreciated, and dreamed of opening day. College had started that fall, and with the campus being an hour away, I couldn't get back to hunt nearly as often. Baseball was another passion of mine, and I carried the love of that game from high school into college. The rigors of the sport were much more demanding and intense at this level, and with a heavy academic load, hunting was taking a back seat. However, as the last few days of September rolled around, fall baseball came to an end, as did my midterm exams. Finally caught up on my collegiate responsibilities, I could pursue my bowhunting ambitions once more.

On the morning of October 15, I was back at the new farm, enjoying a beautiful sunrise from my treestand. The nights had turned cooler of late, with splashes of red, orange, and yellow decorating the timber. After my morning vigil, I planned to hang a new set along an oak ridge brimming with acorns. The *October Lull* was in full swing—or at least that sounded like a good excuse based on the lack of deer sightings that morning. I headed back to my truck and traded my bow for a treestand and twenty screw-in steps before trudging back up the grassy hillside. The day was warm and windy, an Indian summer if ever there was one, and a better day to hang than hunt. The wind would muffle any noise I was sure to make, and the warm weather kept the odds low that any deer would move before nightfall.

I coursed through the lush alfalfa and entered the timber, finding the cluster of oaks I'd been seeking. With a clear view of the valley below, and the oak trees ripe with acorns, I couldn't imagine a more perfect spot. The ridgeline ran east to west, which not only mirrored the bucks' normal cruising patterns, but also allowed me to take advantage of the predominant northerly winds. Slowly but surely, I positioned each step within the oak's bark, climbing with excitement and a bit of apprehension. Before long, I ran out of steps, much sooner than someone blessed with longer legs, but at a height with which I was more than comfortable. I hugged the oak with all I could muster and hauled my stand skyward, with a flimsy rope that was anything but sturdy. Back then, safety belts seemed to be a new fad, and it now makes me shudder to think of all the close calls and wobbly treestands onto which I climbed. Still, ignorance is bliss, at least for the things we escape without harm, and my early years as a bowhunter were no exception. Thirty minutes later, with bruised forearms and shreds of bark coating my collar, I was finished. I looked up at my stand hidden among the limbs and leaves, secured my pull rope, and walked back to my Ford.

Two weeks later, on October 29, I was headed back to that oak ridge stand. The morning was calm and cool, far from the bitterness that November would bring. I climbed the grassy hillside to the alfalfa field atop its crest and was relieved to not see white flags bounding away through the darkness. I reached the timberline, where the woodland's brittle and defeated leaves crunched beneath my boots, making each step sound as if I were walking on cornflakes. Soon, I had reached the stand's platform, and with no snorts or bounding footsteps to applaud my achievement, I felt a great sense of relief. I looked down from my perch and realized the morning was still in its infancy, the forest floor depicting a dark abyss rather than a woodland. I slowly pulled my bow up to the stand, secured my release, and nocked an arrow. It wasn't long before the ebony shadows dissipated, revealing a woodland in the throes of autumn. The hickories and elms had long since been stripped of their foliage, the first casualties of diminished daylight and colder weather. The oaks weren't giving up the ghost as easily, holding onto their leaves as if to rebel against the inevitable.

Not long after sunrise, I heard a pair of wood ducks whistle by, catching only a glimpse of their dancing silhouettes between the tree limbs. A flock of honkers materialized overhead, their classic vocals and V-shaped pattern filling the morning air. I was glancing back and forth across the ridgeline when my ears picked up a faint noise to the east. It was not that of a fox squirrel, whose incessant and clumsy rustling had caused my heart one too many false starts in years past. No, this sound was more fluid and consistent, one that a whitetail walking with purpose would make. As sunlight painted the timber a luminous gold, I saw the first flash of antler coming toward me. The beautiful eight-pointer was cruising down the ridgeline, on a course that would bypass my stand well out of range. I fumbled with my jacket zipper, trying to retrieve my grunt call from the confines of my coat. Each time I pulled on the call's lanyard, it resisted, as if I were playing tug-of-war with a grunt tube. With more effort than should have been necessary, the call finally broke free, allowing me just enough time for a single audition.

"Burp...Burp," I bellowed from the reed-filled tube, doing my best impression of a disgruntled whitetail.

The buck stopped on a dime, his white throat patch and ears now thrown in my direction. Seated and still, I did not move a muscle, straining to control the steam coming from my nervous breaths. The whitetail glared up the ridge in my direction, testing the wind that did him no favors, while turning his ears to decipher the sound. When the buck put his head down, I hit the call again, with the same cadence and volume as before. That was all it took.

With confident strides he began his ascent up the ridge, searching for his challenger, trying to pinpoint what his ears had conveyed. I readied my bow with trembling hands, noticing a mature white oak a mere 20 yards to my left. As the buck moved behind the tree's massive trunk, I came to full draw, following him as he reappeared on the other side. I grunted him to a stop, saw my pin settle behind his shoulder, and my arrow was gone. A flash of orange and white fletching caught my eye as it passed through the eight-pointer, with a stream of crimson in its wake. The buck turned and crashed down the ridge, slowed near the creek bank, and then disappeared over its crest.

I regained my composure and waited for what seemed like an eternity before climbing down to the base of the tree. The sun had now pulled free from the eastern horizon, illuminating the ridgeline with its warming rays. Scanning the timber as I moved down the slope, I saw tines lying among the oak leaves and realized I had done it. I was overcome with emotions and thanked the Lord above as I approached the fallen whitetail. The road to this moment had been a long one, paved with its share of twists and turns, but I wouldn't have it any other way.

One day, I know these memories will fade like the embers of a flame. But as I sit here now, almost thirty years later, I can still remember that chilly October morning as if it were yesterday. More importantly, I remember the people and places that made it possible. Those early years taught me there are no shortcuts in life, and to succeed, one needs a solid foundation built upon hard work, humility, and perseverance. I'm proud to say that bowhunting played a major role in that mindset, and I'll always be thankful for the lessons it afforded me.

Eyad's first buck—October 29, 1995

CHAPTER 2

Decoys and Deception

Watching the clock move like molasses, I was counting the seconds, chomping at the bit to get in my treestand. It was November 1, 1996, and I was sitting through my last lecture of the week. My Friday classes ended at 11:00 AM that semester, which made for the perfect bowhunting schedule. I jumped in my truck a few minutes later, headed north, hoping to be in the Iowa hardwoods by early afternoon. I was attending college at Quincy University, a small school in west-central Illinois. Gaining access to local farms had been difficult, as most were already spoken for. This left Iowa as my only option. Perhaps it was a blessing in disguise. After all, I enjoyed hunting near my home each fall and experiencing the nostalgia that came with it.

My brothers were both still in high school, tremendous athletes who excelled on the gridiron. That night was the last game of the 1996 football season, and I was looking forward to watching the contest under the lights. With the short days of early November upon us, a quick hunt before kickoff wouldn't be a problem. The farm, only a few miles away, was where I took my first buck the previous season.

Over the summer, I had purchased a new set of synthetic rattling antlers, along with a silhouette deer decoy that resembled a doe. The plastic decoy was loud but light and folded up for easy transport. I had never tried to decoy or rattle up a whitetail before. But after seeing the effectiveness of a grunt tube the previous season, I thought I would try it. Numerous articles and videos in recent years had detailed the effectiveness of both techniques, especially when used during the rut. While the jury was still out regarding whether a doe or buck decoy was more effective, I elected to go with the antlerless option.

The archery season had been a challenge up to this point, with few deer sightings and little movement. Toward the end of October, I moved my stand near an interior fence line, where a broken strand of barbed wire created a convenient crossing. From there, the deer followed a creek down a well-worn trail, which seemed to concentrate the movement along its course. There was a white oak within bow range of this highway, perfectly suited to conceal a treestand among its gnarly limbs.

The property was host to a herd of cattle each summer, which the landowner relocated when food sources dwindled. Sometimes they would occupy the timber into October and follow me to my treestand like lost puppies. This season had been free of such encounters, and I hoped it stayed that way. The timber throughout the farm was void of security cover and browse, courtesy of the livestock and mature canopy that dominated the growing season. With the lack of cover and limited food sources, there wasn't much deer activity early and late in the season. The bucks would, however, use this section as a travel corridor during the rut, moving quickly from one section of timber to the next. I was hoping if I placed a decoy along this route that a marauding buck might notice and work toward my setup.

That afternoon, with just enough wind to conceal my approach, I crept through the hardwoods under a clear blue sky. My decoy and rattling antlers had come along for the ride, knowing the bucks were on the cusp of the rut. A serious battle between two bucks could be over anything, from territorial disputes to the first doe in estrus. Such a brawl would draw the interest of other suitors and perhaps lure them into bow range. I placed the decoy along the creek bottom, making sure it was set broadside to the trail. Being a silhouette, the decoy vanished when viewed from the wrong angle, so I had to be cautious with my setup.

Once I was secure in my treestand, I hoisted my bow skyward and nocked an arrow. I placed my bow on the hanger, pulled the rattling antlers from my pack, and took a quick look around. The timber was quiet and devoid of life, the perfect time to pick a fight. I smashed the antlers together before grinding and twisting the tines in rapid succession, trying to imitate two Midwest monsters in the heat of battle. Once I concluded my theatrical performance, I brought a grunt tube to my mouth and bellowed out a long, guttural note, followed by a short burst of tending grunts. I repeated this calling sequence twice more over the next few hours, but the only respondent was an agitated fox squirrel.

With last light fast approaching, I thought about the upcoming football game and catching up with old friends. I looked to my left and caught movement as a buck emerged from the cedars and made a beeline for my decoy. This had me reaching for my bow as the buck circled downwind of the sultry silhouette. The buck, realizing there was something amiss, whirled and bounded to my left, glancing back at the faux form. I was already at full draw by the time he stopped, settling my pin and touching the release in one fluid motion. The buck dropped low at impact, sprinting back down the trail and jumping the fence in a matter of seconds. I listened in the moments that followed but failed to pick up any sounds in the fading light. I feared my arrow had been too low, as I'd seen its orange fletching disappear near the brisket line.

I was anxious regarding the outcome and headed home to call my friend Don. We had become good friends the year before and I trusted his advice. This was a time before cell phones and text messages, when someone had to be home to take the call. He picked up after a few rings and I laid out the story for him. We would meet at the farm in half an hour and hope for the best.

Equipped with a propane lantern and flashlights, we began searching around the impact site. I could see patches of white hair along the creek bottom, with speckles of blood farther down the trail. It was not looking good to start but was consistent enough to keep us moving. We crossed the fence and shined our lights into the night, scanning the pasture before us. Soon, a white belly appeared in the beam of Don's flashlight, revealing the buck had not gone far. A single blade of my Rocket Hammerhead had clipped the heart, initiating what would be a faint but short blood trail. Less than an inch lower, and I would be singing a different tune. The buck's left main beam was shaped like a sickle, growing up and inward with a subtle curve at the end. Likely due to a previous injury, it added even more character to a whitetail I was fortunate to harvest. We still made the game before halftime, a perfect way to cap off a classic hunt.

November 1996

The next year, on October 10, 1997, I took a basket racked eight-pointer at first light, ending my season in short order. I had just got settled that morning when I heard footsteps upon fallen leaves. I hit my grunt tube a few times—only to see a buck approaching my setup. When he passed below my stand, I grunted him to a stop and touched the release. Following a well-placed arrow, I called Don to see if he would assist me, and we met shortly thereafter. A solid blood trail led us to the fallen whitetail, a handsome buck with polished antlers and a gorgeous cape. After hugs and handshakes were doled out, Don mentioned how short my season had been, which got me thinking about the future. I loved every aspect of bowhunting, from the practice and preparation to the setbacks and success. I had yet to harvest one of the giants for which Iowa is known. And if I wanted to accomplish this feat, I would have to let the younger bucks walk. I vowed to adopt this mindset going forward, hoping to gain more experience and a deeper understanding of whitetail deer.

The fall of 1998 welcomed me back amidst another November, and I felt the anticipation of the impending rut. I had hunted hard throughout October, but once again, the sparse cover and resident livestock negated any early season patterns. Trail cameras were starting to gain traction, although it would be nearly a decade before I purchased my first model. This said, I had no clue what the property held, knowing only that a few good bucks would show up come November. The decoy, grunt tube, and rattling antlers were still part of my arsenal, a trio of deception I continued to use with confidence.

On November 4, I awoke to windy conditions and a steady drizzle. There was a big game in town that night, as Keokuk was to host Chariton in the first round of the state football playoffs. My youngest brother, Tameem, was in his senior season and hoping to win a state championship for his town and teammates. I remember standing at the patio door of my parents' house in the early morning hours, watching the wind have its way with an old hickory. With my mind on the game that night, I contemplated going back to bed, but realized no respectable bowhunter would sleep in during the rut.

The conditions did not improve as I made my way down a logging road an hour later. The wind and water concealed my approach, and I moved through the timber without incident. My stand hung in a red oak that resembled a telephone pole, with no branches to speak of until you reached its crown. There was no reason to place a stand in this location, other than seeing multiple bucks cruise through the area in years past. No matter how I dissected the pattern, there wasn't a reasonable explanation—par for the course with big whitetails. Observed movement was reason enough, and the red oak was my only option.

I placed my decoy a mere 15 yards from the base of my tree, ensured it was staked down, and made my way up the oak. The bark of a red oak is sharp and slick, with tiny protrusions that will slice your knuckles to shreds. That usually occurred during the hanging phase, with the slick part coming on days like this. I climbed skyward, working my way up the screw-in steps before bear hugging the red oak at eighteen feet. We danced together in the gusty winds and were finally granted a reprieve, which allowed me to release my hold and turn around.

The weather provided the ingredients for a classic rut hunt, with low hanging, agitated clouds that threatened more rain. The wind continued to blow my tree from side to side as if I were on a chartered fishing expedition. Less than an hour into the hunt, I caught movement to my right. A heavy, long-tined rack materialized through the timber, moving toward me at a steady clip. I could tell he was a good buck, with stout shoulders and a thick neck filling out his frame. Before I knew it, we were sharing the same ridgetop, neither one of us daring to move—but for entirely different reasons. The buck stared at the decoy with unwavering eyes and looked poised to flee at any moment, scrutinizing the situation with a steely disposition. Then I saw his demeanor change as he quartered toward the decoy with an air of machismo in his step. I saw his tongue roll over the bridge of his nose, its pink coloration in stark contrast to the drab surroundings. Gambling on the notion that he was fixated on this lonely doe, I drew my bow and waited for him to turn broadside. Unfortunately, the buck continued to quarter, maintaining his position as he closed the distance on the decoy. I quickly saw the error of my ways as my arm shook rapidly with fatigue, leaving me no choice but to let down.

I brought my bow back to brace, thinking there was no way he would forgive this transgression. I was shocked when he remained focused on the decoy, giving me a free pass as he circled the silhouette. The buck finally turned to his left and exposed his vitals. I came to full draw for the second time, just as two black eyes glanced up at me. The buck hadn't missed the movement this time, but it was too late, as my arrow was already on its way—striking him just behind the shoulder blade. I watched as the buck crashed down the ridge with yellow and white fletching tracing his retreat.

I knew it was Wednesday and that finding help would be difficult. A few hours later, my friend Mike was gracious enough to leave work and help me take up the trail. The rain had stopped in the early morning hours, and I hoped it had not erased too much of the sign. I was worried the arrow had been too high, and I would know soon enough if my concerns were valid. Upon reaching the impact site, Mike asked what had possessed me to hang a stand along this ridge. There were no tracks or trails, no giant rubs or massive scrapes, just a vacant stand in a tree void of cover. I could not argue with the absurdity of the location, but the mature bucks had always gravitated toward it. That was my best answer. We walked through the damp forest without a sound, scanning the timber for blood and bone. As we slid down the rain-soaked ridge, Mike stopped and pointed ahead. Lying near the edge of the creek was a heavy-horned Iowa whitetail. The arrow was still protruding from his chest, evidence he had succumbed to his wound rather quickly. I knelt near his rain-soaked coat, admiring the buck's long tines and perfect symmetry, a trophy in every sense of the word.

November 4, 1998

Chariton defeated Keokuk that night, ending my brother's dream of winning a state title. Regardless of the outcome, it was a privilege to watch his last game under the lights, and I am grateful for the memory. Although the game did not end as we had hoped, neither do most whitetail hunts when decoys are involved. Still, the sheer anticipation and excitement that accompanies each setup, along with the mystery of the unknown, keeps us coming back for more. That alone is worth the price of admission, and everything else is just icing on the cake. I continued to use that old decoy for many years, before it was lost in a move and never seen again. Its disappearance did not bother me, as I already owned the memories it helped me foster. Deception will always be a bowhunter's greatest ally, and should you disagree with this notion, you would only be deceiving yourself.

CHAPTER 3

Arrows of April

I still remember that spring of 1992 as if it were yesterday. The smell of bug spray in the air, the humid weather, and the call of the whip-poor-will all take me back. I was 15 years old and had just started turkey hunting, hoping to harvest my first gobbler. My best friend, Ryan, and his father, Gary, had offered to take me that spring, and after applying for tags we eagerly awaited the opener. A few months later, on a perfect April morning, we parked Gary's truck on a grassy lane and made our way across the field. We placed a pair of Flambeau decoys near an overgrown fenceline, settled back, and let the woods come to life. The cardinals were first to welcome the dawn, their cheery song ramping up with each note. Gary threw out a series of yelps on his box call, and a few minutes later whispered, "There's one."

The gobbler had not made a sound off the roost. But as I peered across the field, I could see a glowing, white head moving toward the decoys. With the anticipation building, I was struggling to keep it together. Clicking the safety off my shotgun, I kept asking Gary if I could take the gobbler, although I had no clue how far away he was. After multiple requests, Gary gave me the green light, knowing I couldn't hold out much longer. My 12-gauge looked

Gary, Ryan, and Eyad—May 2, 1992

like a conductor's baton, spinning in nerve-induced circles, before breaking the morning silence with three resounding booms. I watched the gobbler sail over the treetops unscathed, knowing I should have let him get closer, but I was too excited to care.

One week later, on May 2, 1992, Ryan and I took our first turkeys. A small flock of jakes came in to Gary's calling, allowing us to double-up. It was a moment I'll never forget, and from that point forward I was consumed with spring turkey hunting.

The years passed, and after gaining some confidence with a shotgun, I committed a full season to the stick and string. Many of my friends said it was impossible to take a gobbler with a bow, because their vitals were too small and senses too keen. In the spring of 1999, Iowa allowed its residents to purchase an archery-only tag, which was valid for all four seasons. After years of contemplation and half-hearted attempts, I was ready to give it an honest effort and purchased the tag. I had dabbled with bowhunting turkeys in the past, but I always cashed in my chips for a 12-gauge when things got tough. That was no longer an option, and I would have to make it work.

Few bowhunters pursued turkeys back then, making my quest for information a challenge. Even with my limited experience, I knew a turkey's eyesight was in a league of its own. Drawing on one of these cagy longbeards was akin to walking on water, neither of which I had accomplished. In addition, the farm I hunted was situated on a large hay pasture, with a classic strut zone at its center. This ruled out any natural setups along the timber's edge, which left me with one option. Unlike whitetails, it appeared turkeys didn't care if you brushed in a blind or placed it in the middle of a field. It seemed to be a nonissue either way and could be the Achilles' heel I was looking for. However, if the blind flapped in the wind, made any unnatural noise, or shined like a silver dollar, all bets were off. I purchased a popup blind that winter, which was silent and easy to set up. My accuracy improved as the spring drew closer, and on April 14, 1999, I was fortunate to harvest my first gobbler with a bow.

Setting up my blind the night before, I was surprised when a pair of gobblers came in silently the next morning. It happened so fast that I didn't have time to get nervous, taking the lead bird when he cleared the window. Weighing just over twenty pounds and carrying three beards, he remains one of my best birds to date. Never looking back, I became enthralled with bowhunting

Eyad's first archery longbeard.

turkeys and thought I had it figured out. Little did I know that my education was just beginning.

The next spring, I was raring to go, having scouted and prepared well ahead of time. My bow was shooting great, and after multiple scouting forays I was confident the season would be a good one. Opening day found me setup at the base of a large pasture, awaiting the sunrise with bow in hand. I was not disappointed, as soon a thunderous gobble echoed through the hardwoods. In time, the woods awakened, coming to life with the chorus of spring. I glanced out of the blind's small window and noticed two jakes running at breakneck speed for my decoys. Just as excited to shoot a jake as any longbeard, I attached my release to the string and came to full draw.

My first arrow flew a tad low, grazing the jake at 15 yards before bouncing across the pasture. My second shot found the blind's window, which deflected the arrow to parts unknown. Down in the count with no balls and two strikes, I fired a third arrow harmlessly over the jake's back—striking out on three pitches. Back then, I ran a three-arrow quiver, sold on the notion that if I needed more, I'd surely need my eyes examined. Needless to say, whoever gave me that advice must not have been a turkey hunter. You can guess what happened next. No sooner had the jakes hightailed it out of there than a gobbler hammered in the pasture above me. On the heels of his throaty introduction, the monarch crested the hill and sauntered toward my decoys. The longbeard worked his way to within 10 yards of the blind, then spun and danced before me, as if he knew I was out of arrows. I felt more like a birdwatcher than a bowhunter, shaking my head in disbelief as the gobbler took his sweet time among the decoys.

After his departure, I exited the blind and retrieved the only two arrows I could find. I saw that my broadheads were covered in mud and did my best to clean them off, but it was a lost cause. I walked down to the timber's edge where the jakes had disappeared, and saw that one of them was still there, suspicious but unalarmed. Hoping to take advantage of the jake's inexperience, I nocked one of the arrows I had retrieved from the field and attached my release. I waited until the youngster stepped behind an oak tree before drawing my bow. Once he reappeared, I quickly settled my pin and dropped the string. My arrow did its best impression of a boomerang, curving to the right by at least three feet before burrowing into the ground. As the jake flew off for the county line, I stood there in disbelief as to what had just happened. At the very least, I learned that mud-caked broadheads don't work, and that bowhunting turkeys was anything but easy.

Over the next week, I hunted hard before class, running into roadblocks and mishaps along the way. I felt like I was chasing my own tail—setting up in locations that had worked with a shotgun in years past—only to see the longbeards skirt my ambush. I watched them move in a certain direction each morning, down a steep embankment that housed a few cedar trees at its base. Not exactly your classic turkey setup, but when in Rome, do as the turkeys do. It was obvious they were drawn to this location, so here I would focus my attention on Saturday morning.

Short on both energy and confidence, I planned to hunt all day if I had to, trying to recapture a little of both. Despite the perfect conditions and setup, I heard no gobbles at daybreak. That would not change over the next hour as I nodded off to the sound of songbirds and farm machinery in the distance. At around 8:00 AM, I heard a gobbler hammer in the timber to my left, so close that it startled me back to consciousness. I picked up my bow

April 2000

and peered out the small porthole of the blind, seeing nothing but a vacant pasture and decoys teetering in the breeze. Then the old boy gobbled again, much closer and with enough enthusiasm that I knew he was coming.

I held my bow with shaking hands as the shadow of the gobbler's fan crawled down the hillside. Crescent shaped and fully formed, the shadow loomed larger, evidence that the gobbler was inching closer. I slinked back within the blind and followed his shadow down the hillside, preparing for the shot that I hoped would unfold. In the next instant, his bulbous form filled the space, with a full fan illuminated by the sun's eastern rays. My arrow found its mark, anchoring the longbeard within the decoy spread, where he flopped and tumbled before coming to rest. I escaped the blind to collect my prize, hoisting him in the morning light with a deep sense of pride and fulfillment.

With another tag in my pocket and one week left to hunt, I concentrated my efforts on the opposite side of the farm. The day before I planned to hunt, I ran a quick scouting mission through the area, a section of timber that was greening up rather quickly. Just a few yards into my venture, I heard a gobbler hammer from the nearest ridge, with another bird gobbling soon after. With late afternoon upon us, I assumed they would roost close and made plans to return before sunrise.

The next morning, I parked my truck just off the sharp bend of a gravel road and entered the timber under a shroud of darkness. Although I tried to be cautious in my approach, there was only so much I could do with the dry conditions. I erected my blind in a clearing along a hogback ridge and sat back to await the day. My assumptions had been correct, as a pair of longbeards gobbled in the early morning light, not far from my setup. Within twenty minutes another gobbler had joined the party, cranking up just down the ridge from the other two. Wing beats and muffled gobbles soon followed, evidence that the trio was now on the ground. Over the next few hours, my every yelp and cackle was answered in kind. Unfortunately, the longbeards held their ground, showing no interest in closing the distance.

With the eleven o'clock hour fast approaching, I removed a gobble call from my vest and decided to play the jealousy game. I had nothing to lose as the day grew hotter, making the blind feel more like an oven than an ambush. Hitting the gobble call after an aggressive series of yelps, cuts, and cackles, I heard the trio of longbeards answer immediately. I repeated the sequence, only to have them respond once more with a flurry of gobbles. Placing my calls on the ground, I sat back and decided to play hard to get. Nothing gets the attention of a suitor like the silent treatment. And with all my cards on the table, the waiting game began. The minutes passed with nary a sound, when suddenly I heard a volley of purrs coming up the ridge, followed by rapid footsteps atop the woodland leaves.

I glanced out of the blind and was shocked to see three angry toms encroaching, focused on my jake decoy with disdain. With crimson-colored crowns, the trio flogged and gouged the feather flex decoy, knocking it off the stake. I came to full draw amidst the ruckus, but the birds were so close together that it was impossible to pick one of the longbeards out of the melee. Having to rise above the window for fear of hitting the blind, I saw an opening and released my arrow into the nearest gobbler. As the longbeard hobbled down the ridge, the other two birds shifted their attention, charging their wounded comrade with a vengeance. In the throes of death, I could hear the dying gobbler's last wing beats as they hammered against the forest floor, mixed in with the ill-tempered assault of his former friends.

I waited an hour before beginning my search, hoping to find the gobbler where I'd last heard him. Working my way down the ridgeline, I noticed the woods becoming denser, carrying a shadowy disposition that was absent in the clearing above. After circling the ridge with no luck, I returned to the blind and its open spaces, trying to regain my line of sight. On my next pass, I saw the gobbler lying in the leaves, his ebony feathers veiled amidst the midday shadows. I relished the weight of the longbeard as I packed him out and was grateful for a season that showed me how challenging this endeavor could be. It had all been worth it in the end, and I couldn't wait for April and its arrows to come back around.

CHAPTER 4

Silence on the Athabasca

With turbulent waters and an ominous flow, the Athabasca River winds through the northern tiers of Alberta. I was hunting here in late May of 2000, on my second quest for a black bear north of the border. I had hunted black bears once before in Ontario, waiting six nights for a boar to appear, only to see a sow and two cubs the last evening. While it was a trip that fueled my desire to hunt these ebony giants and created fond memories with two of my good friends, I hungered for more. Not yet having a full-time job and still in college, I worked hard and saved carefully, hoping for another chance. Then one day I read an article by noted author M.R. James in *Bowhunter* magazine. Mr. James wrote of his adventures along the Athabasca and the giant bears he encountered. I was enthralled by his words, and while I had no means to get there, nor any business wanting to go, I vowed to hunt the Athabasca one day. Two years later, fueled by the words of M.R. James and a solid dose of desire, I was drifting down its murky waters in search of a giant bruin.

My first night on the river was subject to Murphy's Law, as a faulty motor forced us to hunt near camp. The mechanical failure set us back two hours but left ample time for an evening hunt. We grounded the vessel on the Athabasca's muddy shore, where I grabbed my bow and headed into the Canadian bush. I walked down a beaten path and came upon a clear cut with multiple trails converging at its center. Before me was a large barrel, filled with succulent sweets, beaver carcasses, and oil. How anything could enjoy such a feast was beyond me, but the bears had not asked for my opinion.

I climbed onto the elevated platform secured to a small pine, nocked an arrow, and prepared for the evening hunt. The hours passed uneventfully, until just before dark, when I saw a jet-black beast moving toward me. I was told that a mature boar would have a broad snout, large paws, and small ears attached to a pumpkin-sized head. This bear was just the opposite, and having no intention of taking a young bruin, I sat back to enjoy the show. It wasn't long before darkness devoured the bear, and fearful the beast would be lying in wait, I found myself not wanting to leave my treestand. Short of a pistol—and the common sense to bring one—I descended the pine and walked nervously toward the river. Like Ichabod Crane on All Hallows' Eve, I kept looking over my shoulder, convinced something was following me. Despite my fears, I made it back to the boat, finding my smile as I drifted down the Athabasca.

Bear camp is a relaxing place, with most hunts taking place in the evening. While you can hunt in the morning, most bears are taken over bait later in the day. Mornings are spent shooting your bow, fishing in local waters, and refreshing bait stations. The next morning, I did just that, accompanying one of the guides to check a few baits. We talked as he drove, and he mentioned one stand where a large boar had been frequenting the bait. Although the bear's patterns were erratic, he appeared to be a true giant based on the sign. The stand was located deep within a swamp and was only accessible by Argo, and even that was questionable with the recent rainfall. After discussing possible stand options for the afternoon hunt, I asked if I could hunt the swamp that evening. He took just a second to think about it, and then said, "All right, I'll take you in tonight."

Loaded with fresh goodies and treats for the bait, we worked our way deeper into the wilderness. I wish I had taken a mouth guard with me as we bounced along in the Argo that afternoon, because the ride was less than kind. Like a rodeo bull on steroids, the Argo dipped and dived in the slippery mud, throwing us from side to side. The smell of gasoline and burning belts soon filled my nostrils and made me lightheaded, giving new meaning to the term *motion sickness*. We eventually reached the end of the trail and parked the Argo, having to walk the rest of the way in. The overcast sky seemed to be on the verge of another shower, a common occurrence since my arrival. As we entered the swamp, canopied by pine and spruce boughs, I noticed the area had an eerie feel about it. It was shielded from the wind and sunlight, and I could see why an old bruin would call this place home. After refreshing the bait station with beaver carcasses and molasses, I climbed into my stand, soon hearing the Argo crank up and fade into the distance.

Refreshing the bait station.

While at least four hours remained before nightfall, the day seemed much darker with the passing front. The mosquitoes, ever present on any bear hunt, were unrelenting. I did my best not to look down at my clothing, where the crawling, dense mass of mosquitoes had given my camouflage a black hue. Donning a bug-tamer jacket, thick gloves and a head net, I tried to protect myself from their onslaught. The blood-sucking insects seemed angry with my attire, as if my wardrobe had robbed them of a meal. Not helping their cause, I had also duct-taped the sleeves of my jacket, preventing the mosquitoes from finding ulterior routes. Not even an hour into the hunt, I caught movement to my left. Scurrying along at a frantic pace, a pine marten was making his way toward the bait. He seemed to miss nothing and was always on edge, grabbing a piece of meat before hustling back to the forest. The marten repeated this process over the next few hours, making the time pass quickly, as if I was attending a matinee at the local theatre. With diminished daylight came a haunting silence as darkness enveloped the swamp. The pine marten had disappeared, along with the whiskey jacks and red squirrels that had lectured him most of the afternoon. As I peered into the darkness with dilated pupils, I saw the outline of a hulking mass and realized that a large bruin was making his way toward me.

I was having trouble focusing in the fading light and kept blinking, making sure the oncoming giant was not an apparition. Unlike the sow from Ontario, or the young male from the evening before, there was no synchronous stride, but a confident lumber and sway. His pumpkin-sized head, small ears, and beady eyes all answered a question that needn't be asked. This was a mature boar, and I hoped to make good on the opportunity. Glaring up as if he knew I was there, the bruin took a long look and then continued his approach. The beast seemed to fear nothing, and his demeanor embodied that notion. I cautiously raised my bow, feeling a mixture of fear and excitement that I had yet to experience in the field. The boar slowly turned his head, his left side exposed, a solid wall of black melting into the looming darkness. I came to full draw and tried to settle my pin but noticed it was spinning in circles far larger and more erratic than normal. The pin finally settled on the bruin's midnight-colored coat, just before the arrow vanished behind his shoulder. With a growl, the bear lurched forward and headed back into the swamp, crashing through the pines and spruce. A few seconds later, a long, guttural moan echoed from the darkness, followed by another. Then, all was silent.

I had heard stories of the death moan but did not expect the emotions that it stirred deep within me. Descending the tree, I eased over to the bait and soon found my arrow protruding from an old log. The shaft revealed ample sign, but I thought it best to wait before taking up the trail. I gathered my belongings and left the swamp, following the same path back to the Argo. Along the way, I came across a small field with a few snowshoe hares scattered about. I was moving past when I suddenly heard footsteps behind me. Turning around, I recognized the pointed ears and gray-colored face of a large lynx stalking toward my position.

I yelled at the feline to scare him off, not sure what his intentions might be. He undoubtedly was hunting the snowshoe hares I'd seen in the field but now appeared to have shifted his focus. The lynx did not seem the least bit afraid and perhaps was upset that I had interrupted his dinner plans. He crouched down as if to pounce, glaring at me, not a muscle moving in his shadowy form. I backed away, keeping my eyes glued to the cat. He suddenly

The camera flash scared the lynx back into the night.

burst into motion and sprinted toward me. Holding my bow like a shield, I shouted once more, and the lynx stopped a mere 10 yards away. I soon got the impression that he was more curious than carnivorous, which eased my concern. I slowly pulled a camera from my pack and snapped a photo, the flash scaring the lynx back into the night. With two bounds he was gone, realizing I wasn't that interesting after all. After catching my breath, still in disbelief at what had just happened, I moved on as well.

Later that evening, we followed a steady blood trail to the fallen bruin. As I knelt beside the giant boar, I recalled the nights I had spent dreaming of this moment and the sacrifices made to get here. Wrestling with feelings that were hard to describe, I gained a deeper understanding of who I was as a bowhunter. Not only did I feel pride and gratitude for a swift death and an accurate arrow, but also a sense of remorse for the life I had taken. Although some give little credence to this mindset, I have since embraced it, feeling that empathy and elation should be found at the end of every blood trail.

I spent the rest of the week with a video camera, watching some younger bears work the baits. A few days after taking my bruin, I was on my way to another stand, when I spotted two cubs scurrying away through the brush. I couldn't help but laugh at their antics as they climbed to nose-bleed heights in a lonely pine. I was aware that their mother must be close, so I took a quick video and moved on. I had just settled in my treestand when I heard rustling behind me. I peered around the trunk and saw a large sow, which I assumed to be the cubs' mother. This seemed to be the case as she made her way to the base of my tree, where she promptly began her ascent. I watched with trepidation as she climbed higher, her claws gripping the pine, until she was within inches of my leg. At this point I was getting concerned, still on the calm side of panic, but knowing I had to do something. With no change in her demeanor, despite my verbal assault, I elected to give her a tap on the nose with my boot. This sent her fleeing the scene, which brought my blood pressure under control. No doubt, a few of my gray hairs resulted from her actions, but who's to say which ones. It was an amazing end to my black bear adventure, but an encounter I could have done without.

Optometry school started that fall in St. Louis, and my time in the field was curtailed. Little did I know how demanding my studies would become, nor how quickly the years would fly by. Now, as I sit here with pen and paper, nearly twenty years later, I have yet to take another black bear, nor am I sure that I ever will. Limited time and a growing family, along with other adventures have thus far vetoed pursuing another bruin. Perhaps one day, the dream that pulled me to the Athabasca will find me again, but if not, I am content with my memories.

Eyad's Alberta Bruin

CHAPTER 5

Land of Lincoln

It was the summer of 2000, a year full of anticipation and change. I was moving to St. Louis in a few months to start graduate school, and in the interim, I was working part-time at a local gym. There I first met Jim, one of the most dedicated deer hunters I've ever met. If you saw Jim, you'd wonder how he had time to hunt, as surely he spent his autumns playing for the Green Bay Packers. Built like a tank and strong as an ox, Jim didn't look like a guy you'd mess with. Still, he was one of the nicest people I've ever met, and we often exchanged deer hunting stories and strategy after his workouts. As the summer ended, Jim offered to take me deer hunting in Illinois that fall. I vowed to return the favor as he had drawn a coveted nonresident Iowa tag. Quincy was only two hours away from St. Louis, and because of Jim's generosity, I might be able to hunt more than expected.

School started with a flurry of work and responsibility, and to say I was busy is an understatement. In addition to my academic obligations, deer hunting was always on my mind. To ensure that I had time to hunt, I spent hours recording lectures and notes on audio cassette tapes, while writing questions on flash cards with their answers on the back. I listened to the tapes while driving back to Quincy and used the flash cards to study in my treestand. Albeit tedious and tiresome, I didn't have a choice if I wanted to excel in the classroom, while still pursuing my passions in the field. While hunting one night, Jim said he thought he saw something white fluttering through the woods and asked if I had seen it too. I played the fool and answered surreptitiously, knowing he probably witnessed a flash card or two falling from my perch.

On November 2, I dropped the string on a huge bodied eight-pointer that chased a doe through a picked cornfield. The shot was just a tad low but captured enough of the whitetail to impede his retreat. A high-pressure system had left frigid remnants of its passing, with cold temperatures and clear skies forecasted overnight. Despite no imminent threats of rain or snow, I felt we should pursue immediately, as his wound appeared more crippling than mortal. We were also contending with coyotes, whose means of death would be far worse than a second arrow. Considering these factors, we decided to move forward, hoping it was the right call.

November 2000

Just a few yards into the timber, we heard the buck rise from his bed, but his departure was cumbersome and slow. As we drew closer, a steep ditch materialized, and at the bottom lie the heavy eight-pointer. He was unable to escape the hollow, his wounded leg grossly evident, so we descended with bow in hand. Once we reached the bottom and stepped forward, I knew we had made a terrible mistake. The enormous whitetail, with long tines and a bull-like physique, swung his head so fast that I was completely caught off guard. Narrowly missing my throat on the first pass, the buck swung back the other way, engaging the weapons with which he was graced each fall. Jim and I tried to escape the beast in close quarters, fearing he would get his bearings and turn on us. After dispatching the monster and realizing how close we had been to being gored, I could do nothing but sit in silence. I shouldered the blame for a less-than-perfect shot, knowing we had been lucky in more ways than one.

With Iowa tags tucked in our pockets, Jim and I made plans to hunt the Hawkeye State in the weeks ahead. I was off on November 10, a three-day weekend, and was going to take advantage of it. Jim couldn't hunt that Friday, so I planned on a quick morning hunt before hitting the books. It was a frigid day for early November, which should get the bucks on their feet. I knew it would be a tough sit and did the best I could to layer accordingly.

I had purchased a new face mask from Cabelas that summer but had never tried it on. It felt warm and quiet upon its arrival and was made with the best material in the industry, at least that's what the tag claimed. I was hunting the same farm near my parents' house and planned to set up in a shallow depression, hoping the wind would be less severe. That plan didn't last long, because two hours into my hunt, and I could barely feel my extremities. I was about to climb down, realizing I wouldn't make it much longer, when I heard walking behind me. Turning to my left, I saw the biggest whitetail I've ever seen in the wild—and that holds true to this day.

The giant was at 15 yards and severely quartering toward me. I was hand-cuffed, only able to study his frame and demeanor. His antlers made his body look disproportionate as he tilted his head back, testing the wind for does and danger. This would be my first lesson in the difficulty of hunting bowls and saddles. The wind currents act more like a pinball, bouncing around the bowl, betraying hunters no matter how faithful they are to wind direction. Areas like this are impossible to hunt, and I learned that lesson the hard way. I was waiting with frozen hands for him to turn broadside, when he finally caught my wind and looked up. Silhouetted against the sky, with no leaves or branches to conceal my form, I knew he had me. He took two quick bounds and stopped at 30 yards, where I was already at full draw. I tried to find my pins in a panic but realized I couldn't see through my face mask. Using my teeth and tongue to manipulate the mask, I saw a hint of green fluorescence and lined up my sight with the monster. I released my arrow, unable to see its flight, then reached up and pulled the mask off my face.

The buck was bounding out of my life, stopping to glance back one last time before disappearing into the cedars. There was a pile of white hair near my arrow, as if he'd been given a haircut, which in hindsight I guess he had. The arrow was clean, falling just short of his heart, the outcome breaking mine. I hadn't practiced with the face mask, and because of it, I lost my chance at the deer of a lifetime. I recall going back to my parents' house, burying my head on the kitchen table and wanting to forget. Mushroom hunters found his sheds the following spring on an adjacent farm, scoring just under 200 inches. Jim would join me in Iowa for a few hunts over the next two weeks, but I just couldn't get him on a big whitetail. Luck and time weren't on our side, and before long the season was over.

October 2001

The next fall, with a schedule full of conflicts and clinicals, I hoped to get a few days in the field. Jim was once again gracious enough to invite me to hunt. My youngest brother, Tameem, now an All-American linebacker at Truman State, was in his prime on the football field. Traveling with my family and watching him play were some of the best times of my life. I knew that missed games were moments I could not get back, and making every one of them was my priority. Unfortunately, the only time I had left between football games and school was an occasional Friday afternoon.

In early October, an unseasonable cold front passed through the Midwest, painting the heartland with a coating of frost. It was hardly typical for this time of year, but I welcomed it with open arms, knowing it would get the big boys on their feet. I was hoping to get a quick hunt in before meeting up with my family for the weekend, and Jim said I was welcome to join him. Just a few hours of tree time were all I needed to get right with the world, and I was looking forward to it. The stand I was hunting was in an overgrown fence line, which bordered a standing bean field. Just as the afterglow of an autumn sunset faded in the west, I saw a huge-bodied deer heading my way. The antlers were heavy and tall, and they kept getting bigger with each passing second. Soon the buck was at 20 yards and angled to my right. I remember seeing my pin hovering in small circles over the buck's vitals, and then my arrow was gone. The buck did not travel far after the shot, crumpling in the beans before darkness encompassed the field. To this day, he remains one of the biggest bodied deer I've ever taken, with solid mass and long main beams. Thanks to Jim, I had collected my second Illinois buck in as many years.

As the fall of 2002 approached, I found myself immersed in my busiest year of training, with the first round of boards behind me. I had somehow passed, removing a heavy burden off my shoulders, which freed up more time to bowhunt. Jim's expertise and deer hunting knowledge had garnered the attention of a national film crew, and rightfully so. I had met few bowhunters with his passion and skill for hunting big whitetails, and I was glad for his success. Any free time Jim had would be tied up with filming, which meant we couldn't hunt together as often. I knew this could be my last year in the St. Louis area before heading to parts unknown, and I was unsure where my training would take me. So, I elected to buy one more nonresident tag. If it worked out and Jim had free time, we might squeeze in a hunt or two.

I hunted sparingly through October, while still catching all my brother's football games and keeping up on my studies. The season passed in the blink of an eye, and before I knew it, we were knocking on Thanksgiving's door. The Illinois shotgun season was looming, which meant I had only two days left to hunt. Jim and Jimmy, ironically the name of the videographer in town that week, had been hunting hard, but had yet to connect on a mature buck. The last thing I wanted was to be in the way, but Jim, with his never-say-die attitude and generous demeanor, gave me permission to hunt a property with which I was familiar. I knew this acreage as the *Flash Card* farm, where I studied the nights away while perched in a treestand. I had last hunted this farm two years ago, and unfortunately, there were no longer stands in the area. Not to worry, I always kept my climber with me throughout the fall if a situation like this arose.

I parked my truck and opened the cab to retrieve my gear. Back then, on a student's budget, I used plastic trash bags to store my hunting clothes. Upon opening the plastic bag, I was greeted with a putrid smell; the mold and stench was almost unbearable. I knew what had happened, as the week before I was back in Iowa for a quick hunt, which was interrupted by a torrential downpour. After the squall, I had stored my wet clothes in a plastic bag and forgot to remove them, hence my current predicament.

Digging through the foul-smelling gear to locate my release was a wasted venture, as the hinges were locked in place with a thick layer of rust. Here I sat during the peak of the rut, in the heart of the Golden Triangle, and I had no way to hunt. After scolding myself with some choice words, which would have gotten me thrown out of most athletic events, I conceded defeat. There were only a few hours of daylight left, and I was out of options. Just as I had given up, a light bulb went off in my head.

I got out of my truck, sifted through the back seat and soon found what I was looking for. Stored beneath the seat was a broken, old rope-style release I hadn't used in years. I remembered throwing it in the storage compartment last season but had since forgotten. The release was not perfect by any means, with a broken throat that didn't allow for much adjustment. I improvised by securing the release to my forearm and thus manipulating the overall length. The next step was to find clothes, which I pulled from the dirty gym laundry I planned to wash at my folks' that weekend. The pair of sweatpants and old Nike sweatshirt I picked from the pile didn't smell great but were a welcome reprieve compared to the moldy plastic bag.

Smelling like a locker room and with a release that resembled a cast, I walked across the picked bean field. The weather was brutally cold and cloudy, as if December had grown impatient and showed up early. The wind was not helping either, blowing out of the northwest with such force that I wouldn't last long with my meager clothing. As I continued my walk of shame, I detected the odor of my attire, which made me shake my head in disgust. I was planning to hunt an inside corner, forged from the junction of an overgrown fence line with the timber's edge. I could see where I sat and studied two years ago, filing through flash cards as I prepared for the upcoming week. It made sense that a marauding buck would run this route. The crosswind would allow him to check for does as he cruised the fence line before cutting across to the adjacent woodlot. I planned to sit along the edge of the field, just downwind of this travel route, which would be my only option.

With as much motivation as a sloth on sleeping pills, I wrapped the climber around the base of the nearest tree and began my ascent. Slowly but surely, I made it up to fifteen feet and felt this was sufficient based on the surrounding cover. I separated my boots from the climber, hoisted my bow skyward, and unhooked the pull rope. Still facing the timber, I looked to my left and almost fell out of the tree. A big buck was parading down the fence line, moving fast with his nose to the ground. I was handcuffed as the buck cut across the inside corner and now stood a mere 10 yards from my tree. This buck was on the move, likely in search of an estrus doe, and I had to act fast. I nocked an arrow without thinking twice, and then hooked my rope release to the string. If he saw me, so be it. I had no choice but to be aggressive.

The buck was working a scrape when I looked back up, still in the same spot my eyes had left him. He raked the ground and flung dirt through the air before thrashing a helpless sapling. I settled my pin and the arrow was gone, passing through the buck with ease. He crashed through the timber and out of sight, after which I began to shake, making the climber feel more like a wake board than a deer stand. Behind me I heard a deer snort, which was directly downwind, interrupting the thrill of the moment. A young buck, a spike no less, was pounding his hooves like a Clydesdale. The bruiser I arrowed had failed to detect my presence, whereas this youngster had done so easily, a testament to how valuable the wind is to their survival and our success. When I reached the base of the tree he was gone, which was fine by me, because I was leaving too.

I jumped off my climber and left it attached to the tree, almost stumbling face first in the bean stubble. I raced in my truck down the gravel to Jim's house and found he and Jimmy had not yet departed for their evening stands. They asked me what I had forgotten, and I explained that I just shot a good buck and needed some help. The laughter that followed was impressive, and while it took some convincing, they finally believed me. I told them that I felt the shot was good and he shouldn't be far. They had been hunting hard all week, so I harbored some guilt in knowing I'd been on stand less than a minute, and in sweaty gym clothes to boot. There was only one explanation for my good fortune, and that was complete, unadulterated luck.

We gave the buck time, as I had not seen him go down, and could not recall if he was broadside or quartering at the shot. I was supposed to meet my family and girlfriend for dinner that night in Quincy before heading to the football game in the morning. I gave her a call, explaining my situation and that I would need to recover the buck after dinner. Foreshadowing at its finest, she wasn't the least bit pleased, which did not bode well for the future of our relationship. After supper, I met up with Jimmy, as Jim had taken a nice doe and was in the process of his own recovery.

Jimmy and I headed back to the timber, where we found the arrow in short order. The sign looked darker and less profuse than I hoped, which curbed my enthusiasm. As we followed a scant blood trail through the timber with flashlights in hand, Jimmy whispered for me to stop. I stood still and listened. Soon I heard a massive animal stand up and start thrashing in the brush. We crept down the ridge and up the other side, scanning the dark forest for my buck. Suddenly, Jimmy's flashlight beam hit a small patch of white, and then much to our surprise, a coal-colored mass took shape. A farmer's cow had escaped and was bedded on the hillside above us, looking just as surprised as we were. We backed out and did a few more circles, but the sign wasn't there. I thought my shot looked good, but arrows and blood trails don't lie—something was wrong. The reality hurt even more, realizing that we may have pushed the buck out of the timber. Dejected and concerned, we backed out, knowing we would have to return at sunrise to retrieve this giant.

The next morning, we found the heavy-horned whitetail a short distance from where we stopped looking. The arrow had done what I feared and exited farther back, thus compromising the blood trail. The buck carried a beautiful mahogany-colored rack, with a unique, mushroom-shaped tip on the end of one tine. He was the last buck I would take in Illinois, and I cannot think of a more perfect whitetail to end on.

November 2002

I'm not sure what to say about Jim and all he did for me, for nothing will do him justice. There was no reason for him to take me hunting, to teach me the things he did, or help me when I had few other options. Nor was there a reason for him to grant me access, to put up with my questions, or assist me on many a trail. Jim never asked for anything in return, and I knew he never would. It just wasn't his way. Perhaps one day, I can return the favor and see that he harvests one of those Iowa giants. I know there is no way I'll ever be able to repay him in full, for the good fortune and memories he bestowed upon me are beyond reciprocation.

CHAPTER 6

Sweet November

The weather was unseasonably warm that fall, with near record highs into November. I had been hunting hard since the opener, trying to fill my tag on a mature whitetail. A giant had eluded me early in the season, ghosting past my treestand just before sunrise. My only other encounter had come in late October, when my arrow sailed high on a nice eight-pointer, the buck no worse for wear. My friend Don had gained access to a small farm near West Point, Iowa, and asked the landowner if I could hunt as well. With a blown opportunity under my belt, I thought a change of scenery would be good and decided to scout the new farm. It appeared the whitetails were fond of this property, as multiple trails, tracks, and rubs tattooed the landscape.

The farm also housed a good number of cattle, which seemed to be my nemesis, ever present on the properties I hunted. I found ways to hunt around them, dodging cow patties and sneaking past the herd. I couldn't escape these obese ungulates but made the best of it. A cedar thicket drew my attention early on; the thick cover bordered an oak ridge ripe with acorns. Rubs and scrapes laced through the area, revealing I was not the first to appreciate its attributes. The proximity of food and cover is always advantageous to predator and prey alike, and I hoped to be the beneficiary. The area looked to hold promise, and on my second scouting mission in late October, I jumped a good buck near the edge of the cedars. His wide rack glided through the thicket with ease, as if he had done this before. The cedar thicket was likely his sanctuary, and I knew he wouldn't abandon his bedroom based on one disturbance. I filed the information away for future reference and moved on.

At the base of the ridge was a creek strewn with colorful pebbles and rocks, making for a beautiful setting. As much as I love aesthetics, I was more intrigued by the crossing the local whitetails had created. Trampled down and laden with tracks, the trail crossed the serpentine course of the creek and then dispersed into the timber. Just above this aqueous crossing was a large white oak, its centuries-old trunk much too wide to comfortably hang a stand. I said comfortably, not impossible, as this was my only option. Unable to wrap my arms around the big oak's circumference, I felt like I was climbing a rock face, using my fingertips to scramble up the tree. Nevertheless, the stand was hung, leaving me with an awkward ambush in a perfect location.

I returned a few days later, on a warm November morning, hoping the deer would ignore the weather and stay on their feet. I was leaning back in the stand as best I could, focused on not pitching forward, when I heard faint footsteps in the timber. Too dark to visualize their maker, I pulled the grunt tube from my jacket and hit the call. The sound of walking ceased, and then resumed its cadence, with a different direction and volume. Soon the buck was within range, his antlers and sturdy shoulders materializing along the creek bank. I laced an arrow through his vitals and watched him crash within sight. My sister Jackie and her friend drew the short straw that day, helping me drag the Iowa whitetail from the depths of the creek bottom. It was the same buck I had jumped near the cedars, his wide rack unmistakable.

Five years later, I was back in Iowa, looking forward to another season in the Hawkeye State. It was now 2004, and I was working six days a week between two jobs, slowly transitioning to a full-time practice. Previous seasons had felt like an endless hourglass, filled with more time than I knew what to do with. Things had changed since then, and with no vacation time amassed, I wasn't sure what the fall would bring. I still had permission to hunt the farm near my childhood home and was looking forward to the opportunity. In early September, I began scouting the property, looking to fine-tune my stand options. The cows were back, always my kryptonite, and I just couldn't seem to avoid them. While walking through a Conservation Reserve Program (CRP) field on the west side, I jumped a good buck bedded within the jungle. Whitetails always look bigger when running away, but this one needed no help. He had a wide, sweeping rack and good mass, and I hoped to encounter him again that fall.

There was a timber strip just below the CRP field, laced with cow paths and deep depressions, their tracks entwined with the whitetails'. I hung my stand near the end of the strip, where a stock pond and hay pasture created a classic pinch point. Two limbs afforded me arm rests, and the cover ensured I was nearly invisible. The stand location was almost too perfect, and I wondered how I missed it years ago. In early November, I returned to the pinch point, optimistic the bucks would be cruising for does. I had just recovered from a bout of poison ivy, courtesy of short sleeves and a vine I thought to be innocuous. As it turned out, hairy vines were no friends of mine, a catch phrase I learned the hard way.

November 1999

Feeling better as I tapered down the Caladryl, I was almost back to normal. The beauty of November is that anything can happen—all I needed was the right five minutes. The morning was calm and cool, with a subtle breeze out of the west. I parked my truck along a gravel road and then made my way across the cattle pasture. The dew from the grass coated my boots like a creek crossing, but the rubber material was impervious to its moisture. I found my stand in the predawn darkness and got settled without causing a stir. The sunrise was slow but steady, creeping skyward from beneath the eastern horizon. I could see the ridgetops and creek bottom before me, a landscape that rekindled memories of years past. I thought back to the first time I hunted this farm, how my life was so different now, and yet, these acres remained unchanged.

The first two hours on stand were quiet, save for the bustling squirrels and raucous woodpeckers filling their cupboards and bellies. The rut ensured that the bucks would be on their feet. I just had to be patient. Unlike the early-and late-season patterns of bed to feed, this time of year held promise from dawn until dusk. That was the nature of November, never knowing and always on guard, making every ounce of energy and patience worthwhile. I turned my head to examine the stock pond, its surface glass calm and not yet covered in ice. Tracks littered its shores, a mixture of fur and fowl, all seeking to quench their thirst.

Then suddenly, a tall set of antlers emerged from the creek bottom, bursting onto the scene without warning. No sound or sight preceded his entry, and I had to decide. Hitting my anchor, I grunted the buck to a stop and my arrow was gone. I would not see him again, not on this morning nor at the end of a blood trail. My arrow was shining back at me, having grazed the buck, its shaft clean and fletching unscathed. The whitetail wasn't a giant, but I would have been proud to take him.

My chest felt deflated, as was my confidence, knowing I had blown a golden opportunity. I sat back with my head pointed toward the gray sky. I had lost all interest in the day. I so wanted to climb down and forget about bowhunting, the long drives and short nights finally catching up with me. If it wasn't November in Iowa, I may well have done that. Still, I stayed the course, knowing I wasn't getting that chance back, doing my best to move on. That mindset is easier said than done, but it had to be found. Pulling another arrow from my quiver, I took a deep breath and snapped it to the string. It was just shy of 10:00 AM when I looked to my left and saw antlers through the barren hardwoods. The way his neck angled up, I could tell he was working a scrape, but that was all I could determine.

I removed the grunt tube from my pocket, positioned the call, and emitted a long, guttural note. The buck glanced in my direction, his response to my challenge still in question. In a matter of seconds, I had my answer, as the buck started his way toward me. I lost him for a moment in a timbered depression before he reappeared on the other side. Moving slowly, but with an agenda, he worked his way up the ridge. Once he jumped the fence, he hobbled toward a scrape 20 yards away, favoring his right side as he approached. I could tell he was an old warrior, with a gray muzzle and a physique trending downward. It appeared age was just a number to him, however, as he thrashed and tore through a licking branch, trying to intimidate his rival.

November 2004

My arrow left the string without a sound, passing through the buck as he worked the scrape. Leaving faster than he approached, his departure was short-lived, as I heard him crash a few seconds later. Before taking up the trail, I called Don to see if he would care to join me, and we met within the hour. It wasn't long before bladed brows and heavy antlers found our gaze nestled among the oak leaves. I realized he was the same buck I had jumped in September, when a scouting mission revealed his bedding grounds. I thought back to the first story in this chapter and how a similar scenario had unfolded. Both bucks had revealed themselves early in the season, erupting from their beds and showing their hand.

Knowing a big buck was in the area, coupled with the frenzy of the rut, had given me the confidence to stay the course. With one thing on their mind come November, a buck's senses are shorthanded, and every bowhunter has a chance to score. More bucks would fall in the next two years, all in the eleventh month and along travel routes in the early morning hours. The rut will always be a bowhunter's power play, their extra man on the ice—November just happens to be the arena. I can't say I'm a big hockey fan, but I've hunted whitetails long enough to know a good thing when I see it.

CHAPTER 7

Tundra Traditions

In late June of 2005, while working at the St. Louis VA Medical Center, life decided to throw me a curve ball. I was finishing my residency, and after ten years of classes and clinicals, I would be done at week's end. I was looking forward to starting my career, along with an upcoming caribou hunt I had booked in the spring. After assisting a patient out of the exam chair, I tried to walk but could not feel my right leg. I ignored the problem, thinking my leg had fallen asleep. One hour later the feeling had not returned. I had trouble walking down the hall but still thought it was nothing. Fortunately, a colleague talked me into going to the emergency room, where further testing revealed that I'd experienced a stroke. I was skeptical until I reviewed the MRI, showing a section of my brain glowing like a flashlight. I was only 28 years old and was speechless.

The following days in the hospital were the worst of my life. Initially, they had no idea what caused my stroke or if more clots were looming. I tried to stay positive but couldn't help wondering why this had happened. I didn't smoke, drink, or use illegal substances, and I worked out religiously. Eventually, the doctors determined that I had a congenital heart defect called a patent foramen ovale. While common in the general population, it is often linked to strokes. A small clot that normally would have passed without incident, escaped through this defect and caused the infarct. When the head of neurology at the University of Iowa came to check on me, the advice I received was crushing. I was informed that because of the small opening in my heart, any heavy lifting or exertion could cause another stroke. I was lucky, she said, but might not be the next time around. I had prided myself on staying in shape and eating right, and yet, here I was.

In time, I regained feeling in my leg, but the progress was slow. I had booked my caribou hunt months before, and despite my setback, the hunt was still on my radar. My priorities may have been short-sighted, but it offered hope and something to look forward to. Not yet able to jog or lift weights effectively, shooting my bow became my release. I found peace in the quiet sounds of the stick and string and slowly regained my confidence. Although it would be many months before I was back to full strength, both physically and psychologically, I was more than ready for my journey to Quebec.

Cruising high above the tundra below, the float plane made its way toward base camp. It was mid-August, and I was embarking on my first caribou hunt in northern Quebec. Over the past few weeks my right leg had regained considerable strength, almost to the point I didn't notice it. I was just happy to be here, knowing this adventure would be good medicine. The view was nothing short of spectacular, with sparse clouds scattered throughout the clear blue sky. I could see distinct paths emblazoned on the ground below, trampled tundra that created a maze of highways for the caribou to follow. These same paths had been used for hundreds of years, timeless trails that laced their way through the landscape.

With beautiful gray-white capes and tall, branching antlers, few animals can match the physical majesty of a bull caribou. Regarded as one of North America's most regal animals, mature bulls carry antlers with palmated tops, bladed shovels, and bez points that resemble Goliath's hands. With August upon us, the caribou's annual migration was about to commence. The bulls' antlers would still be in velvet, but fully formed, and I hoped to encounter one of these tundra monarchs.

As the pilot brought the float plane down, I could see a multitude of small lakes and streams immersed throughout the tundra. Landing on the glass calm waters before base camp, the pilot taxied up to the dock and tied off. Eager to get started, we stepped off the plane and unloaded our gear. Camp was on the shore of a crystal-clear lake and consisted of small cabins, one of which would be my home for the coming week. The aluminum boats and outboard motors that littered the shore were our means of transportation, allowing us to traverse the lake and hunt different areas. My guide, Ben, would accompany me into the field, and was one of the outfitter's most experienced guides. Although I could legally use a firearm, I explained to Ben that I was committed to using my bow and would like to do so for the hunt's entirety. Caribou country is open and vast, often making stalking within archery range difficult. Still, I knew many bowhunters who had accomplished such a feat, and with any luck, I could do the same.

After getting settled in camp and looking over my gear, I got dressed and headed toward the dock. Ben and I would make a quick run to a distant cove where we could glass the surrounding hillsides. The gun hunters had done well the week before but informed us that the migration had been slow. While small groups of caribou were trickling through the area, there was no sign of the large herds for which the migration is known. As we climbed into the boat, I noticed the sky had darkened and the winds were picking up speed, reminding me how quickly the weather can change in the Canadian wilderness. With a strong crosswind blowing from the north, I tightened the straps on my life jacket, hoping the boat would make it across the windswept water without incident.

We hit the mouth of the cove shortly thereafter, where the wind seemed nonexistent, and soon dragged the boat on shore. I threw a few things in my daypack, grabbed my bow, and we were off. While climbing the ridge that led to our lookout point, I glanced over my shoulder at the lake and approaching front. The whitecaps rolling on the water had me concerned, wondering how we would navigate back to camp. Ben seemed unaffected by the weather change, explaining how conditions like this were common on most caribou hunts. We summited the ridge and glanced over the top, hoping to glimpse antlers on the horizon. Unfortunately, our hopes were met by vacant tundra, so we sat down to glass until nightfall. The beauty of Quebec, or any tundra hunt, is the potential to see for miles. I was grateful for the 10x42 binoculars draped around my neck, as without a pair of quality optics, the ability to locate and identify game was diminished. Notwithstanding our great vantage point and excellent optics, the tundra stayed quiet the rest of the evening. Ben and I left the cove just before dark, motoring across the lake as waves punched the bow like a prize fighter. We arrived back at camp, wet and wind-chilled, but were optimistic the morning would bring better weather.

Caribou Country

The next morning, I learned that Mother Nature had other plans, adding a good deal of rain and wind to her arsenal. No matter; we suited up in raingear and headed out, hoping the wind and rain would grant us a reprieve. As we worked our way across the tundra, I noticed the ground beneath my boots was soft and spongy, courtesy of the lichens that call this place home. Numerous rock formations dotted the landscape, with one standing out among the rest. It consisted of large boulders, which would not only shield us from the elements, but also from the watchful eyes of any approaching caribou. With several trails coursing within bow range of this rocky outcropping, it had the makings of the perfect ambush. The weather was showing no signs of improvement, so we cinched down our hoods and settled in, hoping a bull would wander past our setup.

The hours passed uneventfully, with the wind and rain working their way through my gloves and gortex. Then suddenly, Ben tapped my shoulder and said, "Here come a few good bulls." I nocked an arrow as my pulse picked up speed and my breathing quickened its pace. Peeking around the rocky outcropping, I saw four nice bulls carrying gorgeous, velvet-coated racks. Despite the elements, I could hear hooves hammering against the trail, the sound getting louder as they approached. Soon all four bulls were within 20 yards, their massive antlers a sight to behold. I came to full draw and settled my pin on the lead bull, following him as he trotted along. The movement seemed to catch the bull's eye, and in the brief instant he stopped to decipher the motion, my arrow was gone.

The arrow entered just behind the bull's shoulder, buried to the fletching, and I watched as the herd erupted across the tundra. The bull made his way toward the lake, with obvious plans to swim to distant shores. Just a few yards into the windswept water, the broadhead did its job, and I had my first caribou. Words could not describe what I was feeling as I tipped my hat to the skies and said a silent thank you. We headed back to the boat and motored out to claim my prize, pulling the bull back to shore for photos and field dressing. It was an amazing day, but little did I know, the best was yet to come.

Ben and Eyad

The days that followed brought sunshine and diminished winds, along with a different problem in the form of black flies. This made me wish I'd been more careful in my complaints, as the cold and wind seemed less bothersome than the swarms of biting, crawling insects. The migration was still lagging, but enough bulls were showing up to make it interesting. Unfortunately, after two blown stalks and an equal number of misses, the challenges of bowhunting the tundra were becoming apparent. While I could legally fill my second tag with a rifle, I was content carrying my bow until the end. Ben and I continued to cover many miles via land and water but could not close the deal. Caribou hunting can be feast or famine, and as the hunt wore on, there was no doubt we were experiencing the latter.

We took a lunch break on the fifth day, which allowed me to cast for lake trout near camp. I crept up a steep rock to cast, only to slip and slide into the water. No worse for wear, other than being soaking wet, I trudged back to my cabin and changed clothes for the afternoon hunt. The outfitter had warned me that Fish & Game would occasionally show up to check licenses and ensure all hunters were wearing blaze orange. Although I was bowhunting, I was required to wear an orange vest for safety sake, as other hunters were carrying firearms. Ben was scouting some new country and left me to hunt a well-worn trail near a pinch point. After sitting there for an hour, I thought I heard chopper blades in the distance. It only took seconds for my eyes to confirm what my ears had detected, and sure enough, Fish & Game was coasting in to my setup. I thought I had nothing to fear, but that was until I reached into my pocket and realized my tags were gone.

The wardens were professional and polite, at least their tone seemed to be, while they discussed my fate in French. Trying to explain my situation—that my tags were in my wet pants back at camp—seemed to fall on deaf ears. I wished my guidance counselor had pushed me into taking French rather than Spanish, so I could have explained my predicament with more clarity. After the wardens discussed things for a few minutes, they beckoned me toward the helicopter. It would have been nice if my first helicopter ride was under different circumstances, because at this point I thought my hunt was over. After checking my tags back at camp and confirming I was legal, the wardens were kind enough to let me off with a warning. They flew me back to where I was hunting on the tundra, showing me some amazing country along the way. I thanked the wardens as I removed my headset and departed the chopper, grateful they were so understanding. In reality, I'd been granted a free helicopter ride, although I'd paid for it with beads of sweat and rattled nerves. When I met up with Ben later that afternoon, I don't think he believed me at first, but soon he started laughing, and after a few seconds, so did I.

The next morning dawned clear and cold, with the temperature change seeming to keep the black flies at bay. Ben and I once again hunted hard, but the caribou were nowhere to be found. As we worked our way back toward the boat, Ben suddenly brought up his hand and hit his knees. I looked up toward the horizon and saw a large set of antlers moving toward the lake. The bull's rack looked impressive, possessing long tines and multiple bez points on both antlers. We waited until he disappeared below the crest of the ridgeline and then made our move. Sprinting toward the edge of the lake, we then followed the shoreline, trying to get in front of the bull. We hit a shallow depression and stopped to catch our breath, hoping our efforts were not in vain. Then I saw tines coming in our direction as the old monarch angled his way toward the lake. I ranged the bull and came to full draw, settling my pin high on his ribcage and touching the release. Time stood still as yellow fletching spun through the air, their flight culminating in crimson. The bull scorched across the tundra on his death run, soon coming to rest atop a rocky knoll. As I approached the fallen giant, I couldn't believe the character his antlers possessed. The bull's bez points were heavy, his top palms and

shovels distinct. I was blessed to have experienced such good fortune, a surreal ending to a hunt that almost wasn't.

I spent the rest of the trip fishing for brook trout and lakers, capping off an amazing adventure. Quebec will always hold a special place in my heart; and to this day, I can still see that bull standing on the horizon, his antlers silhouetted against a backdrop of blue. Over the next year, I regained strength in my leg, learned to live with the effects of the stroke, and was better for it. The tundra is a magical place, and I am glad that I experienced its beauty firsthand. While the migration never made its way to camp, it didn't bother me in the least. After all, a bowhunter always needs an excuse to go back.

CHAPTER 8

Cypress Shadows

The orange trees flashing past were a welcome surprise, as my northern home was still enveloped in a blanket of ice and snow. It was March of 2006, and my travels had taken me to Zolfo Springs in central Florida, where I hoped to match wits with an Osceola gobbler. Named after the legendary Seminole chief, Osceolas are known to have impressive spurs, dark wing bands, and long legs to better traverse the swamps where they reside. I had been fortunate to harvest the other subspecies of wild turkeys in the United States but had never considered an Osceola hunt until now. I met outfitter David Mills at his ranch house later that evening and could feel the anticipation building, knowing our first morning was only a sunrise away.

Following a great supper and a good night's sleep, we were bouncing along in the pre-dawn darkness toward a cattle pasture near camp. David had seen quite a few birds here in recent weeks, which happened to be a traditional strut zone. I was hunting with Doug Crabtree, a good friend of David's, as well as an accomplished state and national turkey calling champion. He was in town filming with Woodhaven Custom Calls and had already taken a nice longbeard himself. Doug was familiar with the area, and with a limited time frame, I would need all the help I could get. The dawn was slow to arrive and was accompanied by a shield of fog that made it difficult to see. While preparing a natural ground

It was great to be in the Sunshine State.

blind beneath a palmetto tree, I noticed the humidity in the air was stifling, a welcome change from the icy throes of winter I'd left behind. Despite the fog and humidity, the barred owls seemed to care less, greeting us with the familiar melody that turkey hunters know by heart.

"Who-cooks-for-you...Who-cooks-for-you-all," resonated across the pasture.

Much to our dismay, the throaty gobbles that usually follow this classic chorus never transpired, as the foggy conditions had given the gobblers a case of lockjaw. Years of turkey hunting had taught me that on foggy mornings such as this, gobblers will stay tight-lipped until just the right combination of light and mood strikes them. We waited patiently with our backs against the palmettos, listening to the owls chuckle and hoot as the fog burned off the field. The songbirds joined in with a sunrise serenade of their own, just before a thunderous gobble echoed through the morning air. As if making up for lost time, the longbeard continued to hammer from his perch, drowning out a symphony of feathered musicians. We assumed the gobbler wouldn't fly down until the fog cleared, and we were not wrong. Two hours later, we heard wing beats from within the swamp, signifying the gobbler had finally left his roost. Unfortunately, this was the last sound we heard from him that morning. We headed back to the ranch for an early lunch, where we made plans for the afternoon hunt.

A few hours later, we headed into the cypress-choked swamp where the gobbler had flown. David and Doug knew of a clearing in which the birds preferred to strut, and that's where we were headed. We worked our way toward the clearing; each step reverberated through the swamp, making our entry anything but silent. To make our approach seem less intrusive, Doug grunted, growled, and raked the ground, doing his best to imitate the sounds of wild hogs. It seemed to work, as no alarm putts welcomed our approach, which gave us confidence moving forward.

Once we reached the clearing, we set up the blind and arranged our decoys within bow range. We gave our surroundings a few minutes to settle down before Doug began a series of lost calls that emanated through the swamp. Although I had called in many gobblers over the years, my skills paled in comparison to Doug's, who made my efforts sound like a squeaky fence post. Almost immediately, a gobbler hammered back, with a second gobbler following on the coattails of the first. Knowing two longbeards were in the swamp, Doug called more aggressively, hoping to bring them in on a string. The gobblers were reading the script, responding to Doug's calls and getting closer with each response. Then we heard it: subtle purrs and yelps coming from the same direction, revealing a group of hens had joined the party.

Doug motioned for me to pick up my slate and start calling, wanting to fur-ther challenge the hens before they intercepted the gobblers. Doug aggres-sively cackled and cut with his diaphragm, while I responded with soft yelps and clucks on my slate, doing our best impression of good-cop, bad-cop. Our barrage of vocal mimicry continued, as did the hens' agitated rebuttal, with each series drawing the birds closer. Soon my ears picked up the un-mistakable sound of a gobbler drumming, mixed in with the irritated purrs of the hens. I peered through the blind's window, amidst the cypress stumps and green foliage, and could make out four angry hens approaching our setup with full fans in tow.

Side by side, the two gobblers approached the decoys, following the hens on a leash. The hens reached the decoys first, confronting their plastic foes and expressing their anger with body bumps and aggressive purrs. Coming to full draw, I settled my pin on the front tom's vitals and punched the trigger. I knew I had rushed the shot, with my accuracy being as poor as my patience. With feathers and putts flying through the air, we watched the gobbler run back into the swamp. I knew I had struck the bird too low. The odds of recovering a poorly hit gobbler were never good, especially one with his legs and wings about him. We had worked so hard to get here, and I had just let a golden opportunity slip through my hands. Doug and I scoured the swamp and adjacent timber for any sign of my gobbler, but we came up empty-handed.

After spending most of the second day looking for my bird, we had one last evening to hunt and would make the best of it. Late that afternoon, David took us to another property, one with a logging road running through a thick swamp. The area looked like the Amazon, and I wondered how we would ever call a turkey through this jungle, much less get a shot. Within a few minutes the canopy retreated, revealing a clearing surrounded by cypress trees. David said the gobblers would strut in this area before going to roost, and he felt it was our best option.

We set up the Double Bull and arranged our equipment within its spacious confines. Doug would be running a video camera in the hope of getting some footage for an upcoming DVD. I was less than optimistic, feeling more like the poster boy for pessimism. I tried to stay positive but could only think of my missed opportunity. Shadows loomed and grew longer with each passing hour as they fed off the setting sun. I was tempted to pack up, feeling the end of this hunt was a forgone conclusion. Doug had been calling religiously every thirty minutes, hoping a tom would take notice and work his way in. With brushstrokes of crimson and orange painting the western horizon, I looked to my left and almost dropped my bow. A giant longbeard was coming down the logging road, approaching silently as the older toms often do.

I followed the longbeard's steady gait, my fluorescent pin matching his confident stride. Despite the blind's dark interior, the old tom caught the subtle movement of my bow and stopped on a dime. The longbeard raised his head skyward and peered toward the blind, just as I settled my pin and squeezed the release. I saw the arrow spinning through the air, a perfect blur of color and motion, before disappearing into the Osceola's ebony feathers. The tom sprinted off to our right, but within seconds came to rest in the shadow of a cypress tree.

As we approached the fallen gobbler in the fading light, we realized he was an old warrior, with hooked spurs and worn-down wing

Doug and Eyad with their hard-won Osceola.

tips. Doug had captured the entire hunt on video, which I was fortunate to watch on the Outdoor Channel some months later. After a photo session on a cypress stump, I threw the Osceola over my shoulder and reflected on the emotional roller coaster I had experienced. I had given up on the prospect of success and was convinced my first opportunity would be my last. Every now and then, we need a reminder that games can still be won in the bottom of the ninth. I knew this lesson would serve me well, long after the dust had settled on this old gobbler's fan. No matter the species or season, time of year or predicament, I vowed to never again give up on a bowhunt. When I look back on the years since then, I am proud to say that I've kept that promise.

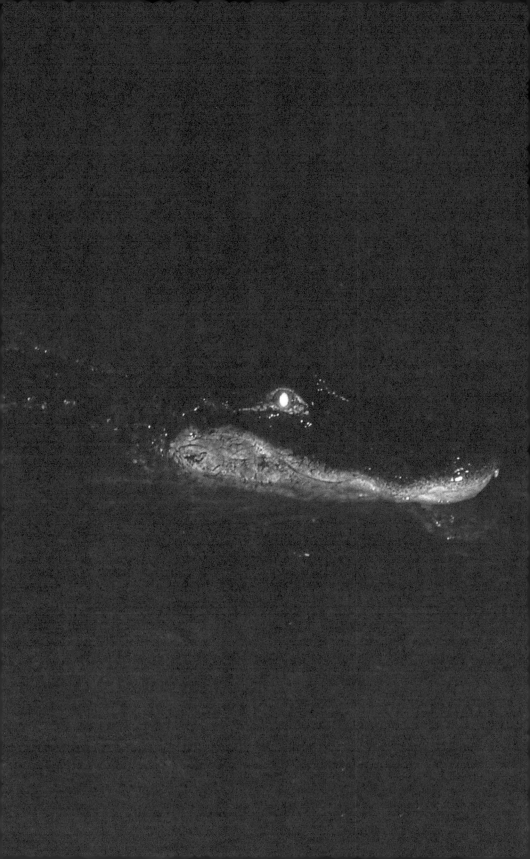

CHAPTER 9

Gator Country

Deep within the swamps and sloughs of Florida, amidst the humid air and cypress trees, swims a reptile of giant proportions. Early Spanish explorers called it *El Lagarto*, but it is known today as the American Alligator. When the temperatures soar, and the heat of summer is upon us, normal bowhunting seasons often close. The southern states, however, still provide a unique bowhunting opportunity for those with an open mind and a sense of adventure.

I had been interested in hunting alligators for some time but could not seem to get away with my busy work schedule. Most of my vacation was used during the fall, when traditional deer and other big game seasons were in full swing. Then, in March of 2006, I decided to push the envelope and make the call. I would be in Florida that June for another commitment and booked the hunt for the same week. Before long I was boarding a plane, awaiting my chance to bowhunt gators in the swamps of Florida.

With powerful jaws and armor-like skin, the American Alligator can grow more than fifteen feet long and weigh nearly a thousand pounds. These cold-blooded monsters are remnants of a time long since past, whose life span can encompass a century. Gators have protective scales called scutes, which act like armored plates. These elevated, spine-like protrusions are arranged in a linear fashion, much like the dragons of fictional lore. Therefore, only two areas are susceptible to arrow penetration: the neck region and just behind the front legs. Both areas comprise softer tissue, which allow a greater chance of penetration. Once arrowed, gators will roll and thrash on the surface of the water before diving into the depths.

Alligators are cold-blooded, which means they can still close their jaws and thrash their tails, even after their heart has stopped beating. This puts your life and limbs at risk, and every precaution must be taken. Securing a gator's jaws with heavy tape and steering clear of its tail are critical after landing one of these prehistoric monsters. Many hunters have suffered broken legs and lacerations while wrestling these beasts, which aren't to be taken lightly.

A few pieces of equipment are necessary before you chase alligators with a bow. Muzzy's Gator Getter kit is a convenient option, as it can be used with your whitetail rig. This kit includes a bobber-like float, specialized reel, and fiberglass–aluminum gator arrows. A heavy-duty line attaches to the barb-tipped arrow, which then leads to the floatation device and reel. It's like watching a rerun of *Jaws* when the arrow strikes home and the bobber is pulled under. Insect repellant and a bug-proof suit, like the Bug Tammer, will make your hunt more enjoyable. Mosquitoes are no strangers to the south, and during the warm summer months they are sure to introduce themselves. A spotlight and headlamp are also critical for nighttime hunts, as spotting the blood-red glow off a gator's retina will point you in the right direction.

Eyad practicing with gator gear.

That June, after my commitments had concluded, I called my friend Brian and picked him up. We had not hunted together in years and were looking forward to the adventure. There are various ways to book a gator hunt, from nuisance tags to special draw units. With time constraints and limited flex-ibility, we chose to hunt with a nuisance trapper near central Florida. The state employs trappers to remove alligators near residential waters, where they pose a threat to humans and their pets. These areas include canals, swamps, ponds, and lakes throughout the state. This would allow us to expe-rience a gator hunt firsthand, learn to use bowfishing equipment, and spend the day on the waters of Florida. Should we succeed and harvest an alligator, the trapper would process the meat and use the proceeds to cover his costs. We were warned that calls may come in while we were hunting, which would require us to remedy the problem, whatever that might be.

Before loading the truck, Brian and I practiced with our bowfishing rigs, making sure they were dialed in. We spent the morning checking various ca-nals and lakes, hoping to catch an alligator bathing in the summer sun. Just past noon, the trapper's phone rang, and he took the call. A large gator was working its way from a canal toward the backyard of a residential property, focused on an elderly woman's Chihuahua. It sounded like a page out of a fictional tabloid, but we were off to investigate nonetheless. As we pulled up to the house, I could hear a woman screaming inside and a dog barking ag-gressively. The trapper grabbed a ten-foot pole with a giant noose attached to the end, which was made to subdue these big reptiles. We headed toward the rear of the house, where a dog the size of a shoebox was yapping at a giant gator. The beast seemed amused as he crawled toward the miniature canine, craving an appetizer before lunch. I don't know if I was more impressed by the gator's arrogance or the canine's courage, but my money was on the gator.

The trapper circled around and lassoed the toothy reptile, which changed the gator's demeanor. The giant's tail whipped back and forth as it rolled across the lawn, hissing and snapping its jaws. Brian and I steered clear, realizing how a situation like this could get out of hand. Soon the trapper was on top of the gator, yelling at us to get back as he taped its jaws shut. Brian and I had no clue what to do but did as we were told, and soon the gator was loaded in the truck. It was an eye-opening experience, and the power these monsters possessed had me shaking my head in disbelief.

The trapper lassoed the gator before it reached the Chihuahua.

The trapper explained that one of the most effective strategies to luring a gator within bow range was to use an alligator distress call. They could become call shy, like any species of game, so he used it sparingly. I had never heard of such a thing, but again, was green as a cucumber in the ways of gator hunting. If the right situation presented itself, it was a tactic we would employ. Our next stop was at a large pond adjacent to a canal. The trapper snuck over the dam and suddenly took a knee. He motioned for us to do the same. We crept over the rise, where I could see a gator's nostrils protruding from the water. The ridges along the gator's back glistened like polished steel in the midday sun as the beast lie motionless near the shore. We retraced our steps, circling around to the far end of the pond, using the cattails as cover. Once we were set, the trapper motioned me forward into the cattails, explaining he would work his way back before turning on the electronic call. We hoped the gator would respond and work along the edge of the shore where I was lying in wait. It seemed like a crazy plan destined to fail, but we would give it a shot. Hidden within the rigid stalks, I heard the most unique sound, as a piercing, high-pitched shriek emanated from the electronic device.

"Eeek Eeek Eek Eek Eek."

I had heard nothing like it. But as I looked back toward the gator, it was coursing along the shore and coming straight at me. It was happening so fast, I didn't know what to do. I came to full draw as a V-shaped ripple announced the reptile's arrival. The gator cruised toward the distress call, now almost within bow range, its vertical, cat-like pupils constricted beneath the midday sun. As the gator slithered past, I placed my pin on its neck and touched the release. The beast vanished into the depths with my arrow, but to my surprise, the bobber showed no signs of submerging.

I reeled my line in with reckless abandon. The spool became entangled, forcing me to retrieve the line hand-over-hand. Wrapping the line across my palm like a kite string, I felt a weight resist my efforts. It was subtle at first, but soon became more evident, which I knew could mean only one thing. Pulling with everything I had, a white object suddenly materialized from the depths. It slowly came to the surface and revealed itself as the pale, white underbelly of an alligator. The arrow had centered the spinal column, directly behind the ear, and the beast had expired within seconds. We drug the 7-foot gator to the shoreline, where we quickly taped its jaws, knowing it was better to be safe than sorry.

As the air cooled and darkness enveloped the Sunshine State, we backed the trapper's boat into the canal. We had the spotlight ready and were hoping to get Brian an opportunity. My eyelids were heavy, but I was looking forward to the experience of a nighttime encounter. We slid along with a trolling motor, checking isolated bays and inlets, looking for the glow of a gator's eyes. A few hours later, we entered a hidden cove where a pair of red eyes found our spotlight.

Eyad with his Florida gator.

Brian filled his tag in the wee hours of the morning.

The motor purred toward the crimson-colored orbs, and at five yards, Brian released his arrow. The fight was on as Brian battled the gator into the night, holding on as the beast dove and rolled through the black water. It was nearly 2:00 AM when we brought the gator in, having to ground the boat and wrestle him to shore. We were exhausted but elated, finding it difficult to hide our smiles as we headed back to the docks.

Brian and I learned a great deal on our Florida adventure, experiencing a side of bowhunting few know exists. It was an incredible hunt, and the privilege of sharing it with a good friend made it more memorable. Alligator hunting is not for everyone. But if summer rolls around and you get the bowhunting bug, these toothy giants may be just the medicine you need.

CHAPTER 10

Waiting on Water

Bowhunting pronghorns had always been on my radar, and in the fall of 2006, I finally got my chance. The speed goats of the West possess characteristics unlike any other North American species, with black horns and shades of white mixed into their tan coat. With speed and vision second to none, they are a worthy adversary for any bowhunter. While many Western states harbor good numbers of antelope, none are as legendary or renowned as Wyoming.

That spring, I called Miller Outfitting in Gillette, Wyoming, and asked about availability for a September bowhunt. Doug Miller, the owner, informed me they had one spot remaining for mid-September and that I was welcome to come. Not needing to be asked twice, I jumped at the opportunity, and before I knew it September had arrived. During my rehab from the stroke, I became immersed in bodybuilding competitions and training, finding myself in better shape than before the incident. The week I was scheduled to hunt with Miller Outfitting was unfortunately a few days before a bodybuilding competition in New York City. I had qualified for this event and wanted to finish what I started. Despite trying to separate each trip by two weeks, it just wasn't in the cards. Along with the stressors of a new job, I was cutting calories and doing cardio in the weeks leading up to the event. Simply put, I was running low on energy.

Although I shoot year-round, I pick up the pace in the weeks preceding any hunt. Fine-tuning my equipment, choosing the appropriate clothes, and situational shooting all become relevant. Yet this year, I was so exhausted from training and work that I found little time to prepare. Still, my bow and arrow combination was shooting well, and I was confident that I could place an accurate arrow.

Various tactics exist to hunt antelope, but the most effective is sitting on water holes scattered across the arid grasslands of the West. Decoying rutting bucks can also be an effective strategy, but one not usually employed this time of year. The weather had been horribly dry in Wyoming, perhaps the best news a waterhole hunter could ask for, as rain can make this tactic a wasted venture. If the weather stayed the course, there was a good chance I'd get an opportunity, even with the limited number of days I had to hunt.

In mid-September, I left Iowa and arrived in Rapid City, South Dakota. There I rented a car and drove west to Gillette. The scenery was breathtaking. Rust-colored rocks, sagebrush flats, and a vast landscape stirred images of the Wild West. I arrived at the ranch later that night where I met Doug Miller and the rest of the crew. To prepare for the upcoming bodybuilding competition, I needed to consume excessive amounts of water and protein in the next two weeks. That need sent me traveling to the local Walmart with one of Doug's guides, where I purchased bottled water, beef jerky, and almonds for the week ahead. With my equipment and cooler in check, I was ready for my first morning in Wyoming.

Welcome to Wyoming

I awoke early the next day and quickly got dressed, finding the temperature cool and the wind nonexistent. Barreling into the truck with Doug and a few other bowhunters, we bounced around until we arrived at the bottom of a large basin. I gathered my gear and worked toward the waterhole, knowing I wouldn't emerge until well after dark. I was setup nicely and knew my chances were good if the drought-like conditions persisted.

As the sun's rays illuminated my surroundings, I saw a bone-dry grassland encasing the blind in all directions. The temperatures approached triple digits each day, and there was no cover in sight. How anything could survive in this country was beyond me. Only thirty feet across, the drinking hole was small but held a decent amount of water. The edge of the water was littered with tracks, proving that quite a few pronghorns had been visiting this oasis with regularity.

After nocking an arrow and placing my bow on the ground, I arranged my stool and pack within the blind. My water bottles, beef jerky, and almonds were removed for easy access, a buffet of nutrition at my disposal. Once settled, I grabbed a water bottle and removed the cap, tipping the beverage back for a quick drink. I leaned into the window as I drank, glanced toward the water hole, and almost choked on my Aquafina. There at the edge of the water was a small doe—and right behind her a nice buck. Cautiously approaching the oasis, the buck paused before proceeding, allowing the doe to test the proverbial waters. With bottles surrounding me like bowling pins, I was hesitant to reach for my bow, fearful a domino effect of water and plastic would ensue. In time, I was able to lift my bow and turn it upright before quickly attaching my release. The buck was now at the water's edge, drinking with his head down, allowing me to come to full draw.

With the sun cresting the horizon and my green, twenty-yard pin floating on his tan coat, I squeezed the release. My arrow disappeared low and just behind his elbow, which saw the buck whirl and sprint across the prairie. Elation was soon replaced with guilt and dread as I watched the buck bed down with his head held high. He remained vigilant, proving my arrow had missed his vitals, and that I was in for a challenging recovery.

With no change in the pronghorn's demeanor, I called Doug, who agreed I should try to close on the buck. In the vast expanse of open country that is Wyoming, there was no risk of visibly losing the antelope, and I wanted to end this hunt as humanely as possible. I exited the blind and circled around, soon finding myself within 40 yards of the buck. As the pronghorn stood and slowly walked away, I steadied my pin on his vitals and touched the release. The arrow arced through the air and settled behind his shoulder, and the buck came to rest among the sage.

I approached the trophy antelope and noticed he carried impressive horns and a gorgeous cape. I was surprised at how small they are, but also how strikingly beautiful. His horns had heavy bases and sharp, curved tips. I could not imagine a more perfect animal. We took some photographs before heading to the locker where the buck was processed and caped. I spent the next day driving through Wyoming, enjoying the sights and sounds of the Cowboy State. Standing before Devil's Tower, I took it all in, realizing how fortunate I was to experience such things.

The New York bodybuilding competition came and went, and while it was a great experience, it was tough to beat my Wyoming adventure. Bowhunting can be the most difficult endeavor to pursue, but at other times, one of the easiest. I try to embrace opportunities when they arise, whether they occur in the first hour or on the last day. This said, I also had the chance to explore new country, share stories around camp, and meet some incredible people—things I couldn't have done sitting in a blind. My only regret is not practicing more, as perhaps my first arrow would have found its mark with a steadier aim. Still, the emotions that followed taught me many lessons, reminding me to practice with purpose and precision, and be prudent in the shots I take. I hope to hunt pronghorns again one day, but the next time around, I bet Wyoming makes me wait a little longer.

Eyad's Wyoming Pronghorn

CHAPTER 11

Tusks and Tennessee

The incessant buzzing in my ear had stopped, which I knew could mean only one thing. Sure enough, the mosquito began its feast, an assault I could do little about. I was in central Florida on the tail end of an Osceola hunt, trying my hand at wild boar. The terrain was best described as open pasture, with thick palmettos and grass surrounding its borders. Rain had been a common occurrence, and when coupled with the humidity, it made for the perfect mosquito breeding ground. The wild pig I'd been stalking was almost in range, hence my inability to rebel against the bloodsucker. I just needed a few more yards and the right angle for an opportunity to present itself. The swine eventually turned in my direction, and I laced an arrow through its vitals. The boar soon expired, ending yet another exciting hunt for wild hogs.

The history of wild boar in North America dates back centuries. There are innate differences between feral hogs and Russian Boar. In 1539, Spanish explorers led by Hernando De Soto first introduced domestic pigs to North America. Thirteen pigs were brought to Tampa, Florida, where they were used for food and trade with Native Americans. These pigs soon escaped into the wild and became feral or wild hogs. Perhaps this is why De Soto is considered the "father of the American pork industry." At the time of De Soto's death three years later, their numbers had risen to nearly 700. It wasn't until 1912, almost 400 years later, that Russian wild boar were brought to the states by George Moore near Hoopers Bald, North Carolina. He was given access to 1,600 acres to build a hunting preserve filled with various game. But only the Russian boars flourished. These Razorbacks escaped and began interbreeding with feral hogs, leading to the hybrid strains so prevalent today. Hogs can vary in appearance and size, with most being dark black or brown in color. Males carry the larger tusks and average 200 pounds, whereas females are much smaller in both body weight and tusk length.

Over the years, I've been fortunate to hunt wild boar a handful of times, mostly in the southern states. Texas and Florida have offered ample opportunity at free-range hogs, but my fondest memories lie in Tennessee. The Volunteer State has seen its share of problems with wild pigs as they have invoked billions of dollars' worth of damage. In 1999, the state allowed year 'round hunting of this invasive species, only to see the hogs spread like Kudzu vines. To expand hunting opportunities, hunters introduced pigs into areas they were absent before—a mistake Tennessee couldn't undo. What once was a fifteen-county problem, escalated to eighty of Tennessee's ninety-five counties having sizable boar populations. Wild boars by nature are omnivorous, eating everything from grain and nuts to small mammals and insects. Farmers took notice as the pigs rooted up their freshly planted crops, harassed livestock, and spread disease. It didn't take long for another policy shift to take place. In 2011, wild boar were deemed a nuisance species in Tennessee, which for the most part, meant only landowners with special permits could hunt. This caused quite the uproar among local hunters, as many Tennesseans have hunted wild boar for decades.

My first experience hunting these tusked beasts took place near Jamestown, Tennessee, long before the regulation changes. Jamestown is in Fentress County, on the edge of the Cumberland Mountains in the northern part of the state. My good friend Don accompanied me on the hunt, one we were chomping at the bit to experience. It was late December and the roads were ominous, coated with black ice that teased the back of my Ford. We arrived at Crooked Creek Hunting Lodge near midnight, where we met Buck Pierce, owner and operator. Buck showed us to our quarters and detailed what time we should be ready to go. The weather front chasing us across the state had settled in, greeting us with a blanket of snow and ice the next morning.

Crooked Creek is classified as a high-fence operation, and like other outfitters, must be to operate legally in Tennessee. Most who have hunted hogs, however, will tell you that fences are little more than a formality. No matter the region, hogs seem to find their way into any acreage they see fit, and this 1,200-acre preserve was no different. Crooked Creek uses various methods to hunt wild boar but prefers hounds to trail these testy pigs. Mountain Curs led our crew; these keen-smelling canines were trained to track and bay up wild boar from a young age. This is a more traditional way to hunt these ebony swine, and being an ardent upland hunter in years past, I was curious to see how the dogs worked. Navigating the mountainous terrain was challenging, with ice-covered hillsides and steep gorges throughout the property.

Less than an hour into the hunt, with snow beginning to fall again, we heard barks resounding from an icy trench. We crested the ridgeline to see a large hog charging the dogs, swiping at them with razor sharp tusks. I was up to bat first, making my way toward the howling hounds with bow in hand. The boar was defiant and kept fighting off the dogs, moving deeper into the thicket. Eventually, I made my way to the bottom, where I saw the pig on the edge of a creek bank, protesting the hounds' assault. In no time, I was face-to-face with the menacing brute, attaching my release as I prepared for the shot. There was a cedar tree to my left, which I used for cover before stepping into the open. I might as well have been a matador with a red cape, because in the next instant, the boar charged me like a bull. I dropped my bow and swung behind the cedar, just as a midnight-colored flash swiped at my leg. I picked up my bow and noticed the hog had turned and was now facing me again. My pin settled between his shoulder blades, and luckily my arrow found its mark.

After getting the hog back to camp, we were back in the bottoms on the trail of another boar. Don was closing in on the barking hounds, trying to position himself for a shot. The hog's raven colors stood out against the backdrop of snow, while crystalline flakes continued to fall. Don made good on his opportunity with a perfect arrow, ending a quick yet exciting hunt. We had taken two nice boars in a matter of hours and experienced a traditional Tennessee hunt to boot.

We were set to leave the next day, packed up and ready to hit the road. We met up with Buck in his office to pay our final tab and asked to whom the check should be made. Buck said that making it out to Crooked Creek or Buck Pierce would be fine. Always light-hearted and quick-witted, Don commented that it was a good thing Buck's last name wasn't *Naked*. With

Don and Eyad with their Tennessee wild boars.

crickets for an audience, the joke fell on deaf ears. We shook hands and left awkwardly. We were sitting in my truck when Buck came walking toward us, with enough gusto that we knew something was wrong. Don rolled down the window to see what the matter was, and Buck questioned, "Is this some kind of joke?"

He handed Don's check back to him, which was written in perfect penmanship:

Pay To The Order Of: *Buck Naked*

Somehow, Don's joke had possessed his hand to write exactly what he was thinking. Don quickly remedied the situation with a new check, and after a few half-hearted laughs we sped out of Tennessee.

Buck must not have been too upset, for he welcomed my friends and me back four years later. This time, I was accompanied by Gary and Ryan, two of my best friends from back home. You might recall Gary and Ryan from an earlier turkey hunting story, and with school starting that fall we didn't see each other much. It was Christmas break, and we wanted to spend time together, so we all decided to arrange a boar hunt at Crooked Creek. Another weather front followed us across the state, this one more frigid than four years prior. Tennessee was supposed to be warmer than our Iowa home, but my limited experience had proved otherwise. Buck was there to greet us and show us to our cabin, where we found much needed rest. The next morning, we saddled up and headed out among the craggy bluffs and ice-covered hillsides.

We wanted Gary to have the first opportunity, and the hounds didn't take long to locate a boar. Gary moved in and settled his pin, only to see the hog move and take the arrow in the shoulder. With hardly any penetration, thanks to the boar's rigid shoulder plate, the hog sprinted out of the bottom. Moments later, Gary's second arrow found the pig's shoulder blade once again, yielding the same result. The dogs could not contain the pig and soon lost him over a cliff face. We scoured the bottom and ridgeline, but with too many pigs in the area, the dogs found it difficult to focus on the wounded boar.

Gary was disappointed and felt terrible about the situation. Buck said they would keep an eye out for the hog, but not to hold our breath, as these critters were tough as nails. The hours passed with little action until sunset encased the mountains. Just then, the dogs bayed and hollered, indicating they had found another hog. Moving down the ridge, we saw a mature boar facing the curs, swiping at the hounds with glistening tusks. Not wanting to take another chance, Gary removed his sidearm and dispatched the boar with a single shot. What followed was one of the most amazing revelations I've ever seen in the timber. Not only was this boar a solid specimen, but it was the same animal Gary had lost that morning. Both broadheads looked like thumb tacks through the boar's grizzled coat, barely piercing the shoulder blade. Wild boar are regarded as one of the toughest animals in the woods, and after witnessing Gary's hunt, I wouldn't disagree. Gary couldn't believe it and was all smiles in the fading light, his disappointment now a fleeting memory.

The dogs were still hammering as we packed up, which motivated me to work in that direction. Sure enough, another large boar was on the ridgeline, batting away the hounds like a fly swatter. I circled around and placed an arrow behind the hog's shoulder, hoping that would be enough. The beast sprinted down the ridge and into a cave, leaving me no choice but to follow. Perhaps foolishly, I worked my way down the embankment toward the cavern, where I heard the boar growling in the darkness. Able to visualize his outline in the cave, I placed a final arrow, which ended the hunt. We processed the boars that night and got some rest, our legs feeling the effects of a long day.

The next morning was one of the coldest on record, with overcast conditions and blowing snow. Ryan had the only tag left, but wanting to experience more of the hunt, I went along to keep him company. I questioned that decision a short time later, because my feet and hands were freezing in the brutal cold. We were stationed in a ground blind made up of old logs and blowdowns, hoping the limbs would shield us from the elements. Wishing I had dressed more appropriately, my thoughts were interrupted by footsteps upon frozen leaves. A single line of hogs was coming down the trail, moving past our blind at a steady gait. Ryan has always been an incredible shot, and his smooth release on the biggest hog was textbook. With perfect arrow placement, the boar didn't go far, soon tumbling in the falling snow. Like my first hunt years ago, we had found success on the Cumberland Plateau, amidst the blowing snow and freezing conditions.

Gary moving in for the shot.

Whether it be free range or high fence, sitting in a treestand or following hounds, wild boar offer something for every hunter. Despite man's encroachment, they continue to thrive, with numbers growing at a steady rate. Although many states offer bowhunting opportunities, my trips to Tennessee will always hold a special place in my heart. Time spent with close friends

Ryan and Gary

and memorable moments are among the reasons why, and I wouldn't trade those icy memories for anything. Sadly, it was the last time I would hunt with Gary, a man who taught me so much, and who was more like a father than a friend. He would lose his battle with cancer years later, a fight he took on valiantly. I remember shooting my bow the afternoon of his visitation, the weather calm and cold, typical of late November in Iowa. The sun was setting in the west, its orange embers painting the barren hardwoods in a golden hue. I stood there in silence, thinking of our fishing trips to Canada, the love of turkey hunting he bestowed upon me, and a deep-hearted laugh I would never forget. I'm glad we experienced one last hunt together, and I know he's in a better place, smiling down with memories of Tennessee.

CHAPTER 12

Lone Star Lessons

I can still recall the turkey hunting videos I watched as a teenager, long before DVDs and Internet shows dominated the outdoor market. One of my favorites was Realtree's *Springtime Memories*, a video dedicated to spring turkey hunting across North America. Every time I watched that VHS tape, I was captivated by the Texas hunts, with their mesquite trees, rattlesnakes, and hard-gobbling Rio Grande turkeys. Prolific and easy to fool, these Lone Star longbeards were the bobber-and-bluegills of the turkey world, gobbling their heads off as they approached with reckless abandon. As a 15-year-old kid, easy was all right by me, and I couldn't wait to practice self-defense on these Texas Rios. My expectations were quickly curtailed, however, when in 1998 my dad and I embarked on our first Lone Star adventure. Although I harvested a jake with my 12-gauge and made lasting memories with my father, it brought me back to reality regarding Texas and its turkeys. These gobblers were anything but easy. And should I ever aspire to take a Rio with my bow, I had a feeling that Texas would make me earn it.

It would be many years before I returned to Texas, this time with more experience and much less naivety. By that time in my life, I was committed to the stick and string and had tasted some success on Midwest gobblers. I would be hunting the Spike Box Ranch in west Texas and was looking forward to the opportunity. The first morning I was hunting in a blind overlooking a large expanse of mesquite. I had moved in on a loud-mouthed longbeard and quickly set up the Double Bull blind. After nocking an arrow and getting situated, I called softly, hoping the longbeard would be interested in a date. Soon the tell-tale sounds of a strutting gobbler found my ears, which caused my heartbeat to accelerate. Catching movement from the corner of my eye, I saw a mature Rio working his way into my setup—spitting, drumming, and side-stepping his way in.

Diamondback Rattlesnake

Eyad's first archery Rio.

Seconds later, I watched as my arrow passed through the gobbler, striking him just behind the wing butt. The longbeard stumbled, regained his composure, and then scurried off into the thick cover. I was told to never leave a wounded gobbler in this part of Texas, predator rich with no shortage of jaws and claws. I did not heed that warning, waiting the customary thirty minutes after the shot. Any arrowed game needed time, and although this mindset would serve me well in the years to come, in this situation it did not. I found what was left of my gobbler nearly an hour later, not far from the entrance to a coyote den, with nothing to celebrate but a few feathers and the promise of another day. On my last evening, despite missing a shot and having an encounter with a testy diamondback rattler, I tagged a jake with a perfectly placed arrow. While I was thrilled to harvest a Rio with my bow, the desire to take a mature Texas longbeard still burned within.

The following spring, I returned to the Spike Box Ranch with unfortunately the same results. Although I was snakebit in Texas and knew that Kansas and Oklahoma had great numbers of Rios, I was bound and determined to take a mature longbeard in the Lone Star State. After talking to friends who had taken Rios in Texas, I decided to try a private ranch near the Mexican border. It would be a change of scenery and a chance to experience something different. The rancher sounded confident that he had enough gobblers to give me a quality hunt, and at this point I was up for anything. In early April, I flew from Iowa to San Antonio, rented a car, and then headed south toward the ranch. This south Texas country was beautiful, with wildflowers painting the landscape in a spectrum of colors. A few hours later I arrived at the ranch, had a quick bite to eat and got settled. Checking my bow, arrows, and broadheads is a ritual any traveling bowhunter can appreciate, and I was glad to see my equipment was in check. The landowner had a friend who lived on the ranch and maintained it year 'round, transporting hunters in search of turkeys, deer, doves, and wild boar.

The next morning, accompanied by a few hunters from California, we loaded up the rancher's truck and headed out. I was dropped off well before sunrise at a permanent blind, with a small water hole within bow range. I was instructed to sit there until noon, at which point they would pick me up and consider our options. This wasn't what I had in mind, but I would give it a chance with the dry conditions. Unfortunately, the morning proved uneventful, as I heard only a few gobbles on the adjacent property. When the truck pulled up just a few minutes past noon, I asked if I could walk the ranch and try my luck in different areas. The rancher said that was fine. They would eat lunch and then check on me later that afternoon.

Although the temperatures were predicted to hit the low 90s, I stayed the course and kept hunting. The ranch encompassed thousands of acres, so I was at no risk of running out of real estate. But I questioned my sanity with a cloudless sky, scorching temps, and anything but good luck on my side. I sauntered through a sauna for nearly an hour before taking a break in the shade of a mesquite tree. Back on the trail a short time later, I soon found what I was looking for. Stretching toward the horizon was a long sendero, painted with purple and yellow wildflowers across its expanse. The area had the makings of a classic strut zone, with a patch of trees offering a shaded sanctuary for my blind. After checking for cactus bushes and rattlesnakes in the grass below, I erected my Double Bull and placed my decoys on the sendero. With hardly a gobble over the past few hours and nothing to lose, I threw a series of calls across the Texas landscape. My first sequence of lonesome, love-sick yelps went unanswered, as did the second, without so much as a courtesy gobble. I scratched out one more series of yelps, purrs, and cuts, wiped the sweat from my brow, and then sat back inside the sweltering blind.

The heat inside the blind was stifling. I tried to ignore it as beads of sweat dripped from my nose. I wondered if the other hunters were toasting my stupidity at the local restaurant, taking bets as to how long I'd last. I looked up and exhaled with exacerbation—then did a double take. Not 50 yards from my blind was a gobbler in full strut. Once I realized the heat was not playing tricks on me, I grabbed my bow, fixated on the full fan pirouetting between the cactuses and wildflowers. Slowly but surely, the gobbler made his way toward the decoys, with worn down wingtips tracing his course. Perhaps I was too hot and tired to get nervous, or maybe my southern setbacks had taught me to keep my emotions in check. No matter the reason for my apathy, I was calm and collected, waiting patiently for the gobbler to turn broadside. With bronze and black feathers illuminated beneath the Texas sun, the gobbler side-stepped before slowly turning to his left. As if on cue, my arrow was gone, cartwheeling the gobbler across the sendero. Drenched and shaking— a combination of the heat and excitement I'm sure—I escaped the blind to collect my prize. The air outside hit me like an arctic blast, a welcome relief from the sweltering heat, although not as comforting as tagging my Texas longbeard.

Carefully setting my camera on the tripod, I programmed the timer and then hustled back for a photo. Texas got the last laugh, as somehow I sat on a clump of cactus while posing for the picture. I doubt the other hunters in town heard my cries that afternoon, but I wouldn't be surprised if they did. It was a fitting end to my Lone Star adventure, one in which nothing had come easily. The essence of bowhunting has always been the challenge, and Texas proved to be no exception. As I admired my gobbler's thick beard and handsome fan, I thought back through the years, recalling the stories and videos that made hunting Rios seem so easy. Filling my tag had gone from a foregone conclusion to an impossible task, but I enjoyed the journey. While I contemplated how to remove the cactus needles from my backside, I heard the rancher's truck rumbling down the sendero. He pulled up beside me, glanced down at the Rio's tail protruding from my pack and questioned, "Looks like you have a story to tell me?" Hobbling into the truck with a grimace on my face, all I could say was, "You have no idea."

Eyad's Lone Star Longbeard

CHAPTER 13

Hide and Seek

The highway looked dark and lonely in the early morning hours as I drove north toward the Hawkeye State. I had slept little the night before, the caffeine and anticipation now masking my fatigue. I arrived well before sunrise and positioned my blind on a grassy knoll, knowing the longbeards preferred this pasture. The weather was perfect, with temperatures just cool enough to keep the mosquitoes at bay. Despite the ideal conditions, the hardwoods remained silent, save for the songbirds that never disappoint. My eyelids grew heavy as the sun climbed higher, the coffee finally running out of steam. In time, I found myself on the floor of the blind, the soft grass feeling like a hammock on a lazy summer day.

A few hours later I awoke, feeling better but surprised I had slept so long. I thought a gobble had woken me from my slumber, but I couldn't be sure. Arising like a periscope, I slowly peered out the blind's window. Five longbeards were marching toward my decoys, a wall of black iridescence against an indigo sky. I picked up my bow and carefully turned the limbs upright, never taking my eyes off the approaching posse. The gobblers were soon parading around my decoy spread, inspecting the lifeless forms as they swayed in the wind.

Coming to full draw, I waited until the flock gave me an ethical opening and then dropped the string. My arrow struck the bird in the lower thigh, which had me scrambling for a second arrow. The tom hobbled through the pasture, not mortally wounded but injured nonetheless. His comrades, seeing an opportunity to reduce the gene pool, pursued with malevolence on their minds, determined to finish the job the arrow had not. With his wings and wits still about him, the gobbler veered left and headed for cover, trying to escape the wrath of the longbeards. He found sanctuary within the shadows of a cedar tree, where he remained still, hoping the toms would cease and desist. The gang seemed satisfied with his exile, moving on to greener pastures, leaving me to deal with my own problems. Delivering a second arrow would be a tall order, so I cautiously left the blind, hoping he would expire.

A few hours later, I returned with bow in hand. The blind was still positioned in the pasture, which provided cover as I crawled back to the scene of the crime. As I approached the blind, I saw the gobbler was still beneath the cedar, his white head erect and aware of my presence. This wasn't what I expected, and just as those thoughts crossed my mind, he stood and raced for the timber. I lost him among the maze of blowdowns and multiflora rose, not having a clue where he went. I crept along, inspecting every bush and shadow, trying to determine where he was hiding. Reaping the rewards of warmer weather, the foliage had come to life, which added difficulty to my pursuit. I had not heard wing beats upon his retreat, nor rapid footsteps atop the forest floor. He had to be close.

As I slowed to step over a deadfall, the gobbler rose from a tangle of branches and scurried away. There was no chance I would catch him, knowing if he made the CRP field at the edge of the property it was game over. I dropped my bow and took a hard left, leaving the forest for the open expanse of the pasture. Cutting back to my right, I sprinted down the timberline, parallel to his direction of travel. Wounded turkeys usually fly or run in a straight line, and I hoped this one had read the playbook.

Once I reached the CRP, I reentered the timber, again surrounded by briars and brush piles. With no bow and little confidence, I sprinted back toward the blind hoping to cut him off. I came over a small rise and met the gobbler head-on, his bewildered expression matching mine. He put on the brakes and spun around, sprinting back toward the field with me in hot pursuit. I felt branches swiping at my face and eyes, like a cartoon running through a haunted woodlot. A cluster of multiflora rose grabbed my left thigh, its thorns ripping my pants and leg in one fell swoop. Even with one good leg the turkey was gaining ground. He was now almost to the field edge where open space and daylight awaited us both.

Tripping on a deadfall, I jumped back to my feet and over the fence, regaining my momentum. The gobbler was in the field now and running across it—a race I joined in short order. My face and arms were a map of abrasions, my chest was on fire, and I could feel an open wound on my left thigh. I was almost within reach of the gobbler, racing across the pasture with "Chariots of Fire" playing in my mind. Then the longbeard did the unexpected: he ferociously flapped his wings until he was airborne. Gliding only a few feet above the pasture, the gobbler tried to gain altitude, leaving me no choice but to throw my own Hail Mary.

Iowa 2003

I dove through the air, cumbersome as a newborn calf, grabbing the tom's tail in midflight. We tumbled together through the pasture, his legs kicking my chest and shoulders as I held on for dear life. The longbeard's powerful wings slapped both sides of my face like a punching bag, their rhythmic assault disorienting. Battling a butterball in an Iowa hayfield wasn't on my bucket list, but I could mark it off just the same. I soon lost my grip, leaving me with a handful of tail feathers, before sprinting forward and tackling the tom once more. With feathers littered about the pasture and more scratches than I could count, I finally had my 2003 Iowa gobbler.

The next spring, after a successful Merriam's hunt in western Nebraska, I was back in the Hawkeye State. A barred owl threw out the morning's first pitch, and a gobbler responded with his own wake-up call. I scratched out a series of soft tree yelps on my slate, which also caught the longbeard's attention. He cut-off my next calling sequence with a thunderous gobble—confirming he was interested. Sure enough, the old boy waltzed in right off the roost, with a confident swagger all spring monarch's exhibit. Once he was broadside, I settled my pin and laced an arrow through the gobbler. He cartwheeled and sprinted back into the timber where I quickly lost sight of him.

I escaped the blind and hurried over to the timber's edge, hoping to see the longbeard lying still. Contrary to my wishes, there was nothing but a vacant forest with no sign to speak of. I was still gun-shy from last year's circus, and if the gobbler was hidden in this timber, I would be better prepared this time. I called Don and his son, Seth, two of my best friends, and explained my dilemma. The plan was to execute a well-orchestrated turkey drive and pin down the tom between us. I had a feeling he was still in the timber, and if Don and Seth could circle around and work back toward my position, perhaps we had a chance.

We were back at the pasture within a couple of hours and set up accordingly. Don and Seth were on the far side of the woodlot, along the edge of the CRP. I was on the other side with bow in hand, lying in wait. There

was a good possibility the gobbler was already gone, as it had been some time since my departure. I nocked an arrow and took a knee, waiting for the drive to commence. A few minutes later I heard Don yell, "Eyad, he's coming your way!"

I looked ahead through the timber and could see a white head bobbing in my direc-

Seth and Eyad—2004

tion. Already at full draw, I settled my pin on his beard and dropped the string; the tom fell a split second later. The drive had worked to perfection, as the tom was buried in a brush pile, flushing when Don slowed to navigate the terrain. Without the help of two friends and a little luck, the gobbler would have remained a mystery.

Eyad set up his blind and decoys the night before.

The following spring, I was back in Iowa, stationed in the same pasture. I was setup near a grove of ancient oaks where a gobbler had been roosting all week. I was using a new broadhead called the Gobbler Guillotine, a four-bladed beast devised for head and neck shots. It was new on the market and an interesting concept. I found the broadhead to be accurate with stiff arrows, long feathers, and aggressive helical. Four colored straws were to be placed over the blades to better control airflow and accuracy. The straws were fluorescent orange, which made them easy to see in the dark confines of my blind. The night before, I had erected my Double Bull under the cover of darkness, placing the decoys within 10 yards of my ambush. I returned early the next morning, entered the blind, and eagerly awaited first light. The gobbler hammered soon after, responding to a train whistle in the distance. He was much closer than I thought, and I dared not make a sound. The decoys were surely visible from his perch, which I hoped would be enough.

Storming in off the roost at first light, the gobbler wasted little time. He slid under an electric cattle fence just past the decoys before returning to full strut. I settled my pin on the bird's wattles, trying to calm my shaking hands. The gobbler stopped on a dime, catching a flash of the fluorescent straws as they hovered near the blind's window. At the shot, I heard a strange sound and then saw the gobbler take flight. This wasn't your casual glide or puddle jump, but full throttle ascent. I stuck my head out the window and watched as he rose above the oak trees and disappeared into the hardwoods. I must have hit the cattle fence, or my ears were playing tricks on me. No matter; the gobbler was good as gone, and there was nothing I could do about it.

Guillotine Gobbler 2005

A short time later the skies opened with a torrential downpour that continued for hours. It was so intense that I had to shut the blind's windows to have a chance of staying dry. Around lunch time, I threw in the towel, but decided to walk out in the direction the gobbler had flown. I thought finding a few mushrooms would help my mood, so off I went. The timber was still fairly open, the limbs dripping like a leaky faucet from the recent downpour. I had gone 200 yards when I looked up and saw what appeared to be a black trash bag. Soaking wet and stiff, the gobbler was lying among the leaves, seeming to have perished in flight. There was a perfect slice across the base of his neck, where one blade had caught him; hence, the sound my ears had picked up. I hadn't seen him fall from the sky, but if not for my morel addiction, I never would have looked.

A few years later, I was back in the heartland on the cusp of the 2008 season. The past few springs had been exciting, but thankfully hadn't included any goal line stands. The farm I was hunting was a good distance away, requiring an early morning wake-up call. The air was crisp and cold when I arrived two hours later, with the sky bathed in an ocean of stars. As I walked across the picked cornfield in the moonlight, I noticed the morning felt more like November than early April. Wearing thermal underwear and a stocking cap, I saw frost glistening off the broken stalks, reminding me that spring was still on the disabled list.

The property consisted of vast cornfields with timber strips along its borders. The turkeys would roost in the timbered areas and then fly down into the agricultural fields. I chose to set up on the highest point in the cornfield, where a gobbler could see the decoys and consider my invitation. The woods awoke a short time later as barred owls and tom turkeys exchanged insults. The owls continued their onslaught, hooting and hollering until the gobblers left the limb.

A short time later, I looked to my right and saw a gobbler in full strut a good distance away. He was alone, a bachelor ripe for the picking. He seemed to favor my setup and sound, gobbling at every yelp, cackle, and cut while slowly zigzagging in my direction. It wasn't fast or smooth, but within the hour he was at 20 yards and closing. I should have been more patient, but his slow and steady approach made it difficult. The gobbler was still working his way toward the decoys when I settled my pin and fired a fastball right over his fan. I wasn't sure what happened, but the gobbler was not sticking around to find out.

The decision I made next wasn't the right one, but in the interest of honesty, I let the excitement get the best of me. A second shot at 40 yards saw my arrow veer left into the gobbler's chest, knocking him backward into the corn stubble. Back on his feet and taking flight, the gobbler looked like a jetliner ascending high above the tree line. Hammering his wings with the intensity of a band saw, he slowed and settled deep within the timber. I knew the significance of his flight pattern and it wasn't good. I had the bird dead to rights but instead fired a warning shot over his head. Fast bows don't make up for bad decisions, and I never should have taken that second shot. I was so upset with myself that I left my blind and marched straight for the timber. On a fool's errand, perhaps, but I had to walk out my frustration and disappointment, giving every effort to find that tom.

Hooks

Over the next three hours, I walked every inch of that timber. I found sheds, ticks, and cockle burrs, but failed to locate my gobbler. Sweating profusely and tattooed with thorns, I'd seen enough and headed back to the truck. When I reached the field edge, I glanced at my watch and realized I had another hour to spare. My clothes were so thoroughly soaked with sweat and burrs that it felt like I was wearing a wet suit made of Velcro. I shed my shirt and thermals, laid my bow down along the creek bank, and entered the timber for one more lap. Following a well-used deer trail to circumvent the cover, I casually walked along its course, glancing through the tangled maze.

While circling back toward the truck, I passed by a small clearing with a lone cedar tree at its center. I thought something seemed out of place, noticing what appeared to be a black, boulder-shaped mass lying beneath its branches. More attentive now and curious, I moved in that direction, walking at a steady pace with no hurry in my step. The curvature and feathers took form as I moved closer, revealing the gobbler's refuge. He was lying under the limbs of the cedar tree, his head tucked against his wing, staring as I passed by. I didn't change my direction or pace, nor did I make any sudden movements—I just kept walking. My masquerade worked as the gobbler remained nestled beneath the cedar, allowing me passage toward the creek.

Once I had retrieved my bow, I nocked an arrow and followed the same route back through the timber. As I approached the gobbler for the second time, I began to get nervous, my mind accepting the reality of what might happen. I drew my bow without breaking stride, bearing down on the unsuspecting tom from a few feet away. The moment I stopped to settle my pin, he rose from his bed, seconds before my arrow found its mark. I hoisted the tom skyward, grateful beyond words, knowing how lucky I was to taste success.

I wish I could say that was the end of my theatrics that season, but the longbeards had other plans. The infamous pasture, where I had tackled and chased gobblers in years past, was where I found myself in late April. The dawn revealed curtains of fog drifting across the field, dissipating just as a longbeard lit up the morning. I had a full strut decoy bobbing among faux hens, intending to challenge any approaching toms. Exceeding my expectations, the gobbler pitched off the roost and raced across the pasture, his white head resembling a lighthouse on a foggy night. The longbeard's colorful wattles bounced up and down as he picked up speed, his bulbous chest threatening to tip him over. The tom was punching my Pretty Boy decoy in the blink of an eye, and still doing so when my arrow left the string. The gobbler flopped through the field after a well-placed arrow and came to rest with his wings splayed. I thought he was done, only to see him rise and hobble into the timber. Bowhunting this pasture had become my *Groundhog Day*, with each hunt seeming to mirror the last.

The arrow seemed well placed, but the gobbler's departure told a different story, raising more questions than answers. I circled around to the CRP and pushed the woodlot back, knowing I was on my own this morning. This timber was no stranger to hide-and-seek, and we were now in the midst of another game. Step-by-step I crept forward, trying to get a jump on the old warrior, looking to discover his hideout. I was nearly to the end of the woodlot, within 30 yards of where the gobbler had vanished, when I stopped to look left. Like a real-life whack-a-mole, the longbeard popped up and sprinted toward the field. I fired an arrow that ricocheted off a hickory limb, followed by another that cleanly missed the gobbler.

Having more arrows, but the common sense not to use them, I dropped my bow and sprinted after the longbeard. I dodged low-hanging branches, jumped a strand of barbed wire, and chased feathers and putts down the fence line before corralling the gobbler near a depression. Normally subdued when I'm alone, content with internal monologues and excitement, I let out one of the loudest shouts I can remember. Every soul within earshot heard my victory cry that day, but with the history I had with this pasture, I think I earned it.

When I replay these hunts in my mind, never once have I thought myself to be anything but lucky. Any higher, and that first gobbler would have been out of reach, gliding off to parts unknown. The second tom would have stayed a mystery, if not for a good friend's slow pace and slight pause. The last three were simply products of persistence and a good bit of luck. Turkeys are one of the toughest targets in bowhunting, making you pay for the subtlest inaccuracies. They are also no different than other upland game, holding tight to cover when threatened, and flushing only when thought to be discovered.

Regarding shot placement, I learned some painful lessons along the way. Although the wing butt is the gold standard on most three-dimensional targets, it is a poor choice for two reasons. It not only acts like an armored plate to arrow penetration, but also lies near the breast, where nearly all these birds were arrowed. This large mass of muscle has little vascularity, and whether it be shotgun pellets or broadheads, damage to this tissue rarely causes death. I've learned to aim farther back, just above the legs, where the margin of error is greater. A turkey's vitals extend well behind the wing butt, and aiming just above the thighs is almost a sure thing. Without both legs, a turkey struggles to run or fly, and removing this asset will greatly enhance recovery rates.

The infamous pasture and Eyad's Iowa longbeard.

Lastly, giving a gobbler time to expire can work to the archer's advantage. Bursting out of blinds to chase wounded birds can give them a shot of adrenaline and just enough motivation to fly away. Don't ask me how I know. While there are always exceptions, it's best to let them walk off and bed down. A big gobbler can disappear when he wants to, so inspecting every blowdown and brush pile is critical. If you can find them before they flush, a stationary target always trumps a moving one. No matter your broadhead of choice, dialing in your equipment and being selective is critical to success. However, if things don't go according to plan, sheer determination will fill its share of tags. Bowhunting is said to be about the chase and the challenge, but when it comes to turkeys, you could say I've had my fill.

CHAPTER 14

Western Dreams

It had been a trying year, and more so for my younger brother Nabeel than anyone. On May 26, 2008, Memorial Day to be exact, my sister called to inform me that our brother had been in a terrible accident. A drunk driver had crossed the median and struck his SUV head on. My brother was alive but critically injured. After many weeks in the hospital, multiple surgeries, and painful rehab, he was finally cleared to go home. In time, he would walk again, but it would be a long recovery. I was planning a trip to Alberta that fall to pursue the giant mule deer that roam its prairies and grasslands. Hunting was the furthest thing from my mind, though, knowing the pain and anguish my brother was enduring. In the days preceding my travels, as if he knew the guilt I was carrying, my brother told me I needed to enjoy this hunt. He asked only that I have fun and be safe. I promised him I would do that, wished him well, and prepared to head west.

Nabeel's car after it was pulled off the highway.

I left on September 13 for Calgary, Alberta, where outfitter Corey Jarvis of Three River Adventures awaited my arrival. I'd spoken with Corey numerous times over the past year and was optimistic we would have a memorable adventure. We arrived in camp near sunset, where I got settled and checked my equipment in the fading light. The next day, we awoke to a breathtaking view of the Alberta landscape, with the Harvest Moon hanging low on the horizon. The luminous orb was a sight to behold as it stood watch over glistening, golden fields.

The Harvest Moon hanging over the Alberta Rockies.

Corey said the mule deer would be on their feet early and late in the day, usually bedding down during the midday hours. The warm weather wouldn't help our cause, forcing the mulies to seek shade much earlier. Our only hope was to watch them bed down or catch a glimpse of antlers above a grassy swale. From there we could initiate a stalk, using the terrain and wind to our advantage.

Traveling between the Rocky Mountains and agricultural fields, we glassed valleys and draws, looking for tall tines above the grass. We caught a few smaller bucks on their feet early, milling around and feeding, but had yet to locate a mature animal. Around midafternoon, we headed for an isolated clump of cattails, where Corey had seen a good buck earlier in the week. I had been dying to stretch my legs, so I volunteered to take my bow and work toward the small patch of cover. As I approached the reeds dancing in the wind, the cattails erupted with antlers. Seven bucks rose from their beds and bounded across the prairie. They had remained unseen, hidden among the reeds and grass until I interrupted their siesta. The mulies disappeared over a small rise, which had me hustling back to see what Corey wanted to do.

We drove to a distant hillside, where we hoped to locate one of the better bucks in the group. Corey selected a vantage point and set up his spotting scope, so we could glass the valley below. It was almost an hour into our glassing session when we caught movement along the edge of a draw. Two bucks were feeding near a thick section of cattails, both mulies carrying impressive racks. We watched them for more than an hour before they bedded down a sizable distance apart. The deer were separated by enough real estate that stalking one would have little effect on the other. With a stiff wind and plenty of daylight, the conditions were perfect.

Corey suggested we locate a few landmarks to use as references during the stalk. He explained that everything would look foreign once I was down there—sage advice for this flatlander. Using hand signals from the truck, Corey would let me know if the bucks changed position or fled before my arrival. Thirty minutes later, now in the bottom of the valley, I located my first landmark. We had identified a barley field from the road, knowing the cattails were on the other side. Just as Corey had said, it all looked different now that I was down here, and I was grateful for his advice. After I reached the barley field, I could see the cattail thicket over the rise, which hopefully contained one of the bucks.

I hit my knees and crawled forward, hoping the strong gusts of wind would mask my approach. The closer I got, the more rattled my nerves became. I had no clue where either buck was located, but after scanning the cover, I finally glimpsed antlers hidden among the dark reeds and grass. It appeared as if someone had placed a European mount in the grassy swale and failed to retrieve it. This had to be one of the bucks, and there was no doubt he was a giant. My adrenals were in overdrive. Beads of salty fluid poured off my brow and into my eyes. This only complicated matters, blurring my vision and forcing me to blink away the excess. Crawling along at a snail's pace, I pushed forward through the dense grass, keeping an eye on the elevated antlers. Luckily, the wind continued to befriend me, masking my approach as I crawled within bow range.

Eyad was finally within bow range of this Alberta giant.

Then, out of nowhere, a large doe rose from the thick grass and looked in my direction. I knew if I flinched this stalk was over, so I dared not move a muscle. The standoff lasted well over five minutes; I took short, shallow breaths, count-ing the seconds until she moved on. Despite the doe's alert demeanor, the buck re-mained motionless, his ant-lers nestled along the edge of the grass. Eventually, the doe turned and moved away, soon vanishing within the cattails. This seemed to make the buck nervous, and he rose from his bed.

Only then did I realize how massive he was, with a tall, spider-like rack and dark antlers. I ranged him at 44 yards, settled my pin, and touched the release. It seemed like a movie in slow motion as the arrow approached his vitals—on course to end this hunt. In a split second; however, the buck lowered his mass, and my arrow sailed harmlessly over his back. Unscathed and better for it, unlike my ego, the mule deer bounded over the hill and out of my life.

Watching his antlers crest the hillside, I experienced a sudden feeling of dismay and discouragement. The emotional high of crawling within bow range had been incredible, but unfortunately, so was my level of disappointment. I knew the other buck was still ahead, unaware of my presence, and I had to keep it together. I slowly moved forward through the prairie grass and found the inside corner I'd been seeking, where the other buck had bedded down. Soon, my eyes found a wide set of antlers framed within the cattails.

Oblivious to my presence, with a sweeping rack and good mass, the buck was in a similar position to the first. I quickly cut the distance in half, hastened by the cattails and cover that shielded my approach. With height not being one of my strongest virtues, I could barely see over the cattails as their brown, oval-shaped pods teetered in the breeze. With every gust they swung right, offering a snapshot of the bedded giant, before swaying back to obscure my view. By the time the cattails ran through their next cycle, my release was on—I only needed the buck to rise.

He stood moments later, and I came to full draw, hoping the wind would grant me one last favor. As if on cue, the next gust pushed the cattails aside, and my arrow was scorching across the prairie. The buck bounded toward the horizon with ivory-colored fletching protruding from his side. I waited for Corey before taking up the trail, and a few minutes later we spotted the buck just over the rise. I thought of my brother as we approached the fallen mulie and tipped my hat to the Man upstairs. The buck was regal in every way, with dark antlers and a stone-colored cape. Surrounded by some of the most beautiful country I've ever seen, I took it all in, so grateful for life's blessings.

Eyad's Alberta Mule Deer

Whenever I think back on that fateful summer, or see prairie grass blowing in the wind, I'm reminded of many things. The power of faith, the importance of family, and the harsh reality of life all come to mind. Separated by distance and obligations, my greatest regret is that I didn't do more to help my brother. I cannot turn back the hands of time, but I hope he knows that I thought of him every day. His courage and strength in the face of adversity was nothing short of remarkable, a testament to the man he is. He never gave up, despite the depth of his struggles, and recovered to build an incredible life. Although those moments and memories changed our lives forever, I thank God every day that we have the chance to forge more.

CHAPTER 15

Ice Age

Driving down the interstate, I smiled as the meteorologist's voice came through the speakers. "Today's high will be –40 with the wind chill, folks. The National Weather Service has issued a winter storm warning and it's advised to stay indoors." Most would dread this brutal cold, but I eagerly awaited its arrival. No, I hadn't lost my mind, nor was I portraying a foolish sense of toughness. I wanted to prepare for an environment in which forty below was the norm rather than the exception. My journey would be a long one as I pursued a prehistoric beast three hundred miles north of the Arctic Circle. The Inuits call them *oomingmak*, or "the bearded ones," otherwise known as the musk oxen.

The musk ox is found north of the Arctic Circle in a habitat not for the faint of heart. They are relics of the last ice age and perfectly adapted to withstand the harsh environment for which the Arctic is known. During the winter and early spring, the temperatures average –40 degrees below zero, making the proper equipment imperative. Leaving your skin exposed can lead to severe frostbite, the loss of fingers and toes, and in worst-case scenarios—death.

Covering every inch of my body was essential, so that the Arctic wouldn't grace me with a reminder of my ignorance. A neck gaiter, ski goggles, full-face mask, and large mittens gave me confidence this wouldn't happen. Layers of wool and polartec thermals, along with 2,000 grams of thinsulate in my boots, would provide flexibility and warmth. A good friend who hunted the Arctic years ago had lent me his beaver fur hat, laced with wool to protect me from the elements. As I bundled up and tried to shoot my bow, I felt more like the Stay Puft Marshmallow Man than a bowhunter. In time, I grew accustomed to my clothing, confident it would not be a hindrance to my accuracy.

My research had led to a spring hunt in Cambridge Bay, on the southeast shore of Victoria Island. Victoria Island is the second largest isle in Canada and is known for harboring large numbers of musk oxen. I had almost booked my hunt in the fall, when a short window of warmth graced the tundra with green lichens and rolling hills. When it came to bowhunting these mammoths, however, I envisioned wooden sleds, frigid temps, and a landscape coated with snow and ice. That environment was the allure for me, and wanting to experience the frozen tundra, I scheduled my trip for the spring of 2009.

I left Iowa on March 28, and after a connecting flight in Edmonton, I spent the night in Yellowknife. The flights were smooth and sleep came easily. Dawn arrived quickly, and with it came my flight to Cambridge Bay. As we approached Victoria Island, the captain reported a severe blizzard had moved in, which would make landing on the island impossible. Rather than returning to Yellowknife, we embarked on a *milk run* in which the aircraft visited three villages to deliver supplies. Although many in the hunting party were disappointed, I was excited to experience these various Arctic communities. Over the next ten hours we landed in Gjoa Haven on King William Island, flew over Pelly Bay, and touched down in Taloyoak on the Boothia Peninsula. Here, I conversed with local Inuits, listening to their tales of polar bear hunts, Arctic char, and eternal winters.

We found ourselves stranded in Yellowknife the next day, but on March 31, we finally made our way to Cambridge Bay. As the plane descended under bluebird skies and frigid temperatures, I caught glimpses of the terrain below. What I witnessed was a sea of snow, endless and vast. The long days of travel had left me drowsy, but the arctic air was like a shot of Red Bull toasting my arrival. We unloaded the plane and made our way to the Fish and Game Department to purchase our licenses. The residents of Cambridge Bay were friendly and kind, welcoming us with open arms. Later that evening, I got settled in my hotel room, made sure my equipment was accounted for, and relaxed the rest of the night. In the morning, we would load our sleds and depart across the frozen tundra in search of a big bull.

We awoke early on April 1 and prepared to leave Cambridge Bay by sled. Although the threat of frostbite was ever present, the journey in wooden sleds heeded its own warning. Far from an April Fool's joke, I soon realized what the guides were talking about. Every crevice, rock, and hump was a jolt to my system as the snowmobiles pulled us across a desert of ice. I felt like Rocky Balboa in the fourth installment as he battled the mighty Russian, Ivan Drago, taking shot after shot to the midsection. Each blow was worse than the last, but soon I grew accustomed to the back-pounding ride.

Traveling on wooden sleds—Eyad was dressed for the Arctic.

The plan was to hit certain vantage points and, with the aid of quality optics, glass the endless landscape of snow and ice. Once we located a herd of musk oxen, I would depart the sled and pursue on foot, being sure to keep the sled in view. Without the aid of a compass and the Inuit guides, getting lost would be akin to walking the plank on a pirate ship. Moon-like in appearance, every direction looked the same, with boulders and depressions amidst a world of white. Two hours later, we located a herd that hosted a few good bulls. Musk oxen are protective and when threatened will form a defensive circle. The calves are pushed to the center as the mature animals form the outer ring. I could see a stationary circle forming, knowing the bigger bulls would be to the outside.

The musk oxen formed a defensive circle as Eyad approached.

After ensuring my equipment was in good condition following our off-road adventure, I departed the sled and closed the gap on foot. I could feel the arctic wind continuing its assault, searching for a weakness in my attire. Fortunately, the adrenaline surging through my veins dampened the frigid temperatures. I was now within 100 yards and focused on the musk oxen ahead. I could tell the bulls were more agitated as they separated from the herd and walked toward me. This made me uneasy, but I continued marching forward, the wind resisting my efforts like an invisible wall.

The other musk oxen fled across the frozen tundra.

I removed my mittens and face shield to prepare for the shot, a decision I hoped I wouldn't regret. My fingers were already numb, and now the only barrier between my skin and the metal riser was a pair of thin gloves. I realized there was little time before I lost all feeling in my face and fingertips, which hastened my approach. Like clockwork, the three bulls lined up and glared at me, daring me to come closer. I called their bluff and closed the gap, knowing I was pushing the limits of their comfort zone. Swaying back and forth, the bulls raised their horns and faced me head on, while the other musk oxen fled across the barren landscape.

I could tell the bulls were growing tired of this game and would let me know in short order. With worn-down bosses and heavy mass, they stood defiant amidst the blowing snow and wind. Now within 30 yards, the bulls began rubbing their noses against their forelegs, growing more hostile as I approached. Others had warned me of this behavior, a sure sign they were about to charge.

Face to Face

I recalled this safety tip and cautiously stepped back, which seemed to ease their disposition. I came to full draw and settled my pin on the older bull, with my arrow finding its mark soon after. The broadhead seemed to have little effect, and just as I questioned my shot placement, he tumbled and was down within seconds. I knelt next to the bull and ran my hands through his thick hair, feeling the stark contrast between the outer wool and soft qiviut beneath.

We took pictures and quartered the bull before beginning our journey back to Cambridge Bay. The bumps weren't so bad this time around as I seemed to embrace them. Upon arriving back at camp, we were invited to the Nunavut Day celebration that evening at the community center. The territory of Nunavut was established on April 1, 1999, and today was its tenth anniversary. It was a memorable night. I witnessed Inuit traditions such as throat singing, dancing, and high-kick exhibitions. I also sampled authentic Inuit foods, such as narwhal, caribou, musk ox, and Arctic char. We visited with the locals all night, shared hunting stories, and ate like kings. It was the perfect ending to my Arctic adventure.

Hunting musk ox is more than filling a tag. It's about the adventure, the challenge of the elements, and the memories of a modern-day mammoth. I was privileged to experience this perilous environment of ice and snow, to traverse a rugged landscape at the mercy of a sled, and to stand face-to-face with a prehistoric beast. What I thought would be an epic journey to the North turned out to be an expedition, and I wouldn't have it any other way. Humility is a precious emotion, and my trip to the Arctic ensured that my glass will always be full.

Eyad's Musk Ox

CHAPTER 16

Nebraska Hat Trick

It was early May, and my good friend Toby and I were headed to Nebraska in search of Merriam's gobblers. While I had successfully hunted these hard-gobbling turkeys before, Toby had yet to harvest a Merriam's, considered by many to be the most beautiful of the subspecies. With cream-tipped tail feathers and a reputation for being vocal, Merriam's are a turkey hunter's dream. Simply witnessing their majestic white fans pirouetting atop the Nebraska sandhills would be worth the trip alone. When you add the chorus and colors that nature brings to the plate each spring, it was obvious why we were eager to get there.

It was late when we arrived at Calamus Outfitters in north-central Nebraska, and after a few hours of sleep, we met up with owner Adam Switzer. Dillon, one of Adam's guides and ranch hands, would join us for the hunt. I was dropped off in a separate pasture, where numerous gobblers had been strutting in recent weeks. I wearily removed my pack and erected my Double Bull blind as the horizon transitioned from black to gray. As if being called to arms by the rising sun, a pair of longbeards began to thunder, lighting up the prairie with a barrage of gobbles. Unfortunately, a small group of hens intercepted the toms, pulling the longbeards away from my setup.

The morning wore on. No matter how much I tried to fight it, frequent head bobs, fueled by the long drive and lack of sleep, took over. It was amazing how my backpack was looking more like a pillow with each passing minute. Fighting the urge to lie my head down on the Nebraska prairie, I stayed vigilant, hoping to be rewarded with a deep-throated gobble. The turkeys seemed to have other plans, however, as the prairie remained silent over the next few hours. Adam's truck came bumping down the road around 10:00 AM, which meant it was time to move on.

I climbed into the pickup and was informed that Toby had shot his first Merriam's, a jake that came sauntering into his decoys. Despite a well-placed

Merriam's will often roost in giant cottonwood trees.

arrow, the jake sought refuge in a cedar thicket and could not be found. Adam's Labrador Retriever, Honkie, had come along for the ride, and we hoped he could solve the mystery. A golden beast with a penchant for finding wounded fowl, Honkie covered the same thickets they had combed through earlier and found Toby's Merriam's in short order.

After congratulations and handshakes were exchanged, we elected to grab lunch just before noon. We departed the restaurant an hour later, looking for a lovesick Merriam's to lure within bow range. Rather than waiting them out near roost sites, Adam thought we should stay mobile and look for a hot bird. We scouted some beautiful country that afternoon and finally spotted a sizable flock in the distance. The gobblers were parading around their harem in full strut, their white fans silhouetted against the western sky.

Adam didn't have permission on this tract but spoke with the landowner and was granted access. We circled around and formulated a plan, trying to get a bearing on the Merriams' direction. I was optimistic at the prospects

Spring Monarchs

before us but leery of the hens that could make or break our efforts.

We set up our blind and decoy spread, which consisted of two hens and a full-strut gobbler. Adam and Dillon drove off to observe from a distant hillside. Once things settled down, Toby and I began calling. We yelped, cackled, and cut, sounding like two hens desperate for a date. Convincing one longbeard into a shock gobble, we grew more alert. But as the minutes passed, only the sounds of meadowlarks and cackling pheasants filled the air. The silence was deafening, but we stayed the course, hoping our patience would be rewarded.

Our excitement and confidence were waning. I leaned over to Toby and said, "I'm glad you got your first Merriam's and…" I stopped midsentence as two hens came running down the lane.

I whispered, "Don't move. Two hens are on their way and I bet the gobblers are right behind them."

No sooner had those words left my mouth than a triple gobble erupted from behind the blind. With shaking hands, I clipped my release to the string and watched as three gobblers sprinted toward the decoys. I had attached a feathered-fan to my full-strut decoy over the winter, donated from an Iowa gobbler I took many years ago. Not only did the feathers add a hint of realism, but the fan acted like a sail on an ocean bound vessel, causing the decoy to bounce and bob in the wind. Confronting their foe, the trio of longbeards were open and honest, letting this *Eastern* gobbler know he wasn't welcome. As they unleashed their fury, I came to full draw and picked a spot on the nearest tom.

The arrow was on its way, dropping the first longbeard in his tracks. The other two were thrashing their fallen friend when Toby laced an arrow through a

Ring-necked pheasants were also in the midst of their spring ritual.

second gobbler. With two longbeards on the ground, I nocked another arrow, focused on the remaining tom. I can only imagine his mindset, realizing the value of his inheritance, a priceless harem at stake. I waited for the right angle and watched as the gladiator continued to flog the toms, emitting aggressive purrs with each kick.

Eventually, the gobbler spun around, the pocket opened, and my arrow was gone. This sent the tom into a torrential tailspin, which ceased shortly thereafter. Feathers and arrows were scattered about, and we were speechless. The chaos had occurred in a matter of seconds and neither one of us could believe it. As I was shaking hands with Toby, I glanced out at the carnage, only to see the first bird stand up and race across the prairie.

I tried to nock another arrow, but the gobbler was running off too quickly. Picking up speed and taking flight, he glided over the hill and was gone. I jumped out of the blind and crashed through a cedar thicket, where an empty field greeted my gaze. Luckily, Adam was glassing the field from a distant hillside and saw where the tom landed. While we formulated a plan, I noticed Honkie was resting comfortably in Adam's truck. In Nebraska, dogs are legal to locate turkeys after being shot, and although Honkie had been the hero this morning, his skills could not help me now.

After discussing our options, I decided to close the distance on the gobbler's location, hoping to deliver a final arrow. Crouched down and creeping toward the wounded tom, I prayed he would stay grounded. Resembling a speed bump on the prairie, the longbeard held tight, confident in the grassy swale he had chosen as his refuge. With a low profile and my release on the string, I continued to shorten the distance. The sheen off the gobbler's back became more evident as I approached, and soon I was within bow range.

The tall prairie grass prevented an unobstructed view, but I was now within 20 yards and could go no farther. I came to full draw and settled my pin on the tom's ebony form, slowly adding tension to my release. The arrow traveled across the prairie and connected with the longbeard's wing butt, a mistake I wish I could undo. Striking the wing butt of a gobbler is recovery suicide, and like a sword to a shield, my broadhead glanced harmlessly off the tom. With massive wing beats he took flight, heading for a distant cedar thicket. I dropped my bow and ran after the resilient longbeard, giving it everything I had. Each step between us grew longer as my glimmer of hope began to fade. My legs followed suit, seemingly of their own accord, conceding defeat with each wing beat.

Then I saw Honkie, Adam's giant Labrador, blowing past me like a gust of wind. I watched as the distance between Honkie and the gobbler shortened before they both disappeared over the hill. Drenched in sweat and sucking wind, I crested the rise a few seconds later and couldn't believe my eyes. Honkie was walking toward me with the longbeard in his mouth, his eyes gleaming with pride. He looked up as if to say, "Here you go, buddy. I was hoping you'd make the shot, but I had your back either way." Unbeknownst to me, Honkie had been following the entire time, and as the giant bird took flight, he must have decided he'd seen enough. I bent down to take the gob-

Nebraska Hat Trick—Toby and Eyad

Toby's gobbler had four beards.

bler from his mouth and noticed his tail wagging back and forth, a smiling dog if ever I saw one.

Adam usually wears a poker face, but you could see how proud he was of Honkie. We would be hard-pressed to repeat such a hunt, and that was just fine by me. As we drove back to Iowa early the next morning, I stared across the endless sandhills, thought of Aldo Leopold's writings, and realized how fortunate I was to be here. Although we had spent many hours practicing and embraced the opportunities given, there was no doubt we had been lucky. As I pondered this realization, I recalled a saying by the Roman philosopher Seneca: "Luck is what happens when preparation meets opportunity."

I'm sure turkey hunting did not inspire that sentiment. But on this hunt, truer words have never been spoken.

Adam, Honkie, Toby, and Eyad

CHAPTER 17

Glacier Ghosts

Regarding the multitude of big game species in North America, mountain goats are in a league of their own. With beautiful white coats, ebony horns and scenic mountain landscapes, few can match their grandeur and mystique. Harvesting one of these mountain dwellers with archery tackle is a daunting task, often more dangerous than other big game hunts. No, they don't carry the razor-sharp claws of a grizzly or the hostile demeanor of an enraged cape buffalo. What these white ghosts do possess is a beauty much like the sirens of ancient lore, luring bowhunters toward the jagged cliffs and mountaintops they call home. Once on a slope too steep or a ledge too narrow, a bowhunter's worst fears can become reality.

Alaska law requires nonresidents to hire the services of a licensed guide before hunting mountain goats. After tireless research into the outfitters who would guide a bowhunter to the tops of these peaks, I chose Dennis Zadra of Lonesome Dove Outfitters in Cordova, Alaska. Dennis has a solid reputation and welcomes bowhunters into his camp. He explained that two factors will often determine the outcome of a mountain goat hunt: physical fitness and the weather. I never forgot those words and vowed to be ready for my Alaskan adventure.

I booked my hunt for September 2010, as the coming fall was committed to moving and other family affairs. Unfortunately, in careless haste to grab something from my car, I lacerated my forehead on August 5. My brother-in-law was in town helping us move and drove me to the doctor's office, as stitches might be in order. I lay my head back, feeling exceptionally stupid for what I had done, when I noticed that my cell phone was buzzing. While trying to keep blood off my phone, I looked down and saw it was a call from Lonesome Dove Outfitters. I thought that was unusual as my hunt was still over a year away. Unable to resist, I grabbed a tissue and checked the message. To my surprise, one of Dennis's clients could not make the hunt this year, and he was hoping I could take his place in six short weeks.

I have always believed in fate. That summer, my youngest brother, Tameem, had talked me into running a 10K. He is a tremendous athlete and competitor, running three marathons the year before. I played speed-specific sports in college, so endurance was not my forte. Whether it was the allure of the race or the persistence of my brother, I'll never know, but I accepted the challenge and had been training for the past three months. I had completed the 10K one week before Dennis's phone call and couldn't believe the irony. Still, I had a decision to make. My conditioning was solid, and if I cranked it up a notch, I would be ready for this once-in-a-lifetime hunt. After a few phone calls, work schedule alterations, and equipment checks, I was scheduled to leave for Alaska in September.

Training for the mountains.

To prepare for the hunt, I used a training regimen that included running, hiking, lifting, and target practice. I ran four miles three days-per-week, after which I loaded up a heavy pack and swapped out my running shoes for Meindl hikers. I hiked up and down the Iowa hills near home, with the only break being the turnaround at the top. Following the ninety-minute cardio session, I picked up my bow and started shooting. By that point my legs were weary and my heart was racing, simulating the conditions I might face on the mountain.

The rest of the week I lifted weights and shot at the local archery range, imagining fictitious horns and a white cape on each target. I also placed a

Cordova, Alaska

photograph of a mountain goat at work, with anatomical illustrations, to engrain perfect arrow placement. Hard work doesn't guarantee success, but without it, I didn't stand a chance.

Before I knew it, September 20 had arrived, and I was off to the small fishing town of Cordova, Alaska. Cordova sits on Prince William Sound, infamously known for the Exxon Valdez oil spill on March 24, 1989. Notwithstanding this catastrophe, Cordova still sustains a strong commercial fishing industry. The scenic harbor and numerous fishing boats near shore were a testament to that fact. Cordova was beautiful, with mountain peaks in the distance and otters playing near the shore. We weren't scheduled to fly out until the next day, so I visited the Cordova Fishermen's Memorial. Erected in memory of those lost at sea, it was a sad reminder of how unforgiving the ocean could be.

After a good night's sleep and a solid breakfast, we were off on our float plane, flying across Prince William Sound and the Chugach Mountains. As the float plane descended, I watched the fog envelope one ridge before revealing another, the exchange almost rhythmic. Once the plane was unloaded, we set up base camp and organized our gear. The skies were clearing and tomorrow looked to be a beautiful day.

The sun crested the eastern slopes the next morning as we awoke from our slumber. We quickly loaded our packs, taking only the essentials up the mountain. A few extra pounds would feel a lot heavier at the top so packing carefully was vital. We pulled waders on to cross a raging river and, after safe passage, hid them along the shoreline to be retrieved later. Lacing up our boots once more, we attached crampons to our soles, spikes that improved traction and stability up the slope. A climbing ax completed our arsenal, and with cinched down packs we headed up. With each hour the pack grew heavier and my legs wearier, testing my physical and mental endurance with

Flying over Prince William Sound

each step. I kept reminding myself of my training, the struggles and pain I had endured. Time stood still as I willed myself up the mountain, through labored breaths and devil's club, along narrow ledges that dropped into raging creeks below. Dennis didn't seem to break a sweat, and I kept waiting for the Energizer battery to fall from his pack.

Eyad taking a break near the alpine.

Four hours later we hit the alpine, where spike camp was located atop a rocky plateau. After unpacking our gear, I helped Dennis erect the small tent that would be our home for the next few days. Beat down and exhausted, the climb had been brutal, but we were here and it was time to hunt goats. We spent the evening glassing, seeing numerous goats, including one billy that Dennis thought was too young. Dennis explained what we were looking for: a mature billy with heavy bases, a stained rump, and a gentle curvature to his horns. The nannies, or female goats, would lack this coloration change on the backside due to a different posture while urinating. The nannies would also have a more aggressive curvature to their horns and much narrower

The terrain was steep and slick on the mountain.

bases. If they had young goats with them, known as kids, it was a sure sign of their gender. We made our way back to camp near sunset just as the rain began to fall. Little did we know it wouldn't stop for three days.

The next morning, we awoke to dark skies, high winds, and steady rain. Getting dressed was like crawling into an ice bath, as my clothes were still soaked from our ascent. Having only one extra base layer and a set of thermals for sleeping, I had to ration my clothing. I was warned about wearing Gore-Tex on the rain-rich mountains of Alaska, its material no better than a spaghetti strainer. My clothes looked like they had missed the spin cycle in a washing machine and, with low humidity, there was no such thing as drying out. Luckily, I had a Helly Hansen rain suit along for the ride, which couldn't breathe to save its life, but was impervious to the moisture.

After finishing our freeze-dried breakfast, we laced up our boots and began our march up the mountain. The traction afforded by the dry weather had dissipated, replaced by a glazed and slippery slope. Still, we climbed higher, searching for goats along plateaus and shale-laden hillsides. Dislodging baseball-sized boulders revealed the steepness of the terrain, as the sound of rolling rocks echoed down the mountain, long after their departure. We eventually reached the apex of a long incline and stopped to rest, fueling up on Snickers and glacier water. Although my legs were grateful for the respite, it wasn't long before chills and chattering teeth forced us back on our feet, courtesy of the wind and our soaked undergarments. While packing up my wrappers and water, I noticed Dennis standing still, staring over my shoulder. I turned around to see a young billy staring at us, a mere 20 yards away. He must have heard us and crept over the ridge to investigate, studying my shivering form before retreating down the mountain.

Gaining elevation, we noticed two goats on an adjacent hillside, just as the rain changed to snow. We broke out the spotting scope and identified them as mature billies. With the snow and wind increasing in magnitude, the duo slid down the backside of the mountain, never to be seen again. We worked our way up the slope, where a violent gust almost blew me off my feet. Visibility was getting worse, and with each step I became more religious, praying I wouldn't lose my footing and tumble down the mountain. We shielded ourselves from the elements behind a large boulder, but that did little to combat the storm. Moments later, Dennis said he had seen enough and decreased our elevation, hoping to find better conditions.

Halfway down the mountain, Dennis stopped and motioned me to do the same. He pointed down to a shielded plateau that harbored four mountain goats, two of which were nice billies. If the wind cooperated, perhaps we could maneuver above and get archery close. Down the slope we went, crossing an ice bridge before navigating a boulder-strewn hillside. As we drew closer, Dennis knelt and instructed me to remove my pack and crampons. We approached the edge of the cliff, where Dennis leaned forward with his rangefinder before turning around. The look on his face told me it was time.

"The back one, Eyad, 47 yards. This is your chance and may be as good as we get with this weather. Make it count."

I leaned over the windswept ledge, the sheer force of the elements wreaking havoc on my balance, and came to full draw. The snow and sleet continued to bite my face like miniscule shards of glass, adding to the treachery of the storm. Steadfast while settling my pin, I added tension to the release and my arrow was gone. The broadhead arced through the air, twisting through an ocean of ice and wind, striking the billy farther back than I intended.

Mirroring a kick-off formation, the mountain goats exploded off the plateau, staying shoulder to shoulder before scattering into the squall. Crimson painted the side of the wounded billy as he and the others vanished over the ridgeline. All but one white coat reappeared, none with a cherry stain. Following a short wait, we went to investigate, only to see a vacant mountain on the other side. My stomach felt hollow knowing what this recovery would entail. Those who have hunted mountain goats will tell you, unequivocally, they are one of the toughest animals to bring down. While wounded whitetails will seek thickets and CRP fields, mountain goats use tree lines near ominous cliffs to avoid danger. These areas drop off into thin air, and if the goat sought refuge as such, there would be no recovery.

With optics to our eyes, scanning back and forth, Dennis finally spotted the billy. Surrounded by a fortress of stone, the goat was lying in a rocky depression just below a cliff face. If he rose from his bed and moved to our right, he would be lost to a crevasse. Our only hope was to take the billy in his bed, where even if he fell, we could still recover him. Looking at our options, we decided I should circle around and try to get above the goat. Dennis would crawl to the top of a small rise and keep watch, using hand signals to let me know if the goat was moving toward the abyss. Off I went, moving quickly, praying the billy would stay bedded. I scaled a steep slope, moved down across a stream, and then ascended a subtle incline. I thought the goat was just ahead, below the crest of the ridgeline, which I hoped to use as cover. With cautious steps I climbed higher, peering over its apex, only to see a white coat lying below. The billy rose to his feet as I came to full draw, which allowed me to place an arrow behind his shoulder. I rushed toward the edge of the cliff, peering over the side, just as the goat tumbled and fell three stories to the valley below.

I remember saying a silent "thank you" as I heard Dennis yelling, "You did it … you did it!" What seemed like an impossible endeavor months ago, and a nearly tragic ending moments before, turned out to be the bowhunt of which I am most proud. We descended to the fallen billy, where I admired his beautiful white cape and impressive head gear. His hair was soft and much thicker than I imagined. His horns were heavy and sharp as daggers. We spent the next hour taking photos and boning out the meat, with plans to celebrate over fresh backstraps in camp that night. After loading up our packs, I turned and glanced up the mountain one last time. There, standing at its highest peak, peering down through the blowing snow and gusting winds stood a lone mountain goat. How he had reached that peak or stood so statuesque amidst the violent gusts, I'll never know. Losing him in a sea of white, I tried to regain my focus, only to be greeted by a barren, windswept cliff. Like a specter on Halloween, the goat had vanished before my eyes. Smiling beneath my hood, I adjusted my pack frame and headed down the mountain, bidding farewell to the white ghosts of Alaska.

Eyad's mountain goat in the Chugach Mountains of Alaska.

CHAPTER 18

Midday Magic

Of all the seasons here in the Midwest, few can rival the springtime. With emerging mushrooms, spawning panfish, and strutting gobblers—there's something for everyone. While a mess of morels and crappies is tough to beat, turkey hunting has a special place in my heart. Memories of first light, subtle tree yelps, and gobblers hammering from their oak limb roosts draw me back each spring. I always look forward to the sunrise hunts, but when it comes to filled tags, the midday hours have been more kind. Never was this more evident than two magical springs many years ago.

In the fall of 2008, my good friends Rich and Monte asked me to join them on a lease in southeast Iowa. It was closer to home than my previous haunts, so I thought it would be a great option. The lease extended through 2009, so we planned to turkey hunt there that spring. The weather opening day was brutal, better suited for crab fishing on the Bearing Sea. Despite the hurricane-like conditions and driving sleet, we would try it anyway. I walked across the pasture in the darkness and couldn't believe what I was doing as rain continued to hit my face in droves.

I staked down my decoys and hustled into the blind, just happy to be out of the elements. With the pounding precipitation, the acoustics inside the blind were impressive, booming like a bass drum. The moisture rendered my friction calls useless, so I pulled out a mouth call, which still sounded muffled in light of the storm. A few minutes later, my ears picked up a gobble, so I opened a window to look. Racing toward my setup was an old longbeard, the weather not affecting his desires. Grabbing my bow in a panic, I calmed my pin just as he got to the decoys and then touched the release. Save for a few ruffled feathers, the gobbler remained unscathed, retreating through the gale in a frenzy. Grazed gobblers don't fill many tags, and this one would survive to see better weather.

I hunted the property hard over the next week but did not hear another gobble. I called my buddy Danny, who owned land about an hour west, and asked if I could try my luck on his farm. Danny is an accomplished bowhunter and I trusted his opinion. He said I was welcome to try my hand on his turkeys and gave me a rundown of where I could hunt. For nearly twenty years, I had tried to harvest a turkey on my birthday, April 22, which fell in the heart of turkey season each spring. It also was Earth Day, a day designated to supporting environmental protection. I was the one member of my family with an affinity for the outdoors, and the irony made me smile.

I hadn't been sleeping much with a busy week beforehand. My mom was recovering from open heart surgery, I was driving back and forth to hunt and help at home, and work was hectic as usual. With family members helping and life calming down, I tried Danny's farm on the 22nd. The first two set-ups showed little activity, leaving me with one option: a scenic hillside filled with old hickories and oaks. Danny said the gobblers would strut through this area midday, and he advised me not to discount it.

I crossed a CRP field just before noon, weighed down with a blind, decoys, and my turkey vest. Surely a few ticks would tag along for the ride, but I would deal with them later. Having a good book always helps the time pass, and I was currently reading *Lone Survivor*. As I approached the clearing, I saw a red head fleeing the scene—a gobbler I spooked, no doubt. Knowing it was out of my hands and committed to enjoying the day, I erected my blind in the shade of the fence line. The area was just as advertised, with green grass, wildflowers, and open spaces throughout the mature hardwoods. I placed a full strut decoy facing the blind, accompanied by two hens. I let things quiet down before throwing a few calls through the springtime air. About an hour later, through a few more chapters, I sat up to call when a gobble erupted to my left. I didn't need to look; I knew he was close and picked up my bow.

I was hunting in a new blind with a diamond-shaped opening in the front. Offering ample room to shoot, it was ideal for bowhunters but allowed too much light into the blind. I leaned to my right and peered outside as the tom paraded down the hillside in full strut. He came right into the decoys, spinning around the Pretty Boy, giving him the evil eye. Once he was focused on his nemesis, I came to full draw, waiting for the right angle. The gobbler caught the movement, the midday hours revealing my intentions. I buried the pin on the tom's back as he scurried away, and my arrow was gone. The broadhead took him cleanly, dropping the gobbler in his tracks. My birthday wish was finally fulfilled. He remains my heaviest bird to date, and I was all smiles on Earth Day.

Earth Day—April 22, 2009

Two years later, I was back on Danny's farm. I had tasted success early in the season, taking a good bird on my own property. The temptation to buy another tag got the best of me, so I loaded my gear and drove south to spend the night at my sister's. It wasn't until well after midnight that sleep found me, and leaving the warm confines of my bed at 4:00 AM wasn't easy. When I stepped outside, I noticed the morning air had a mild chill to it, accompanied by calm winds and a sky littered with stars. Everything felt perfect and, with the help of a little caffeine, I was ready to go. Parking my truck in a grassy swale along an old farm lane, I went through my mental checklist, feeling sharp now that the coffee had navigated through my veins. Weighed down with my blind, decoys, and a few calls, I headed out across the field, eager to see what the morning would bring. A full moon shined down on me like a spotlight, as if I were a suspect in an interrogation room.

Despite the moon's revealing rays, I slipped in undetected and was positioned atop a small rise well before dawn. Living more than two hours away, I could not roost a bird the night before and knew this setup would be an all-or-none affair. If the gobblers were close, I would be in business. But if not, I would have to pursue other options. I was not disappointed, as soon three gobblers bellowed through the cool spring air. A barred owl chimed in with his own vocal audition, expressing the culinary question with which every outdoorsman is familiar.

"Who cooks for you? Who cooks for you all?"

With daylight fast approaching, the owl showed no signs of slowing down, catalyzing more gobbles as the spring woods awakened. Just as the first rays of sunlight broke the eastern horizon, I heard subtle tree yelps in the gobblers' direction. I had played this game long enough and knew this was a problem, as few gobblers would abandon a harem of willing hens. Still, I remained vigilant and enjoyed the morning, taking in the sights and sounds around me. Shortly after fly down, I saw full fans atop a distant bean field, pirouetting around their hens. I conceded defeat and moved on to another farm, where a scenic strip of hardwoods overlooked a cattle pasture. Here, I had taken my birthday gobbler two years before and felt it was worth a shot. I stepped down from my truck and took a deep breath, hitting my crow call with all the emotion I could muster. Rewarded with nothing but silence, I drove to yet another spot that had boded well for me in the past and once again exhaled through my crow call. Ironically, the only bird to respond was a large crow that flew over to investigate, proving I wasn't worthless in the art of deception.

Just past 8:30 AM, I ventured into the local gas station and purchased a giant cinnamon roll. After completing my carb-loading experiment and reading up on the Iowa Hawkeyes spring football game, I knew I had a decision to make. With a full stomach and dark circles under my eyes, I questioned whether I should call it quits and go home. I had already filled one tag this season and just enjoyed a beautiful spring morning, so there was no need to push the envelope. On the other hand, the spring wouldn't last forever, and with one last tag in my pocket, I elected to keep hunting.

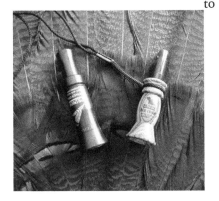

Owl and crow calls will often reveal a gobbler's location.

I headed to an area I knew well, a classic strut zone in the back of a large field surrounded by timber. Strut zones are areas that gobblers can see and be seen, displaying their full fans and brilliant colors for the hens to take notice. Earlier that spring, Danny had called in a nice gobbler for his son at this very location. They had left their blind setup along the field edge should I make it down to hunt. With the sleep-inducing effects of the cinnamon roll now in full swing, I was grateful for their generosity, knowing I wouldn't have to tote a blind across the picked bean field.

Although hunting this time of day can be productive, gobblers are generally less vocal. Notwithstanding this midday vow of silence, breeding remains a top priority for these longbeards. Hens will leave their gobblers as the morning progresses, needing to lay eggs and tend to their nests. At this point, the gobblers become bachelors once more and head to their strut zones. Running and gunning had never worked well for me, and I realized early on that I was educating more gobblers than I was taking home. Waiting in strut zones, however, had been the demise of many longbeards through the years. And as a bowhunter, I didn't feel there was a better strategy. If I could be patient and stay awake, I might have a chance.

As the sun rose higher in the clear blue sky, I made my way across the bean field. I placed my decoy spread within 15 yards of the blind and then scurried back into its dark confines. Once I was settled, I picked up my slate and yelped softly. Every thirty minutes, I scratched out a series of calls—sometimes aggressively with loud yelps, cuts, and cackles—and other times with soft purrs and clucks. About half an hour after my last calling sequence, I heard a crow cawing in the hollow to my right. A gobbler hammered back from what sounded like the same location. I naturally got excited and cut back on my slate but received no answer.

Twenty minutes later, long after my last series of seductive yelps, I again heard a shock gobble to the crow's raucous calls. Now approaching 10:30 AM, I became more aggressive with my calling sequences, cutting and cackling with gusto. Unfortunately, my efforts failed to garnish a response yet again. Not holding out much hope, I called it a day and exited the blind around 11:00 AM. Just before heading back to the truck, I wanted to see if I could elicit one more gobble from the old longbeard. I walked over to the green pasture above the hollow and pulled a crow call from my pocket.

Not expecting much, I took a deep breath and did my best impression of the gobbler's ebony foe.

CAW CAW CAW......GOOOBBLLEEEEE!!!

He's still there, I thought.

The gobbler hadn't budged since his first gobble, but all turkey hunters will tell you the same thing:

Never leave a gobbling bird.

I had to try something different, and all I could think was to move the blind closer to this stubborn old longbeard. It would only be 200 yards from where I was stationed earlier, but to a turkey it might as well be a mile. By positioning myself closer, in the green pasture where I now stood, the gobbler might commit.

I didn't want to move Danny's blind without his permission, so I walked back to my truck and grabbed the Double Bull stashed inside. I shook my head as I threw the blind over my shoulders, realizing my attitude was less than optimistic.

"This is a waste of time and all you're doing is burning off that cinnamon roll," I mumbled to myself.

With the sun nearing its peak and sweat pouring from my brow, I again reached the pasture above the hollow. I lazily erected my blind and decided not to stake it down, leaving my portable ambush to the mercy of the wind. To put things in a different light, I wasn't emitting a great deal of confidence in my current setup. After staking my decoys down among the green blades of grass, I readied my mouth call, and then cut and cackled with as much enthusiasm as a pack mule.

GOOOBBLLEEEEE!!!!!!!

I was surprised the old boy was still in the hollow. I climbed into the blind, now more alert, and called again. No answer. Twenty minutes passed before I repositioned the diaphragm in my mouth and called once more. Still no response. I knew better than to get excited over a *shock-gobbler* like this, a longbeard that toys with the emotions of turkey hunters, with no intention of ever coming in. Minutes passed before I convinced myself that I was playing a losing game. Just before the noon whistle, I reached up, placed my hand on the hub of the blind to break it down, and thought to myself, *I better call one more time*. I cupped my hands around my mouth, prepped the call, and cut loose.

Yelp, Yelp, Yelp, Yelp.......GOOOBBLLEEEEE!!!!!!!

Almost knocking me off my stool, the gobbler was so close that I could hear the rattle in his throat. I knew he must be within bow range as I scanned the rolling hills before me. Then my eyes caught a flash of white, followed by the contrasting red and blue colors of a lustful longbeard. I noticed he was running, not toward the decoys as I had hoped, but away from my position.

What is going on? I thought to myself.

Was it the blind I had placed in the open pasture? Not often are turkeys alarmed by this setup, and while deer usually aren't accepting of newly

erected blinds, turkeys seem to care less. Perhaps it was the decoys? It was not uncommon for a gobbler to shy away from a decoy spread now and then, but I still felt it was something else. Then I saw the culprit, and the reason for the gobbler's paranoia became all too clear. With slivers of light playing peek-a-boo with my feet, I realized the wind was picking up my blind like a buoy on the ocean. While blinds and decoys rarely spook these cagy birds, any unnatural movement will. In my haste to get settled, I hadn't staked down the blind, and its subtle movement had cost me. With each head bob he descended farther beneath the crest of the hill, headed for the deep hollow from which he came. Then, something changed in the old tom's demeanor. Unable to ignore the jake decoy's transgressions, for which the gobbler thought to be anything but a farce, he turned on a dime and hit full strut.

As the tom worked his way back toward the decoys, I noticed his iridescent colors and confident swagger. It was an amazing sight as the midday sun beat down on the gobbler's plumage, showcasing a spectrum of colors. The old monarch continued to work closer, his every step a masterpiece of courtship. I stretched my leg out to hold down the blind as best I could, trying to ensure that a gust of wind wouldn't sabotage my hunt, this time for good. Despite my efforts, the blind wiggled free, continuing to bob with the rhythm of the wind. The tom hung-up well past the decoys, his head raised high in periscope fashion. I knew he had seen enough. I ranged him and prepared for the shot, just as the gobbler dropped his fan and turned to leave. With a solid thump and an explosion of feathers, the tom disappeared over the rise. Stumbling within the confines of the blind, I found my footing and rushed out, trying to get a direction on the wounded tom. What I saw was not a vacant field, but rather, the gobbler's dark plumage lying still against a sea of green.

His tail fan fluttered in the breeze as I approached, and I took a moment to admire the longbeard's striking colors. Every bowhunter knows the uncertainties of this endeavor and how quickly the tides can turn. But on this day, I was grateful to experience the better side of bowhunting. Glancing across the field, I took one more look around, knowing it would be another year before I returned to the spring woods. I knew these moments were fleeting, and I enjoyed every second. Undoubtedly, I was lucky to experience such a hunt, and that this old gobbler seemed to appear out of thin air was not lost on me. An hour ago, I was doing cardio with a blind on my back and complaining about the delirious effects of cinnamon rolls. Now, I was toting an Iowa longbeard under a beautiful bluebird sky. The great magician Houdini could not have conjured up a trick better than this. Then again, I doubt Houdini ever hunted turkeys with a bow.

Midday Magic

CHAPTER 19

Not So Easy Africa

The blinking light on the flight tracker seemed frozen in time as the Boeing cruised over the Atlantic Ocean. Destined for South Africa, I was halfway across the pond, feeling the excitement and anticipation building. I had dreamed of this trip for years, a long-awaited bowhunt to the Dark Continent, pursuing the legendary animals that call Africa home. After tireless research and countless questions, I chose Tshepe Safaris, booked through Bowhunting Safari Consultants and Neil Summers. Neil is a leading expert in international travel and bowhunting adventures, so I felt confident my trip would be safe, memorable, and the experience of a lifetime. Nearly all bowhunts for African game are over waterholes during the fall and winter seasons, which for those in the southern hemisphere take place between May and September. While spot and stalk hunts are an option in some areas, this hunt would find me near a waterhole, waiting for a plethora of species to wander in for a drink.

Like so many bowhunters before me, I had created a list of animals I hoped to encounter. Anyone who has ventured to this storied land has returned with Hemingway-like tales of giant, spiral-horned animals roaming the grasslands, and I hoped to be no different. These thoughts continued as the wheels touched down in Johannesburg, South Africa, where I was greeted by Cobus Mouton, owner of Tshepe Safaris. Tshepe Safaris is a family-owned operation in the northern tier of South Africa, with opportunities to hunt plains game in two ecosystems. Kudu, impala, and warthog are found in the Bushveld concessions, which consist of dense vegetation and limited visibility. On the other side of the coin is the Highveld, an area that resembles the plains of North America, where blue and black wildebeest, blesbok, springbok, eland, and gemsbok abound. We arrived at Tshepe Safaris main lodge where I was shown to my living quarters: a beautiful room with a shower, bed, dresser, and ample space. We had a great dinner, and soon I was fast asleep, dreaming of my first morning in Africa.

Daybreak found us on the Highveld, hoping to intercept a herd of thirsty plains game. Tshepe designs all their blinds to resemble termite mounds and their realism was impressive. The area surrounding the blind was just as I imagined with sprawling grasslands and scattered trees. Before us was a large water trough with numerous tracks around its circumference. I felt our wait would be short-lived, but as the sun climbed higher, the waterhole remained a ghost town. I realized this was bowhunting, and I had not come to Africa for a guaranteed hunt. Still, I hoped a parade of animals would come to quench their thirst.

Hours passed before Marius, my professional hunter for the week, put his hand on my shoulder and whispered, "Slowly grab your bow." With heightened

Tshepe blinds are made to resemble termite mounds.

Springbok at the waterhole.

adrenaline, I watched as two gorgeous springbok, South Africa's national animal, cautiously approached the water. They were much like the pronghorns that roam the grasslands of North America. Sharing the same size and demeanor, they drank from the waterhole, cognizant of their surroundings. Marius, stoic as a Greek philosopher, stared at the springbok, with me wondering if I should draw my bow. As the minutes passed, his eyes never left the small antelope drinking in front of us. Marius finally leaned over and said, "Too young, they need more time." Although I was disappointed, I knew to trust his judgement and placed my bow back on the hanger. In exchange, I grabbed my camera and took photographs of what were my first African animals. The waterhole was quiet the rest of the morning, but it was a great start to my adventure.

After a quick bite, we were back on the Highveld for our afternoon vigil. We had switched locations to where a large group of gemsbok had been watering. With ebony horns, beige sides, and a painted face, few animals are as striking. Considered one of the Dark Continent's toughest residents, perfect arrow placement on Gemsbok is critical. Their vitals are smaller and farther forward than most North American game, which must be accounted for. Time passed, with the waterhole seeing nary a visitor. No matter the continent, if you're waiting on water with bow in hand, your emotions tend to be cyclical. Optimism and hope rise with the sun each morning, peaking at midday, until evening shadows spawn disappointment. We were on the tail end of this spectrum, conceding defeat as the last rays of light found the Highveld.

I was collecting my belongings when Marius whispered, "Don't move." Heeding his warning, a clippety-clop soon found my ears as a steady cadence of hooves met Highveld. Marius whispered, "Carefully reach for your bow, Eyad, gemsbok are coming and there's a good bull." The contrasting black and white mask, the signature of these regal animals, is what first caught my eye. Mesmerized by their long, black horns, sharp as swords with heavy bases, I could see why they are one of Africa's most stunning animals. I slowly reached for my bow, attached my release, and waited for the bull to approach. The female gemsbok also carry horns, albeit longer with less mass, so I had to be sure before dropping the string. Marius confirmed the bull was approaching the oasis, but just as I came to full draw, the herd exploded from the water. I thought I was to blame, but Marius reassured me and said, "It's ok, you did nothing wrong. These animals are wild and sometimes get spooked for no reason. We have time. Stay positive."

My adrenaline subsided as the grassland became quiet once more. With the prospect of their return in question, Marius leaned over and said, "They are coming back. Get ready." I grabbed my bow just as the first gemsbok crossed in front of the blind, followed by two more, before the big bull appeared. The bull was facing the blind at a poor angle, so I waited with shaking hands, hoping he would turn before nightfall. Almost on cue, with one step to his left, the bull finally gave me the shot I was looking for. Entering straight above his leg—the arrow found its mark. A dust cloud followed the herd as they sprinted across the landscape, with the bull falling soon after. We were ecstatic as we approached the trophy gemsbok, without a doubt one of the most beautiful animals I've ever seen.

That night we celebrated over steaks and stories, seated next to an open flame. We decided to spend another day on the Highveld, moving to a differ-

Eyad took this Gemsbok at last light.

ent area with good numbers of blesbok. These spiral-horned antelope are native to South Africa and were a species I hoped to encounter. With reddish-orange coats and a striped face, they are a sight to behold. The next morning, we were hidden within another termite mound, awaiting the waterhole's first visitors. Zebra were the first to arrive, their black and white stripes encasing the drinking fountain. The herd was short on stallions, which kept my bow on the hanger, the mares being the wrong gender for this archer. Gemsbok and ostrich soon followed, posing for the camera throughout the day. That evening, with the sun already consumed by the horizon, I caught motion to my right as a small herd of blesbok worked their way in. When they dropped their heads to drink, one of the better bucks found my arrow, a shot I pulled too far back. The buck sprinted across the Highveld, where he bedded to watch his back trail.

The arrow would do its job overnight, but with jackals abounding in large numbers, my decision was easy. I asked Marius for his rifle and dispatched the blesbok in the fading light, a fate kinder than jackals or their kind would elicit. After supper that night, we made plans to hunt a different concession in search of kudu, warthog, and impala. This hunt would take place on the Bushveld, where thick vegetation and limited visibility were the norm. We left early the next morning, driving past impoverished villages, where *Tin Can* towns abounded. I was reminded of the privileges we take for granted and carried a guilty conscience as we drove away.

In time, we arrived at our concession, now in the heart of the Bushveld. Open expanses were no more as thick areas of jungle-like vegetation devoured the country-side. We were positioned on a waterhole within a scenic acreage, in a blind fit for a king. The concession owner told of a kudu bull that frequented this oasis, and he felt our chances were good. Within an hour of getting settled, Marius tapped his ear and whispered, "I hear warthogs behind us. Get ready." Few animals scream Africa like these tusked beasts, and I hoped for an encounter. With large teeth that emanate from their mouth like a sickle, these pigs are common in most areas of South Africa.

Sneaking into the water atop anxious hooves, the warthogs appeared to have a caffeine addiction, jittery and jumpy on approach. As their heads dipped down to drink, I settled my pin on the largest hog and released what I thought to be a perfect arrow. As if rehearsed, and faster than greased lightning, the warthog dropped and took the arrow above the shoulder. I knew the shot was high and north of the spine—a flesh wound at best. Even with persistence and the aid of expert trackers, we lost the blood trail within 100 yards. We continued our search, but it wasn't meant to be. Our bad luck continued over the next few days as record rainfalls ensured little activity at the waterholes. Complaining about the weather was akin to using a glass hammer, useless in every way. Another day on the Bushveld would be foolish as the animals did not need to water on a regular basis. It was difficult to accept, but after three all-day sits, I had to leave my dream of taking a kudu behind. Our one option was to return to the Highveld, hoping our luck would change for the better.

We were back on the prairie at sunrise, stationed in a luxurious termite mound. A few gemsbok approached the waterhole, smiling for the camera, but little else seemed thirsty. A crafty jackal came trotting in mid-morning, Africa's Wile E. Coyote. Having to judge the distance and shoot quickly, I saw my arrow sail harmlessly over his back. If jackals could laugh, I would have gotten an earful as he scampered across the Highveld. We switched locations after lunch, focused on a herd of blue wildebeest in the area. Marius and I stood watch over the waterhole, but only a few cows paid us a visit throughout the morning. Not long after lunch, two franklins worked their way into the water. These grouse-like birds are prolific across the African landscape and are remarkable table fare. I got the green light from Marius and anchored two of the tasty fowl, adding an à la carte option to the dinner menu. It was a welcome change to the tough hunting over the past few days. With renewed enthusiasm, we sat for the rest of the day, but nothing else quenched its thirst. Again, we tried to stay positive, but that had become an arduous task. Before drifting off to sleep that night, I stared at the ceiling, wondering how anyone could think Africa was easy.

As the sun rose on the final day of my African adventure, I took in every subtle detail. The morning hours passed, lunch was consumed, as was the last book in my daypack. Before I knew it, my weary eyes noticed the sun descending on the horizon. Taking in the cascade of colors with a reflective sigh, I was surprised when Marius said, "Big blesbok coming to the water." Like a shot of caffeine, I was wide awake, grabbing my bow as I focused on the waterhole. Three blesbok, one supporting giant bases and curved tips, made their way toward the water. The blesbok lowered their heads and drank at a fevered pace, allowing me to draw my bow. Without warning, a gust of wind spawned a dust devil and instantly they were gone. Having witnessed this before, I stayed vigilant, knowing there was a chance they would return. A few minutes later, Marius tapped me on the shoulder and said, "They are coming back. Get ready." As the blesbok returned to the water, I tried to settle my pin, but the ember flame on the horizon blinded my efforts. Subjecting my eyes to the effects of solar retinopathy, I bore down on the blesbok and my arrow was gone. Upon impact, the buck bolted from the water, did a short circle and expired. I gave Marius a celebratory hug and handshake before escaping the blind to admire my trophy. Throughout the week, we had exhausted all options, endured setbacks, and found success despite the conditions. I was proud of our efforts and the friendships made, neither of which could be bought.

Eyad's last night Blesbok.

I met my father and fiancé at the Johannesburg airport the next day, where we embarked on a weeklong safari to Kruger National Park. There we forged more memories, laughed the nights away, and saw more animals than we could count. I even got to shoot the *Big Five* while I was there, with a camera of course, but every bit as rewarding. When you bowhunt any species, you add to it a level of uncertainty that is unsurpassed, and Africa proved to be no exception. My first trip to the Dark Continent was remarkable, and looking back, I realize what I thought would be an easy hunt turned out to be quite the opposite. It reminded me that the challenges we face are the essence of any bowhunt, no matter the species or continent. It was the adventure of a lifetime, and perhaps one day I will find my way back to this special place, nestled near a waterhole, waiting for whatever Africa has in mind.

Eyad's dad at Kruger National Park.

This baby giraffe was adopted after its mother was killed by lightning.

CHAPTER 20

The Halloween Ghost

Growing up in Iowa, I had always dreamed of owning my own farm, a sacred place to pursue my passions. That dream became a reality in 2005, when I purchased a small acreage right out of school. The farm was over-run with ATVs, had little cover, and was heavily gun hunted each season. Still, I felt it had potential, knowing that sound management and time could yield tremendous results. With the help of good friends Don and Seth, we planted food plots and established sanctuaries, slowly building the property. It wasn't long before the whitetails took notice, making our farm their own. Bucks, on the other hand, were as scarce as hen's teeth back then. Two years into our venture, and we had yet to harvest anything with antlers.

On January 9, 2008, the tail end of the 2007 campaign, I was shivering high atop a hickory, overlooking a small clover plot. The ground was blanketed in snow and ice; the temperature was bitterly cold. We had no grain to speak of, much less hunt over, but I wanted to finish the game. Does and young bucks funneled out of the hardwoods well before dark, with a good buck bringing up the rear. I stopped the buck just inside the timber, where my arrow found a broken strand of barbed wire. With frozen hands, I walked over to retrieve a clean arrow, closing the door on my season.

In 2008, our hard work continued to pay off. More bucks were showing up and the farm was coming together. The adjacent landowner had granted us hunting rights through a lease, which allowed us to access both properties. We couldn't wait to start scouting and hanging stands on the new acreage and got right to it. In early March, while shed hunting a cornfield on the new property, I found a matching set off a giant eight-pointer. The sheds were heavy and distinct, proving big bucks were using the area, and we hoped others would follow. Over the next few months, we drew up and carried out plans regarding sanctuaries, food plots, timber stand improvement, and native grasses.

The matching set off a buck Eyad called *The Big Eight*.

Habitat development was at the core of Eyad's management plan.

The center of the property became *The Sanctuary*, a large tract of timber we designated as a bedding area. We also increased the use of trail cameras, invaluable tools that allowed us to monitor the property. In late August, Don, Seth, and I set out to hang stands for the coming fall. A local farmer had planted the west side of the farm in alfalfa, a fan favorite among whitetails. The east side remained in switch grass and clover, giving us a nice combination of cover and food. Stands were hung along the edge of our food plots, trying to keep our intrusion at bay. One of our favorite sets was on the north side of The Sanctuary, where we cleared a small opening and seeded down clover. The plot was perfect for a south wind and access was easy.

A few weeks later, while looking over trail cam photos, I noticed two unique bucks. They were impressive, one having long tines and a perfect frame, with a sticker coming off his left beam. The other buck carried heavy palmation and character, almost moose-like. Although the cameras captured other bucks, previewing the approaching fall, I wondered if we would see this duo again. We called them *Sticker* and

Palmy   Sticker

The Big Eight

Palmy, signatures their antlers earned. Along with *The Big Eight*, whose sheds I had confiscated in March, we awaited the opener with optimism and excitement. September flew by, equipment and stands were fine-tuned, and soon October was upon us.

Seth's first archery whitetail.

After taking a doe early in the season, I focused my attention on Sticker, Palmy, and The Big Eight. The October Lull came and went with little movement as usual. On October 25, while having dinner with my family, I got a call from Don near sunset. I knew it could mean only one thing and answered the phone. Seth had shot a nice buck in the north side food plot, and while they didn't recognize him, Don said he was big bodied and mature. They both felt the shot was good but hadn't found the arrow yet. I wanted to head down that evening, but we agreed it was best to give him time. The next morning, we found the buck at the end of a sparse blood trail not far from the stand. He was an awesome animal with thick beams and a perfect rack. I can't express how proud I was of Seth, and seeing him beside his first archery whitetail is a moment I won't forget. After four years of hard work, Seth had taken the first buck on our farm, one any bowhunter would be proud of.

I planned to hunt that night on the east side of the farm, knowing the wind was perfect for the clover plot. We had pictures of Sticker and Palmy in that general area but hadn't seen them in weeks. The shagbark stand was setup nicely and positioned downwind of two major trails. Just before nightfall, I heard deer approaching from the east timber, heading for the clover. I knew this was a good sign, especially if the young bucks and does were moving early. As darkness fell, I saw tall tines coming through the timber and knew who it was. Sticker stepped across the fence and walked parallel to the tree line, working the edge of the food plot. I settled my twenty-yard pin and dropped the string, hearing a loud crack echo through the night. Sticker burst for cover and soon disappeared into The Sanctuary. There was no blood along the arrow shaft, just greasy tallow and fat. I knew I'd hit the brisket and that my search would be in vain. No matter; I spent the next day looking for any sign of the buck but never found a trace. I captured one last photo the following week, on a rainy, windswept night. But I never saw him again. What became of Sticker is still a mystery. Stories abound of his death, from the hands of another hunter to the brutality of winter. What led to his demise I'll never know, but it wasn't my arrow.

I continued to hunt my farm religiously, but buck sightings were rare. We captured a picture of The Big Eight in early November, cruising in the dead of night. He was a beast in every sense of the word, but like most giant whitetails, was reclusive by nature. There was another farm I was hunting with my good friend Monte and thought a change of scenery would be good. I was down and dejected, but as a bowhunter, it was something I had to get used to. On a blustery, cold November day, with a climber on my back, I entered the timber and shimmied up a lonely hickory on the new property. Not long after getting settled, I saw a massive buck chasing a doe across a food plot, perhaps 100 yards away. I had nothing to lose and hit him with everything I had: rattling antlers, tending grunts, even a snort wheeze. I lost sight of him shortly thereafter and waited with bow in hand, but nothing came of it. The wind was howling out of the northwest, and as I went to hang up my bow, I noticed the buck standing there at 15 yards—looking at me. He had circled downwind after my calling sequence and caught me red-handed. We both knew how this would end, but that didn't stop me from trying to lace an arrow through his vitals. The giant jumped the string and my arrow sailed harmlessly over his back, embedding itself in a dead limb. Despite my best efforts, the broadhead was impossible to retrieve, a memento to a tough season.

With Sticker gone and question marks surrounding Palmy and The Big Eight, I didn't know what 2009 would bring. Time passed, and while on a shed hunt in March, coursing along a hardwood ridge, I noticed white tines protruding from the oak leaves. The shed had become the property of the woodland mice long before I discovered it, but the palmation and mass were obvious. Palmy was alive, and with this realization, I found myself enthralled with the giant once more. The warmer months soon arrived, and in late July, we captured a fleeting photo of a palmated beast. The identity of the buck was never in question—Palmy had returned once more. As I prepared for the opener, I thought back to my scouting forays, feeling good about one spot in particular. I had discovered a deep hollow that would make the Headless Horseman cringe, with a perfect crossing near the east end. Whitetails prefer the head of a hollow, where the divide narrows, and this one was a classic. It happened to border a cedar thicket and, with an agricultural field to the east, I couldn't imagine a more perfect setup. A south wind would be ideal to hunt this location, and if I eased in here when the conditions were right, I might catch a big boy cruising.

The seasons changed, and near the end of August a new buck entered the scene. I had placed a camera near the ditch crossing, along the edge of the cedars, and caught the bruiser leaving his bed. He seemed to possess character with heavy beams and a solid frame. The Big Eight from last year remained a recluse, as did Palmy, although both were in the back of my mind. I decided against hanging a permanent set near the cedars, choosing instead to hang and hunt should I return in November. My attention was on Palmy and The Big Eight, but once I got the wind and weather I was looking for—I would be back. On October 25, I headed south along Interstate 380, destined for my farm. The Weather Channel was calling for a storm front that afternoon, and I watched the clouds roll in.

Bleeding Iowa Hawkeye blood, I had survived the football team's thriller against Michigan State the night before and was exhausted. I thought about lying my head back to take a nap, but that was nothing more than a fleeting thought. I wasn't planning to hunt the ditch crossing until November, but Don said he had a feeling, and I've learned to heed his advice. The clouds were looming as I carried my portable stand toward the timber, feeling the weather change as I approached. I walked along the edge of the bean field and then cringed as I entered the hardwoods. Waking the dead with each step, the brittle oak leaves crunched beneath my boots, no doubt alarming every whitetail within earshot.

With meticulous care, I made my way toward the cedars as a south wind brushed my face. I had prepped the site that spring, trimming branches and clearing lanes should I return. My deciduous ally was still there, a white oak with perfect branches to conceal my presence. As I drew closer, I felt a rain drop hit my cheek before a steady drizzle began to fall. This worked in my favor, depressing the sound and scent of my approach. Soon I found myself twenty feet above the forest floor, ready for my evening vigil. I scanned the area for the first time in months and took note of my surroundings. The leaves throughout the hardwoods had changed, trading their green coats for hues of orange, red, and yellow. A gray squirrel was grabbing acorns like a greedy child, grocery shopping before the storm settled in. There were a few more saplings I should have cleared that spring, but hindsight is 20/20.

The hours passed uneventfully, and I questioned my sanity as cold rain-drops soaked through my clothing. Just before nightfall, I saw a decent eight-pointer ghosting through the cedars. Soon after, a doe followed, and my heart raced as she passed by. If the young bucks and does were moving, perhaps the big boys would follow. Minutes later, I glanced to my right and saw a giant rack materialize through the mist and cedars. I immediately noticed his mass and dark-colored rack, attaching my release without hesitation. The buck passed through the timber and stopped to check the wind behind a small sapling before continuing his course. With a sagging belly and thick neck, his maturity was never in question. I pulled my head back and looked for an opening, finally seeing an opportunity if he stayed the course. I bleated sharply when he hit the gap, stopping the buck mid-stride. My arrow was on its way, disappearing behind his shoulder in the diminishing light. The buck bounded off and stopped, his ivory flag flickered back and forth, and then he stumbled. Raindrops continued to pat the leaves like a drum roll, drowning out my footsteps as I approached the fallen beast. Holding his chocolate-colored rack in my hands, after two years of missed opportunities and countless hours, was rewarding beyond words.

The months flew by with no sheds or sightings of Palmy well into 2010. We heard of a large buck being shot on the adjacent property, which unfortunately was not recovered. We wondered if Palmy or The Big Eight was the wounded giant, and the question remained whether they had made it through the harsh Iowa winter. Soon, the short, brutal days of winter transitioned into spring, and it was time to prepare for another fall. We were excited because two distinct bucks were showing up on camera, seeming to call our farm home. Much to our dismay, neither was Palmy, and the hope he was still roaming the hardwood ridges and cornfields began to dwindle.

Eyad's 2009 Buck

While scouting my farm during the off-season, I was intrigued by a certain location on the backside of a ridge. I had seen bucks traverse this area before but never gave it much consideration. This was a classic edge, where secondary growth met mature timber. As the bucks cruised in late October, looking for the first does in estrus, they would use terrain such as this to mask their travels. The ridge also gave them a clear escape route to the valley below, which would appeal to their survival instincts. If I could place a stand along the downwind side of this ridgeline, where the two habitats blended into one, I might catch a big buck with his guard down. An east wind would be essential to make this plan work, but in this part of Iowa, that was a rare occurrence. I hung the stand in late August, when the resident hornets and wasps were less likely to set up shop. Seth agreed to assist me that hot, humid day, and he was a tremendous asset. When we finished, covered in mosquito bites and poison ivy, I noticed a problem. A hickory tree with a large branch was obstructing one of my shooting lanes. I knew the stand must be higher to negate this problem and told Seth what we needed to do. He was less than amused, but helped me nonetheless, even as the mosquitoes and humidity continued their assault. The stand was elevated, and while I thought it might be overkill, little did I know how important that move would become.

On October 30, the Iowa Hawkeyes again defeated Michigan State, which had been a good omen the year before. My wife, Melinda, and I were just leaving with our homemade Halloween costumes on our way to a party. Disguised as the *Tortoise and the Hare*, I had dyed my hair green, painted my face, and donned a shell, always getting the raw end of the deal. I was off the next morning, October 31, and was hoping to be in the stand before daylight. My wife had arranged to get a ride home with her friends, so I could leave early and get some sleep. We had a great evening, and at midnight I said goodbye and left the party.

I arrived at my parents' house two hours later, making sure not to wake them as I unpacked my gear. Still having my costume and makeup on, minus the shell, I removed my bow and boots from the trunk, and then my clothes… wait…where were my clothes? Leaving in a rush that night, I'd forgotten to grab my travel bag on the way out. After some choice words that need not be repeated, I decided what to do. I jumped in my car and headed for the

Tortoise and the Hare

sporting goods department at the local Walmart. Once I arrived, I grabbed the cheapest camouflage I could find and rushed to the checkout. With a cotton Realtree jacket and matching sweatpants, I had to laugh at myself, realizing it was the same outfit I wore almost twenty years ago. Sometimes simple rules the roost, and if there was ever a time to test that theory, this was it.

After I got home, I took a quick shower, threw my new clothes in the washer, and tried to lie down for a quick nap. That didn't work so well, because I tossed and turned through most of it. Rather than risk oversleeping, I got dressed, grabbed a Diet Coke, and headed out the door. An east wind was forecasted that morning and there was no question where I was headed. With baggy sweat pants and remnants of green hair dye beneath my cap, I was at the base of my tree in no time. The first hint of gray was already cresting the horizon, giving shape and substance to the hardwoods around me. I knew the dawn wouldn't wait, so I tied my bow to the pull rope and began my ascent. Climbing into the stand we had hung in August, I felt a northeast breeze hit my neck, carrying my scent over the valley below. As I hoisted my bow skyward, I heard a melody of footsteps coming toward me. A young ten-pointer was cruising down the ridgeline, moving past my stand with his nose to the ground. He was a nice buck, but one I had no intention of taking. Once he was out of sight, I placed my bow on the hanger and got settled, hoping the bucks would stay on their feet.

Approximately one hour later, my ears brought me to attention as I heard subtle footsteps atop the autumn leaves. My eyes followed suit, picking up long tines and a small, streamlined body cruising through the hardwoods. Getting a good look at the approaching whitetail, I realized he was too young and would get a pass. I understood there were no guarantees for his survival, but my decision would help his cause. A few minutes later, I noticed the young buck's behavior changing. He was nervous and staring up the ridge, poised to flee at any moment. Once again, my ears picked up the faint sound of a deer walking—a steady gait that grew louder with each passing second. Frozen like the young buck before me, I dared not look up, fearful the approaching whitetail would catch the movement and flee. The young buck then bolted down the hillside, and unable to maintain any more discipline, I, too, made my move. Regaining my focus as I looked up, I could see palmated beams ghosting over the ridgeline. The buck was walking with authority, possessing broad shoulders and a thick, muscular neck. His ears were laid back and bristled, revealing his lack of amusement with the youngster. The mass, the palmation, it was all becoming clear as he drew closer. It was Palmy, and he was coming right at me.

Realizing the young buck had heeded his warning, Palmy veered to my right and continued down the ridge. I was lifting my bow off the hanger when Palmy stopped on a dime. I could tell something was wrong and then realized what it was. That morning, in a haste to get to my stand, I had walked through an area I shouldn't have—a cardinal sin when hunting big whitetails. Palmy had cut my entry trail and was now aware of a human presence. Although they are constantly surrounded by humans, mature bucks have a low threshold for intrusion, and surely my fate was sealed.

The minutes passed. My heart was racing. I hoped the giant would ignore my mistake. He stood so still that I would have lost him among the forest floor, if not for his head tilts, ear turns, and flaring nostrils. With my eyes darting back and forth, I saw an opportunity, a small opening that might afford enough clearance for a shot. The arrow must travel over a large hickory branch, the same one that motivated the stand elevation back in August. Just as this irony became obvious, I noticed Palmy's demeanor had changed. His tail flickered, and he began walking down the ridge. With bow in hand, I began side-stepping on the tiny stand, turning 90 degrees to my right, needing to turn that much to make this work. Once turned, I attached my release to the string and came to full draw. As his vitals centered the opening, I let out a subtle grunt with my mouth, which stopped the giant in his tracks. My arrow was gone, passing through the monster in a blur of color and sound.

In the throes of a solid hit that echoed through the hardwoods, Palmy raced down the ridge and disappeared. Not hearing a crash, nor seeing him come to rest, I elected to wait thirty minutes before descending the tree. The arrow was nowhere to be found, so rather than push the envelope, I decided to leave and give him time. I was certain of the hit but had seen enough through the years to be cautiously optimistic. Had I struck bone, such as the shoulder blade, it would have been audibly evident. While it was possible the buck was already down, I wanted to call Don and Seth to get their opinion. After I told them the story, they were in their car, leaving their Missouri youth hunt to help. I tried to talk Seth out of it, but he wouldn't hear it. Don, Seth, and his Uncle Bobby were on their way, and truth be told, I needed all the help I could get.

We were back on the trail a few hours later. Failing to locate the arrow after a thorough search, we meandered in the direction Palmy had run. On the trail of a ghost, we took our time, looking for subtle clues left behind. A few minutes later, Don said, "I have blood." It was sparse and much darker than we expected, indicating the arrow may have exited farther back. Being patient had been the right call, because once you bump a buck from his first bed, the chances of recovery are greatly reduced. That possibility weighed heavily on my mind, and at one point I considered backing out, but Don convinced me to keep going. The blood trail was steady, but after traversing two hills and one ditch, I was getting nervous. We worked down into a creek bottom where I heard Bobby say, "Well, you can keep blood trailing if you want or just go look at your deer."

I crested the bank and there was Palmy. He had an incredible twelve-point frame with massive beams and palmation. To be standing before such a whitetail was surreal, and I realized how fortunate I was. We huddled around the giant, telling stories and reminiscing, before dragging Palmy out of the hollow. Sharing those moments with Bobby and two of my closest friends was priceless, and to this day it remains a bond unbroken.

One week later, on November 7, I was perched over a clover plot in an old hickory. I was still relishing Halloween's harvest, but with one more tag in my pocket, there was nowhere I'd rather be. My last opportunity in this stand had taken place two years ago, when I made a poor shot on Sticker. This day would be different, or so I thought. The morning dawned cool and crisp, with the Iowa hardwoods in the midst of the rut. Just after sunrise, I saw a doe crashing through the woodlot, knowing the reason for her panic. Sure enough, an Iowa bruiser with tall brow tines and heavy mass was on her tail, dodging deadfalls and zigzagging in hot pursuit. The doe ran past my stand at 20 yards, with the buck not far behind. I turned to my left and felt the safety belt coil around my midsection like a snake. No matter how hard I tried, I could go no farther. Feeling confident nonetheless, I held my draw until the buck approached and then bleated him to a stop. My arrow was on its way, striking the buck with such force that he coughed aloud and crashed through a brush pile on his exit.

Palmy

Surely he was down, as only a mortally wounded whitetail would act as such. Walking toward the farm house with a smile on my face, I called Don to report the good news. It took awhile to convince both of us it seemed, because I still didn't believe it. Never had I heard of such good fortune, two monsters in as many hunts, after going years without an opportunity on this farm. We were back at the stand two hours later, finding the impact site, with sparse blood soon after. My arrow was lying where the buck had stood, with white hair surrounding the area. I didn't like the looks of that, nor the fat coating the metallic shaft. We pressed on, again finding blood, this time more profuse. Following along at a steady pace, I decided I must have hit one lung, for any whitetail losing both would already be down. We crossed a hollow and then a CRP field, still finding drops consistently. Once we left the grassland, the blood became sporadic, and we struggled to find more sign. We split up, with Don heading toward the timber, and me north through the CRP. Soon, I heard him holler and rushed to the sound of his voice. Don had picked up the blood trail and followed it into a creek bottom, where he saw a red-tailed hawk take flight.

When he glanced over the edge, there lie a massive buck, with huge brow tines and a heavy frame. Moments later, I was peering over the edge myself and could see the giant with my own eyes. I gave Don a big hug as we celebrated before making our way to the bottom. As we approached, I noticed pockets of chilly water surrounding the beast and couldn't believe we had found him. Laying my bow on his chest, I tried to find the entry wound but was unsuccessful. I called Don over, where he too inspected the buck, finding the same result. I couldn't believe what I was about to say, but I knew it to be true. This wasn't my buck. What caused his demise I'll never know, as no visible wounds or signs of foul play existed. Had I found him weeks later, maybe even days, I would have thought him to be mine. We never found another trace of blood, nor did we hear of a giant being found. I kept replaying the events in my mind, knowing I'd never believe them if I hadn't experienced them myself. I asked two local teenagers to try and find my buck over the next two weeks, promising them my Mathews bow should they come up with a miracle. I never had to part with that bow.

To this day, I have no idea what became of that whitetail, nor do I have any clue to his identity. There was no history behind him, and all I remember are giant brows and a massive frame. I trust he made it, the arrow flying low, lacerating his brisket and nothing more. Maybe it was due to my safety belt, or an eager bowhunter dropping his arm to watch the flight of his arrow.

The mystery buck Eyad and
Don found in the creek.

The bottom line and painful reality is that I missed my mark—no fault but my own. As for the mystery buck we found in the creek, the European mount now sits in my home, a buck I never took with an arrow, but a better story because of it.

In the weeks that followed, Seth uncovered a trail cam photo from the fall of 2006, our second year on the farm. It showed a

Don and Eyad—First bowhunt
on the farm—October 2005

young buck with palmated antlers, angled brow tines, and a lean physique. Just shy of his second fall, who could have guessed what he would become, or the tales he would inspire. Neighboring landowners would later add to the story, handing me Palmy's 2009 sheds. They were found over a mile apart and under unique circumstances. I was grateful to have them.

Then, on a cold February day, Seth found The Big Eight. We had been shed hunting the lease, splitting up and taking different ridges, when I heard Seth shout a few minutes later. It was difficult to tell how long he'd been dead, or what from, but The Big Eight had grown into a monster. With a curved main beam and large drop tine, he was a sight to behold. Nature had finally collected him, a fitting end to a long journey. The Big Eight would later grace the cover of this book, his skull and antlers perfectly illustrated by artist Kathy Marlin.

Palmy was the last buck I would take on that farm before I had to sell it and move away. He became a legend through the years, a ghost only spoken of among close friends, and one never to be forgotten. Every hunter aspires to pursue such a whitetail and share that experience with those closest to them.

I feel honored to have been that bowhunter, and even more so to share it with Don and Seth. Those years were some of the best of my life, and I'll never forget the memories we built together.

Palmy 2006

Palmy 2010

CHAPTER 21

The Curse of the Longwalker

Nocturnal by nature and silent as the grave, the cougar roams the canyons and forests of western North America. Better known as the mountain lion to some, these reclusive cats are nearly invisible to man. Lore and legend only add to their mystery, as stories abound of these apex predators. With powerful jaws, sharp claws, and yellow-green eyes, these giant cats are masters of their craft, stalking unsuspecting elk and deer with precision. Because hounds are often used to track and tree these phantoms of the forest, many refuse to hunt them, feeling that the ethics of fair chase may be compromised. I would be remiss if I didn't tell you I was one of them, concerned that using hounds would be too easy. Little did I know how those words would come to haunt me in the years ahead.

After discussing a cougar hunt with a few of my close friends and mulling it over, I decided to give it a try. I was intrigued by these elusive predators and drawn to the ruggedness of the terrain they called home. Over the next few years, I traveled west, embarking on three cougar hunts: from the canyons of Utah to the Rocky Mountains of southern Alberta. From sunrise to sunset, we coursed through canyons and mountain passes but could not locate a runnable track. This hunt, which had seemed so easy in theory, took on an entirely new light. While packing my bags after my third unsuccessful trip, I recalled a conversation with a store owner in Utah. After ringing me up at the register, he looked at my attire and asked, "What are you hunting?"

"Cougars," I replied. "Do you see many out here? We've been hunting for days without much luck."

The old man took a moment to respond, and then said, "Son, I have lived here my entire life and never seen one." With wheels up on my way home, I lay my head back, realizing I'd gotten into more than I bargained for.

Utah Cougar Country

In January of the following year, I decided to give it one more shot. I was headed farther north to hunt with Byron Stewart of TNT Outfitters in northern Alberta. Byron is a well-respected outfitter and has a reputation for taking big toms. When I arrived in Edmonton, I was greeted by Jeff, one of Byron's guides and houndsmen. Jeff is one of the funniest and most energetic guys I've ever met, and I could tell the week ahead would be a good one. We arrived at Byron's and unloaded my gear into the cabin where I was staying. Soon after, we prepared the equipment for the week ahead and ensured everything was functional. In the harsh environment of the northern Rockies, Byron leaves nothing to chance, especially mechanical failures that could leave you stranded. The first morning of the hunt, we awoke to temperatures more akin to the Arctic Circle than Alberta. I did a double take when I looked at the temperature gauge, but it was indeed –38 degrees Fahrenheit. Byron explained that when it got this cold, the big toms would stay holed up on a fresh kill, which they make about once every six days. If it's a big cat, and they kill a moose or an elk, it may last longer. We pushed through the brutal cold and wind, trekking mile after mile across the Alberta landscape. From the paved roads with our trucks, to the mountain passes on quads and snowmobiles, we hoped to cut the track of a giant.

As the week progressed, we experienced warmer weather, courtesy of the Chinook winds that continued to blow. Byron felt the mild conditions could be good and bad. Coming into a meltdown was fine, as we would have a few days to find tracks and follow them before losing our snow. The cats would also be more active in the warmer weather, versus holing up on a kill. The temperatures were scheduled to plummet toward the weekend. When that occurred following a meltdown, it could be tough tracking. The tracks would diminish with the warming temperatures during the day, and then freeze overnight, a double-edged sword for a houndsman. Over the next few days, we covered a great deal of country but failed to locate any tracks worth running.

Near the end of day three, Byron unloaded the snowmobile and ran a stretch of road we hadn't checked yet. He returned just as darkness settled in and said, "Got him." Byron had found a large print running into a track of timber, and with no evidence that the lion had left, we believed he was still hidden in the coniferous jungle. We checked into a hotel that night, grabbed a bite to eat, and awaited the sunrise for what we hoped would be the end of my curse. It was exciting; after three years in cougar country without running a track, I might get my first opportunity. During the night, the cougar would leave the timber and hunt the mountains and valleys to the east. At first light, we merely had to find where he vacated his sanctuary and pick up his tracks from there. If only it were that simple.

On the trail of a lion.

The next morning was the warmest day of the week, going from −38 degrees Fahrenheit on the first day, to the upper twenties. We looked for tracks

along the timber section from the night before, trying to find where the lion had left on his evening vigil. It wasn't long before Byron and Jeff found where he crossed the road and headed into the mountains. After determining we could access the country where the big cat was headed, Byron collared up the dogs and turned them loose. The hounds took off like rockets and soon sounded off. Within minutes they were out of earshot, which was disconcerting considering the number of wolves in the area. If a pack of wolves located Byron's dogs, there would be little left if we found them. Byron, calm and collected, like the Bobby Fischer of cougar hunting, again showed no emotion. I could tell the mountains and drop-offs concerned him, but we hoped the dogs would tree the cougar in an area we could access.

We made our way to a logging road where we stopped to listen for the dogs. Although they had gotten confused at one point, they now seemed back on the cougar's trail. The scent these dogs were following was made the night before, and there was no telling how far the cat had gone. Cougars are known to travel 30 miles in one night, thus earning the nickname *longwalkers* in some circles. Byron took the snowmobile to access the dogs, while Jeff and I followed along on the ATV. Soon we were coursing through the vast forests of Alberta, one of the most beautiful areas I've ever seen. There was no wind, temperatures were in the high twenties, and our anticipation was at an all-time high. This was what cougar hunting was supposed to be, and Jeff was optimistic the dogs would tree the giant tom.

Great Gray Owl in the woods of Alberta.

We soon got to Byron, who had surged well ahead of us, and the look on his face told the story—something was wrong. The map showed a river in the direction the dogs had gone, and we noticed they kept moving back and forth along its bank. While the dogs continued to comb the shoreline, trying to unravel the mystery, Byron explained what had happened. The cougar, despite the raging rapids before him, had crossed the river the night before. We knew that trying to cross the treacherous stretch of icy water would put us all in jeopardy, and just like that, our hunt was over. Bowhunting can take you to the highest of highs, and the lowest of lows, and this was a prime example of the latter. Cougars will often hunt along waterways, such as rivers or streams, but swimming across is almost unheard of. In twenty years, Byron had only seen this behavior a few times, and the earlier humor at my perceived curse no longer seemed so funny. Still, the dogs would not concede defeat, and Byron had to walk down to the river to retrieve them. We returned to the trucks long after dark—wet, tired, and humiliated. Everybody was down and not saying much. It was a long and quiet ride home. We headed back to Byron's house to rest the dogs and regroup. I had little time left, and after so many days in the field, it was difficult to stay positive. Lying in bed that night, I couldn't believe what had transpired. And with rain and warmer temperatures forecasted, it didn't look good.

We started looking for fresh tracks in the morning, but our morale was down. Driving all day and not seeing much didn't help matters either. I was exhausted and wish I could say I had high hopes, but it was almost T-shirt weather and we were losing snow. Then, at 3:00 PM, Byron's cell phone rang and he picked it up. Jeff had found a track—and it was a good one. With clouds moving in and little daylight remaining, I knew Byron had a big decision to make. This late in the day, Byron would normally wait until the next morning to start a fresh track. But with forecasters calling for dropping temperatures and a massive storm, threatening to erase all sign, Byron went for it. At the very least, we could get a direction of travel and know where to start the next day. The fresh snow would help in the coming week, but with two days left to hunt, I wouldn't have time to reap its rewards. This track was our last hope, if it wasn't already too late. We drove as fast as we could to where Jeff found the last track, arriving just as small raindrops coated the windshield. Walking over to evaluate the large depressions in the snow, Byron suddenly became unglued. Up to this point, he had shown little emotion regarding the tracks we had found, but when he saw the large depressions in the fading snow he shouted, "Whoa…What a giant…Let's Go…Let's Go!"

We collared up the dogs and turned them loose, hoping they could find a hot trail. Up the hill they went, disappearing into the dark forest, where echoes of their howls soon faded. The dogs were having a difficult time getting any scent from the cougar's prints, as the warm temperatures and recent rainfall had evaporated the spoor. It wasn't long before they were back at our side, which brought our excitement level down a notch. Still trying to puzzle out the trail, Byron and Jeff decided we should walk down a logging road and into the woods, where the dogs had lost the scent. We hadn't gone far when suddenly, Byron said, "There."

A faint track was outlined in the soft snow, and I'm still shocked Byron saw it. The cat had come onto the frozen road where he could walk with little effort, and then moved back into the timber on a whim, leaving a subtle print in the slush beneath a spruce tree. We drove around at dusk looking for any exit tracks but found none. No doubt the giant cat was still in the timber. We returned to the cabin that night with guarded optimism, hoping that our fortune was about to change. Still, I tossed and turned most of the night, questioning whether my bad luck would continue to follow me like a shadow. If the weather held, we had a chance. But if it rained or snowed, and we lost the tracks, we would never know what might have been. Time would tell.

A mixture of sleet and rain greeted us as we departed the next morning. We drove down the icy highway, hoping the tracks were still fresh enough to follow, because this was our last chance. We located the freshest tracks from the evening before and started there. Byron collared up the dogs and headed into the timber to help them work it out. Jeff and I waited at the truck in case the dogs lost the scent and had to return. This was a good possibility considering the weather and deteriorating conditions. We waited in suspense at the drop-off point, hoping the dogs would figure this out. Just as I was losing faith, Byron radioed in and said,

"I found the tom's bed, and it's fresh."

I had my bow and pack ready to head into the timber when another call came in, but this one wasn't good.

"Jeff, get the gun. I can see the lion up ahead through the timber. He's big and bayed up on a log a foot or two off the ground. This could be a problem."

After being with the dogs all week, I had grown to appreciate and admire their courage and will to keep going. Over the years, Byron has lost a few dogs to these big cats, and that possibility is always present. The dogs, who had given their heart and soul to us all week, had one passion in life, and that was to hunt these giant predators. No matter the cost, they would push on until the end, often risking their lives to do it. As we prepared to move toward Byron's location, he called back and reported the cougar had left the log and was in a *leaner*—a tree that was broken and at an angle. I threw the bow sling over my shoulder and grabbed my pack. After three years in cougar country, I would finally get my chance.

Heavy flakes welcomed us into the dark timber as the forecasted snow began to fall. With each step the barks grew louder, and soon I could see the dogs through the vast forest and falling snow. I ducked under a spruce branch and saw Jeff looking straight up. There, twenty feet off the ground was the giant tom, glaring down with yellow eyes and contempt at the noisy creatures below.

If it desired, a cougar could kill each dog with ease. But not wanting to waste energy or risk injury, they often took to the trees and waited them out. It's when these giant cats choose not to tree, and instead face the dogs one-on-one, that the houndsman is left to carry his best friend home for the last time.

I waited for the right angle, and then my first arrow was on its way. Considering the size of the animal and risk to the dogs, Jeff told me to place one more. The second arrow found its mark as well, and the big cat was down. The emotions coursing through me were overwhelming, but I wore them on my sleeve, embracing this moment as the snow continued to fall. Byron and Jeff walked over to congratulate me. Standing near the giant tom, they both agreed I would be hard-pressed to take another of his caliber.

With the weather deteriorating, we decided to field dress the cougar back at camp. Just as we finished packaging the meat, Byron called me over to look at something. He held a clump of hair in his hand and smiled as I tried to figure it out.

Jeff, Eyad, and the Hounds

"It's horse hair," he said. "You took down a horse killer." The cougar's stomach was full of horse hair, and the stories and urban legends of missing horses and slain livestock now seemed all too real. At 180 pounds, with a skull pushing 15 inches, it was easy to imagine this giant taking down anything he desired.

That evening, the snow fell harder, the wind picked up speed, and the conditions worsened throughout the night. It was surreal to think that all the tracks we had located would be gone the following day. As I look back on my travels through Utah and Alberta, remembering the people and places I was blessed to encounter, I couldn't imagine a better ending. While this old tom will be the only lion I ever take, perhaps one day I'll accompany a good friend into cougar country, where I hope to hear the singing of the hounds again. And should I ever hear someone say, "I'm not sure I'd want to hunt cougars, it just seems so easy." I'll be sure to walk over, introduce myself and say, "Let me tell you a story."

CHAPTER 22

The Apex

When I started bowhunting three decades ago, my mind was filled with images of faraway lands. One stood tall at the apex of my wish list, a journey north into the Alaskan wilderness on a bowhunt for bull moose. I decided to pursue that dream many years later and booked a hunt for September of 2011, with Eric Umphenour of Hunt Alaska. Eric's operation is based in the heart of the Last Frontier and caters to gun and bowhunters alike. I trained hard, fine-tuned my equipment, and stalked four-legged foam at the archery range, doing all I could to prepare. My first-born son, ZJ, had other plans, though, as my wife and I welcomed him into the world the week I was scheduled to leave. While nothing could surpass the feeling of holding my baby boy, I still aspired to fulfill that dream. I pushed my hunt back to the fall of 2012 and waited for the cool winds of autumn to return. Soon, it was time to leave for Alaska.

After spending the night in Fairbanks, I boarded a small plane that would take us to base camp on Dry Creek in the Alaska Range. I knew that Fred Bear had spent many years hunting this area, and it was hard to contain my excitement as the plane lifted off the tarmac. The colorful changes of the fall foliage, the rivers and streams glistening throughout the landscape, and the mountain peaks on the horizon all made for an incredible flight. Banking as we neared a mountain peak, the plane began a rapid but steady descent into the creek basin below. Any concerns I had regarding a rough landing were curtailed as the wheels settled on the gravel bar. Because I would be bowhunting, Eric asked that I arrive in early September before the dominant bulls acquired their harems. This would ensure we had the best opportunity to get archery close, with fewer eyes and ears to foil our stalks and setups. We would try to lure a big bull within range by raking trees and bushes with Eric's *high-tech* call, which consisted of a plastic oil can taped to the end of a stick. On the verge of the rut, these bulls were becoming more territorial and agitated, challenging any adversary they viewed as competition—even an oil can. This would make calling an effective strategy and one we hoped to employ.

Descending on Dry Creek

I slept well the first night in camp, awakening to brisk temperatures and a clear sunrise. The small fire I had built in the wall tent the evening before had long since abandoned me, making the departure from my sleeping bag a tall order. I got dressed and loaded my daypack, once again inspecting my equipment to ensure that travel and time had left well enough alone. As I left the confines of my tent, a wolf howled from the mountains above Dry Creek. Resonating through the valley with haunting undertones, it reminded me that I was not the only hunter on this day. In the midst of the Alaska Range, a combination of foothills, mountains, and valleys comprised the terrain we would hunt. Our plan was to make our way to the higher elevations, which would afford us a better view with our optics. Once we spotted a mature bull, we could move in from the downwind side and close the deal.

We began our day near the top of Iowa Ridge; being born and raised a Hawkeye, the irony was not lost on me. Reddish-purple hues brushed the tundra below, while gilded aspens and green spruce trees dominated the hill-sides around us. The skies opened with a steady rain a few hours later, accompanied by strong winds and dropping temperatures. After glassing the area for some time, Eric spotted a big bull down in the valley. We had no chance if we stayed in the high country, so we loaded our packs and headed toward the palmated giant. Although the scenery was picturesque, getting across it was a different story altogether.

The tundra had the consistency of waterlogged sponges, filled with numerous bogs, shrubs, and tussocks. I felt like a drunken sailor as I stumbled across the expanse, the terrain far from what I expected. The tussocks resembled mushroom-shaped molehills, with clumps of sedge grass atop their crowns and trenches surrounding their bases. While attempting to use the tussock-tops as stepping-stones, I learned that Mother Nature designed them as obstacles rather than allies. Each step was more treacherous than the last, and the combination of steady rain and soaked tundra ensured that my clothes and boots were drenched. The wind was also picking up speed, aiding the cold rain's momentum as it pelted my face like bird shot. Still, we closed the gap, and soon I made out the bull's massive rack through the brush. Cautious of each step and every movement, I nocked an arrow and continued toward the bull.

My excitement was short-lived, for just as quickly as this hunt transpired, it ceased to exist. With long strides the bull disappeared into the tree line, consumed by the mist and vegetation. Whether it was his sixth sense, a fickle gust of wind, or just bad luck, the result was still the same. With dripping clothes and hanging heads, the journey back to camp was a long one. We awoke on day two to foggy conditions and limited visibility. This was Alaska, and one comes to expect changes in the weather, sometimes by the hour. We glassed between screens of fog throughout the morning, hoping to catch a shooter on his feet. In time, a brisk wind escorted the fog from the valley but grew stronger with each passing hour. Donning multiple layers and hunkering down, we tried to escape the gusty assault. Other than spotting a few small bulls, the afternoon was uneventful, and before long the sun began its descent. Taking one last look through his spotting scope, Eric noticed movement to the north. With silver-tipped hair and massive shoulders, a giant grizzly was gorging on blueberries in the valley below. I was fortunate to witness such a spectacle and watched the grizzly until the fading light devoured him.

Rather than returning to base camp for the night, we chose to set up a spike tent on Iowa Ridge. The small tent was a welcome reprieve from the fierce winds, and I could hardly wait for dinner and a change of clothes. A warm meal was not meant to be, however, as Eric found the propane tank in our stove was empty. Settling for granola bars and cold soup, we tried to get some rest, hoping our tent could withstand the blustery conditions. Despite the wind's best efforts, our tent held its ground, and by first light we were ready to go.

After loading our gear in the Yamaha Viking, we worked our way down a steep embankment. I was searching for my gloves in the console when I noticed the vehicle's warning label, illustrating two stick figures flailing their arms in despair. Wanting to get my attention, my subconscious also pointed out deep ruts and potholes along the hillside. Not being the world's lightest bowhunter, I mentioned to Eric that if we found one of these depressions on the downhill side, we might take a tumble. In the next instant, as if my warning conjured it, I felt the front tire sink into a rut—and the Viking rolled. I pulled my arms and legs into my body, hoping to keep them, just as the Viking landed on its side.

The Viking after rolling on a steep slope.

With the UTV's frame buried in the tundra and our gear scattered about, we were both speechless. Had I not heeded the vehicle's warning label, and instead kept my limbs extended, they would have been crushed. Shaken up and bruised, we quickly righted the Viking, loaded our gear, and silently searched for flatter ground. We headed to a vantage point farther up the valley as the wind continued to pick up speed. With powerful gusts over 50 mph, we didn't expect to see much movement, and two hours later that prediction became reality. While a few caribou dotted the landscape around us, it appeared the moose had vanished, perhaps swept away by the gale force winds. Hours passed as we continued to battle the elements, our faces wind-burned and fingers numb. With midday drawing closer, and my hopes far from high, I thought I was hearing things when Eric said,

"I see a couple of cows, Eyad, and there's a good bull with them."

High above the valley below, near a rocky point on the adjacent ridgeline, stood a big bull with two cows. Even with my binoculars, I could only catch flashes of the bull's white antlers against the honey-colored hillside. How Eric had seen them I'll never know, but his glassing skills were impressive. Rather than following the cows along the ridgeline, the bull bedded down on the steep slope, where I noticed a trio of spruce trees near his sanctuary. Surrounded by a sea of yellow, they stood isolated and alone, as if hostages of the aspens and willows. Although the spruce trees served as landmarks to locate the bull, the hard reality remained that he was a good distance away and in a very difficult spot. We would have to cross a creek, climb a pair of hillsides that would make a mountain goat cringe, and then maneuver through the tangled maze within which the bull was bedded. It was crazy to consider, but within minutes I had my bow in hand, and we were headed into higher country.

Wind can be a bowhunter's best friend or worst enemy, and today I wasn't sure which it would be. We knew the bull would not leave his bed under these conditions, and the strong winds would silence our approach. On the other hand, a change in direction or a swirling gust could give us away, revealing our presence without warning. Side-hilling, grabbing trees, and digging in our heels, we made it up the first incline one hour later. With labored breaths and weary legs, we continued to climb, soon spotting the rocky precipice and spruce trees near the bedded giant. Confident we were now above the bull, we circled around and descended, hoping to glimpse his rack in the cover below.

The spruce trees above the bedded bull.

Step-by-step, with the wind in our favor, we crept down the steep terrain, hoping to see him before he sensed us. Soon the contour of the slope changed as solid rock replaced the leaf-choked hillside. The trio of spruce trees we sought soon revealed themselves, and I knew we must be close. Looking for the subtlest nuance in color or motion, we noticed tines protruding from a willow thicket a mere 30 yards below. The bull's rack rotated back and forth like a scythe, mirroring the giant's movements as he surveyed his surroundings. Neither one of us said a word as we stood motionless on the rocky knoll, knowing we had not only found the bull, but happened to be in his bedroom.

Eric stayed back as I pulled an arrow from my quiver and secured it to the string. Creeping closer, now within bow range, I attached my release and took a deep breath. The bull still had no clue I was there—oblivious to my presence. Shifting my weight on the steep incline, I felt a small stick break beneath my boot, and the bull rose to his feet. I hit my anchor and waited for the bull to clear the willows, only needing him to take one step forward.

Then, without warning, as if by a cruel twist of fate, a strong gust of wind blew my arrow off the rest like a feather. The wind, which up to this point had been my greatest ally, betrayed me, changing its mind as to whose side it was on. I grabbed my arrow and placed it back on the rest, noticing the calm demeanor I had exuded before was nowhere to be found. With shaking hands, I attempted to attach my release to the D-loop, but the harder I tried the more difficult it became. Finally, the jaws of the caliper swallowed the loop, but I feared my efforts were in vain. Looking up as my eyes strained to refocus, I watched as the giant walked toward a thicket, taking with him the little hope I had left. Then I heard a noise from behind me. Eric, realizing what was happening, started grunting like a rut-crazed bull.

"Uggmf … Uggmf."

The bull stopped and looked up, hypnotized by the challenge he heard from above. Coming to full draw once more, I tried to find an opening among the leaves and limbs, my eyes desperately searching for daylight. Soon, my eyes found what they were seeking and, within seconds, my arrow did too. With a solid hit echoing in my ears, I watched as the bull disappeared into the valley below. The wind made it impossible to hear anything else, and all I could do was hope for the best.

To say I was thrilled is an understatement, but I knew this hunt was far from over. Although I was confident of my shot placement, I also understood that looks can be deceiving, and the need to evaluate the sign was critical. We walked down to where the bull had stood and soon found my blood-soaked arrow lying on a clump of lichens. Passing through the bull, the razor-sharp broadhead had done its job, but I wondered if I had done mine. The sign looked good as the length of the arrow was coated, yet the blood was darker than I liked to see. I spun the shaft in my hand and noticed a greenish tinge, which had me concerned. We needed to give the bull time, but leaving him overnight was not an option. The wolves and grizzlies would soon claim the bull as their own and, as most bowhunters can attest, the rack would serve as no consolation if I lost the meat. We would wait until late afternoon to begin tracking, and I prayed that patience and sharp blades would reward me before nightfall.

Four hours later, with the sunlight promising little more time, we took up the trail. I was confident we had done everything right by backing out and being patient, but I also realized there were no guarantees. Finding little sign at the impact site, we had to be slow and methodical if we were to find this bull. Weaving through the jungle of willow, aspen, and birch that resided on the steep Alaskan slope, we finally picked up blood. With renewed enthusiasm, we found more sign, staring intently at each sapling, rock face, and leaf. Suddenly, Eric stopped and pointed toward a clearing ahead of us.

"There he is, Eyad!"

Lying before us, in the shadows of the Alaska Range, was one of North America's storied animals. The bull had come to rest among the aspens and willows, with golden leaves scattered upon his side. Carrying long tines and defining character, the monarch was regal in every way. After nearly three decades, my dream of taking a giant Alaskan moose had finally come true.

The next day, we headed back to the kill site to pack out the rest of the

Eyad's Alaskan Moose

meat. Eric had driven the Viking to where the moose had fallen, offering un-matched assistance. After taking care of the meat and removing it from the field, Eric and I hoisted the rack and secured it to my pack frame. The UTV was full to the brink, so Eric would head back to camp and then meet me at a creek crossing in the next valley. He wished me well and was off, soon disap-pearing over the ridgeline. I could tell another front was on its way, blowing over the Alaska Range with ferocity. Securing the straps on my pack frame, I headed out across the tundra, trying to balance the meat and antlers atop the tussocks. Soon I made it to the ridgeline, but rather than following the UTV's route, I took a short-cut to hasten the trek. I dropped off the ridge into the valley below, in time regretting my decision. The fortress of pine, spruce, and willows pushed me around like a pinball, forcing me to bob and weave through the jungle. How these bulls worked their way through this tangle was beyond me. Eventually, I tore through the shrubbery, only to emerge on a ridge I didn't recognize. By this time, I was soaked with sweat and blood, courtesy of my recent hike and field dressing efforts. Feeling my body temperature cool, with legs that felt like rubber, I realized that I was turned around and getting low on energy.

In my rush to get going, I had left my pack in the Viking, not thinking I would need it. I looked over the landscape, realizing there were now two streams flowing through the valley. Picking the right one would be akin to a coin toss—not the best option. What concerned me most was the cold working its way through my body, and the knowledge that I had no compass, radio, change of clothes, food, water, or lighter. I was shaking my head and feeling foolish, knowing I had done this to myself. I headed downhill into a stream bed, hoping to see the rendezvous point around the next bend. Once I was in the bottom, the antlers still digging into my side and shoulders, I lost sight of the horizon. The temperature was dropping, along with my confidence, as I prepared myself for a cold night in the bush. Trudging through the sand and water, I could smell blood on my forearms, hands, and clothing, the iron scent wafting through the air. I rounded a corner, and what I saw turned my face a shade of white.

Fresh grizzly tracks coursed through the creek bottom, zigzagging back and forth. They weren't just any grizzly tracks, but a trio of bears, two of which were much smaller. A bad situation just got worse, as I realized a sow and her cubs were also using this waterway. If I could detect blood, to them I would smell like a meat locker, and there would be no hiding my presence. Interfering with a sow and her cubs is bad enough, but covered in blood and with antlers on my back, I'd be low hanging fruit. Eric had laid a pistol on the ground while we were field dressing the bull, in case a grizzly questioned whose kill we were on. That did me little good now, and I was kicking myself for not being prepared. If I followed the creek, it may be in the wrong direction, and perhaps into the waiting claws of bedded bears. Neither were good options. I was more concerned about the bears than the elements, knowing I could stay on my feet and keep warm, but I wouldn't stand a chance against an enraged grizzly. Breaking out of the bottom and back up the ridge, I felt better about my vantage point but still didn't recognize the landscape on this side of the mountain. I contemplated dumping the pack to return later but knew that would only complicate matters.

With Eyad's clothes soaked in blood and antlers on his back—
this grizzly track wasn't a good sign.

I said a quick prayer and worked down a steep embankment toward the other stream. This one had more turbulence but wider banks, which would allow me to move much faster. Not 10 yards into my decision, drenched and weary, I heard three rifle blasts. They came from the exact opposite direction, behind me, over a ridge I hadn't considered. Sprinting up the incline, as fast as a man with a moose rack could run, I crested the hill. Farther down the valley, I heard more shots and again hurried along. Soon, I had my bearings and worked down a steep incline to find Eric and the UTV. To pass the time while waiting for me, Eric had decided to fire a few practice rounds with his rifle. Why he had done so just before I descended to the other stream remains a mystery. Once among the rapids, his shots would have fallen on deaf ears, making the timing even more ironic. I have no doubt the Man upstairs had something to do with it, letting me suffer just long enough to teach me a lesson.

While waiting for the plane to touchdown on a secluded air strip, we walked along the banks of Dry Creek, where a cabin stood near its shore. Once frequented by Fred Bear, I entered the rustic sanctuary, wondering what stories it could tell. An old arrow hung on the wall, a worn shaft with tattered feathers, still armed with a menacing broadhead. Inspecting the blades with a hint of nostalgia, I thought of the bowhunting icon, his adventures on Dry Creek, and what it meant to walk in his footsteps. A short time later, after loading our gear in the plane, the pilot spun on a dime and accelerated down the runway. Taking one last look at the peaks and valleys in the distance, I felt a sadness envelope me. I realized that I may never return to this place, walk through its streams or wade through its tundra. Strangely though, I was at peace with this notion, knowing I was leaving with memories that would last a lifetime.

Chase Your Dreams

Larry Zach's *Broken Solitude-Whitetail*

CHAPTER 23

Broken Solitude

Grasshoppers scattered like buckshot as our boots shuffled through the alfalfa. It was late summer in southeast Iowa, and I was walking my farm with good friend Rich Waite. Rich was a land specialist in the Midwest and was advising me on a CRP program. As we moved along, I brought up a topic I'd been meaning to discuss. With a growing family, I knew the two-hour drive to my farm would be difficult in the coming years. I explained my dilemma and asked if he could keep his eyes open for a property closer to home.

Rich stopped abruptly, as if my question was a joke, and then said,

"I just listed one today, Eyad. It might be something you want to look at."

Fate has a way of presenting opportunities, and I wasn't blind to this one.

The listed property was a mixture of hardwoods and CRP, with streams, creek bottoms, and thickets interspersed throughout. It had never been managed for deer hunting per se, but in Iowa, the potential is always there. I found it difficult to let go of my first farm and the dreams we had worked hard to fulfill. Still, it was the right decision for my family, and I sold my property in the coming months. Fresh dirt would be exciting, but I knew the challenges that starting over would bring. I took possession of the new farm in early January and scouted the acreage, trying to get a lay of the land and its inhabitants. Aerial maps were great tools, but good old-fashioned boot leather was tough to beat.

One morning, while walking a steep ridge on the new farm, I came across a clump of basswood trees. Multiple trunks erupted from the forest floor like pillars of a coliseum, with several gouged and rubbed clean. Through the years, more than one buck had left his signature on these sign-post rubs, marking his territory each fall. I thought of a keepsake in my office: a framed

Basswood trees in the Iowa hardwoods.

print by legendary wildlife artist Larry Zach. *Broken Solitude-Whitetail* depicts a monster buck standing tall along a hardwood ridge as sunlight filters through the timber. A clump of basswood trees, shredded and scarred, sits in the foreground, while the painting's rustic colors and tones stir images of autumn. My parents had given me this print as a gift in 1992—the first year I started bowhunting. I cherish it to this day, and as I stared at the tattered basswoods that morning—the inspiration for Zach's masterpiece—I couldn't help but smile at the irony.

After weeks of walking the property, I envisioned a habitat plan that I wanted to implement. The first step was to meet with state foresters and identify areas conducive to Timber Stand Improvement (TSI). TSI would kill two birds with one stone, by maximizing both habitat and mast production. The foresters agreed that the understory was struggling, suffocated by a canopy of ash, hickory, and ironwood trees. Hinge-cutting these shade-tolerant species would create a fortress within the woodlands, providing immediate cover and browse. With increased sunlight to the forest floor, oaks and their acorns would thrive, along with wildflowers, blackberries, and forbs. Ancient trees were off limits, no matter the species, having earned that right through the centuries. Not only were they aesthetically pleasing, but they represented living monuments of history; they were treasures to be preserved and protected. Old shagbark hickories serve another purpose as well. They provide housing for the endangered Indiana bat. These flying mammals prefer to roost beneath the plated bark of this deciduous tree, and we ensured there were plenty of vacancies. Don and Seth, along with good friends Monte and Travis, all helped to meet the demands of the forestry plans and schedules. However, it was my father-in-law, Russ, who took on the brunt of the work.

One of the toughest and hardest-working guys I know, he partook in the TSI project like it was his own. I'll always be grateful for the work he put in that winter, helping me chase a dream. Equipped with chainsaws, helmets, and chaps—we hinge-cut ridgelines, dodged falling limbs, and prayed that *widowmakers* wouldn't live up to their name. We always started early, took a quick break for lunch, and then it was back to the salt mines. After a long day in the field, we would work our way to the local Pizza Ranch, where we caught up on

Eyad's father-in-law was instrumental in completing the TSI project.

lost calories. Those days created great memories, but it wasn't all fun and games. On one occasion, I almost bought the proverbial farm. A small tree went rogue and turned on us, falling in a direction we had not anticipated. I recall sprinting down the ridge in a panic—with the widowmaker in hot pursuit. One branch, no bigger than a pool stick, found the top of my head and dropped me like a sack of potatoes. Not wearing a helmet was a fine example of stupidity, and all I remember is seeing stars. A larger limb would have ended my life, and if not for my newborn son, my wife would have too. Scolded like a toddler by my better half, I vowed never to be so foolish again. In time, I was back in her good graces.

With the TSI project complete, I turned my attention to native grasses and food plots. Monte and Travis took the reins and prepared the fields, seeding down switch, big blue stem, and Indian grass. These natives spend their first year growing down and establishing roots, only to emerge skyward the following summer. This ocean of grass would provide cover for all wildlife: from cottontail rabbits and quail to turkeys and whitetail deer. We also established clover plots to enrich the soil and create a perennial food source. Although I didn't see many deer that first season, I did capture some nice bucks on camera. Two in particular had my attention, both carrying impressive antlers. One was a broad-shouldered beast with eight points and a spider-like rack. The other buck was a perfect ten with solid mass. They were frequent visitors to my cameras during the late season, becoming more consistent as the cold days of winter settled in.

As the fall of 2012 approached, we saw the fruits of our labor unfold. The native grasses and food plots were flourishing, while the TSI had created a jungle of secondary growth within the forest. I hoped the two bruisers would return, with larger head gear to boot. I was not disappointed, as by the end of October both bucks had reappeared. The eight looked like a bull, with a hulking neck, curled tines, and heavy bases. The ten-pointer had also become a giant, with a 6x7 frame that reminded me of a picket fence. *Spider* and *67* were on my radar, and I was looking forward to the challenge.

With a young son at home and work responsibilities, my time in the woods was limited. I watched the wind and bounced around, trying to get a fix on either buck. Free-range whitetails have no loyalty, and as they made their rounds through numerous properties, I could only hope our paths would

Shed hunting and scouting in the off-season.

cross. 67 had vanished by late November, making me wonder if his breeding range was concentrated elsewhere. Spider, on the other hand, was a homebody and passed through more frequently. Nevertheless, with the shotgun season looming, I was running out of time. Throughout the fall, I had noticed multiple deer favoring the inside corner of a clover field, but there wasn't a suitable tree for a stand. Still, I had to try something in the eleventh hour and chose the best of the bunch.

A walnut tree would work, if crooked counts, so I hung my stand and chuck-

67

Spider

led as I walked away. I might as well wear a clown suit if I hunted this set, because I couldn't be any more exposed. It was my only option, though, and I had to play the hand I was dealt. On November 25, I was sitting in that eyesore of a stand, on the last weekend of the early archery season. I nocked an arrow and got settled, feeling like a panda in a bamboo tree. Near nightfall, I received a call from my wife that she and my son had come down with a stomach flu. Any parent can imagine the play-by-play on that exchange, and I had to get home soon. I went to grab my pull rope when I caught movement to the south. Spider was heading my way through a narrow section of the field. With my bow in my lap—all I could do was watch.

He worked his way to my left before feeding, now well within bow range. Darkness was encasing the clover plot, so I had to act, and without thinking I hastily turned my bow upright. Spider's eyes locked onto my position; I was busted and knew it, like a kid with a cookie jar. Frozen in place and without a prayer, I thought it was over, when suddenly I caught movement to my right. A small buck had entered the field and was casually feeding along. Spider's reputation as a bully was well documented, and he did not disappoint. He lowered his head and trudged through the green field, his hair bristling, making his way toward the youngster. I seized the opportunity and came to full draw before stopping Spider with a grunt.

The arrow was on its way but was quickly devoured in the fading light. In that instant, I heard a subtle *slap,* as if I had swatted a piece of clothing. Spider whirled and sprinted through the narrows, his white flag soon vanishing around the corner. My phone had been chirping since my wife called, and rightfully so, because it appeared they were getting worse. Nervous as a cat on a hot tin roof—for a multitude of reasons—I hustled down the tree to where Spider had stood. My arrow was embedded in the ground with a faint trace of blood on the shaft. You know what they say about assumptions, and my biggest mistake was making one. Based on the blood trail, or lack thereof, I assumed my arrow had merely grazed him.

Fifteen minutes later, I was back at the truck, having coursed through the field with my flashlight. There wasn't a hint of blood or hair in the direction he ran, nor any sign I could appreciate. I was eager to get home to help my family but vowed to return the next day. Home was worse than I feared, and over the next two days everyone struggled to get better. Not until November 28 did I make it back to the farm, convinced I had grazed the big eight. I had marked the impact site and confirmed my yardage estimation was correct. While working through the narrows and around the bend, I saw a coyote erupt from the creek bottom. He sprinted across the field and into a large tract of timber, which piqued my curiosity. I walked toward the creek but saw nothing of interest along its banks. I spent the day combing the rest of the farm but came up empty-handed. In addition to covering ground on foot, I hung multiple cameras throughout the property, hoping to get proof of life. Spider loved the lens, but over the next two months, I failed to capture another photo.

I kept replaying the shot and sound in my mind, but I couldn't understand why he had disappeared without a trace. The situation wasn't sitting well with me, so I returned in early February, hoping to find his sheds. Four hours later, I had yet to find any bone and decided to cut down a steep embankment. That plan was foiled when I hit a patch of multiflora rose that was impenetrable. Reminiscent of a Stephen King novel, the sharp tentacles wrapped around my body like a serpent, biting into my clothes and skin. Bloodied and frustrated, I burst through, cursing the prickly shrubs with each step. As I tried to navigate the torture chamber, I looked to my right and saw antlers through the thicket. Eight tines lie still in a shallow depression, attached to a skeleton that was weathered and worn. The field where I shot Spider was just across the creek, but the briars and deadfalls made his sanctuary nearly invisible. Shaking my head in disappointment, I recalled the coyote that had burst from this bottom and realized I should have looked harder. Mother Nature ensures that nothing goes to waste, and the clean skeleton proved that Spider had been here for some time.

I sat there in silence and thought about the events following that fateful night, trying to find solace in what lie before me. If it weren't for the coyote or the absence of pictures, the blood on the arrow or his final resting place,

I would think differently about Spider's demise. Closure can be bittersweet, and this ending fit the bill. I called the local game warden, and he graciously offered me a salvage tag, which allowed me to recover the rack. It now sits downstairs among other memorable whitetails, conjuring up stories I won't soon forget. Spider was the first buck I encountered on the new farm, a whitetail I pursued for two seasons, and whose story ended on a cold winter day. While I'll never know what happened after my arrow left the string, I am grateful for the lessons and memories I gained in his pursuit. I didn't feel good about the outcome but would learn from my mistakes. In bowhunting, that's sometimes all we can do.

CHAPTER 24

Big Mountain Bison

Centuries ago, long before the first Europeans set foot upon these shores, an icon roamed the Great Plains of North America. Estimated to once number more than fifty million, with a range that extended from Alaska to Mexico, the American bison ruled the grasslands and prairies. Perhaps no animal is surrounded with as much lore and regret, nor been so entwined into the history of the United States and its settlers. First described by French explorers in the 17th century as *les boeufs*, from which the word buffalo is derived, bison are the largest land animal in North America. Although they share many of the same characteristics as the true buffalo of Asia and Africa, bison are entirely their own species. Sacred to the Native Americans who first inhabited these lands and vital to their culture, bison were worshiped and respected. This mindset did not carry over into those who crossed the Atlantic.

Despite a population thought to be limitless, the slaughter that ensued throughout the 1800s left fewer than a thousand bison remaining by the turn of the century. Thankfully, a select few who feared the bison's extinction preserved the resource a nation took for granted. Now, more than a century later, the bison are secure once more. With numbers throughout the United States and Canada at nearly 500,000, they have made a strong comeback.

Hunting these legendary animals in the wild is a different story. Arizona, Alaska, and Utah offer the only free-range opportunities in the United States, and these tags are difficult to acquire. One other option exists along the Sikanni River in the northern tiers of British Columbia. In this western Canadian province, nonresident tags are allocated each year and are available through select outfitters. It was this option I pursued, and in October 2013, I headed north to bowhunt the American bison.

Nestled in the shadows of the Rocky Mountains, along the banks of the Sikanni River, Mike and Dixie Hammett own and operate Sikanni River

Outfitters. Located just outside of Pink Mountain, British Columbia, nearly 2,000 bison roam the mountains and valleys surrounding this area. With a solid reputation and tireless work ethic, Mike and Dixie have been outfitting bison hunts for nearly two decades. As many before me can attest, I knew this hunt would be challenging, and I couldn't wait to get started. After a long day of travel, I finally arrived in Fort St. John, British Columbia, where Mike greeted me. Soon we were headed toward the lodge, where I checked my equipment and flung a few arrows downrange. Having practiced religiously all summer with sharp, fixed-blade broadheads and heavy arrows, I felt prepared. On the first day, we hunted in the general vicinity of the lodge, glassing the surrounding foothills and drainages. Bison rubs, tracks, and droppings were prevalent throughout the area, and yet, nary a bison was seen.

British Columbia Bison Country

Ty, my guide, and I tried various tactics, one of which included waiting on trails leading to natural salt licks on the Sikanni River. Although there were treestands over these salty wallows, we chose to use a natural ground blind composed of pine boughs and blowdowns. What we perceived to be the perfect ambush was merely speculation, as the bison failed to read the script. The next morning, we were high atop a ridge at first light. Glassing into the basin, my optics picked up large shapes and contrasting colors against the conifers below. A herd of bison was scattered among the pines and prairie, and we formulated a plan. We worked our way down the ridge and around the basin. Our goal was to get in front of the grazing herd and then lie in wait. The bison, however, were moving faster than we thought, and eventually we conceded defeat.

That evening, after a long day of glassing and covering ground, we located another herd. We had to move quickly in the fading light, so we used the tree line as a travel route and worked our way to the downwind side. Concealed by the cover, with our footsteps masked by the wind, we continued to inch closer. Ty stayed back as I hit my knees and crawled the last 100 yards into the herd. Giant humps and dark-colored hides soon appeared as I glimpsed the bison feeding. The sun was dipping lower with each passing minute, and just as I got within 45 yards, one of the cows spotted me. In my haste to get within bow range, I had moved too fast, a mistake the bison would not forgive. Thundering away in a dust cloud, the herd vanished into the pines, and just like that my stalk was over.

Ty warned that I would have to contend with the cows to get within bow range. The cows, acting as sentries to warn the others of danger, are the matriarchs and leaders of the herd. Fighting off grizzlies and wolves, raising calves and enduring hard winters, these cows are masters of survival. All I had done was solidify that notion. Walking back as darkness loomed across the Rockies, I realized this was going to be a challenging hunt.

Upon returning to the lodge for lunch on the third day, Mike approached me and asked if I wanted to go for a "little walk." We had spent the morning glassing new country, and although the scenery was spectacular, we saw no bison. Mike and Dixie had an outpost approximately fifteen miles from the main lodge called *Big Mountain*, which they shut down after moose season. There were no longer horses at this remote outpost, but Mike felt

Hiking toward Big Mountain

it was worth a shot if we had the legs for it. We could use the quads for half of the journey and then walk the rest of the way in. I told Mike that I was interested, and within twenty minutes I had my pack loaded and ready to go. The trek was breathtaking, coursing through streams and mountain passes. Arriving at camp just before dark, we unloaded our gear and got organized. Without electricity or running water, it was a stark contrast to the warmth and comfort of the main lodge. Still, we were here to hunt, and the remote nature of an outpost camp always carries a sense of mystery and adventure.

Sleep found us easily that night, with the morning dawning cold and clear. We departed camp just before sunrise, but it wasn't long before we encountered our first hurdle. Crossing the Sikanni's icy waters is usually a non-issue at the Big Mountain camp, with the aid of horses to stride across its frigid flow. However, with our four-legged friends resting back at the ranch, we were on our own. Stripping down to nothing but our underwear, we shuffled across the river, the ice-cold water electric against our skin. The water climbed higher and became less tolerable with each step, quickly reaching our waistlines. Soon we found ourselves on the other side, where we rushed to get dressed and regain the feeling in our extremities. Throughout the day, we covered some amazing country, all of which held ample bison sign, and yet, we could locate no animals.

Unbeknownst to me, on the hike into Big Mountain, my boot had torn a seam in the heel area. What started as a mild discomfort quickly turned to pain as the blister grew and ruptured. To add insult to injury, Ty, who had suffered a traumatic rock-climbing injury years ago, was also limping badly. We settled in for the night and hoped our symptoms would resolve by morning. Unfortunately, Ty's ankle worsened overnight, and he had to be flown out. Luke, a young guide and wrangler who had come along to help with camp duties, took Ty's place. After talking to Mike and confirming Ty's fly out, we worked our way toward a meadow where Luke had seen quite a few bison. I had covered my blister with moleskin and duct tape, silencing the angry lesion for the time being. Glassing the meadow for an hour without seeing any sign of activity, I noticed a spruce grouse along the timber's edge. The horses weren't the only thing to leave the outpost when it was shut down, as nearly all the food was gone. I was excited when my arrow found its mark, knowing we had fresh grouse breast for dinner.

As I prepared to clean the grouse, Luke, who had stepped over the hill to an-

Eyad arrowed this spruce grouse for dinner.

swer nature's call, was running back toward me. I was concerned at first until he whispered, "Big herd of bison just over the rise." This hunt had been challenging, with opportunities few and far between. Having three days left, I realized this might be my best chance and hoped the odds were in our favor. There was one way to find out. We grabbed our gear and headed toward the bison.

The sun loomed high overhead as we glassed the bedded herd from a distance. With a swirling wind and no shortage of eyes and ears, it was obvious the bison had the advantage. We crawled through the dark timber until we reached a deadfall on the edge of the sun-soaked prairie. Through our optics, we noticed one of the bison possessed curled horns with heavy bases, most likely a mature bull. Although the horns of some older cows can have similar characteristics, they lack the overall mass the bulls carry throughout. With the bull bedded behind a tangle of willows, we knew it was time to move. I took note of a large tree above the bedded giant, knowing that once I hit my stomach, everything would look different.

Luke wished me well and I was off, pulling my body through the willows like a snail. Soon, the slow and monotonous motion began to wear on me, not knowing if I'd been winded, heard, or seen. Continuing through the tangle like a mouse in a maze, I inched closer, my bow and broadhead struggling to maintain their freedom. Then, just like that, I was out of cover. I had hit a small opening and made eye contact with a giant cow. The stare down ensued as the herd master, with a broken horn, peered in my direction. I knew this stalk was over but stayed motionless nonetheless, hoping for a chance at redemption. Lying stone-still on the prairie that day, I received a second chance. The old cow gave me one last glance, turned her head, and then meandered off.

I rolled to my right and began crawling, back within the willow maze and the cover I had foolishly left. The bison continued to move in a single file, not knowing something was amiss, unalarmed thanks to the careless cow. I rose to my knees, realizing the bison were moving out of range. A young bull passed by, followed by two cows, before a large hump and curled horns materialized over the willows. Grabbing for the rangefinder around my neck, I was surprised to find an empty neoprene case, as if my optics had shed its skin. Panic-stricken, I looked behind me and saw the rangefinder glistening in the sun. I rolled back and grabbed the device, came back to my knees, and brought the ocular to my eye. The sun, unrestrained in the cloudless sky, shined down from above and made focusing nearly impossible. Somehow, I found the high-hump and curled horns through the eyepiece, ranging the giant at 45 yards.

With my pin dancing high on the bison, I pulled through the shot and my arrow was gone. The shaft arced across the prairie, its yellow fletching against a bluebird sky, before disappearing over the willows. The sound of a solid hit found my ears as the herd erupted across the prairie, leaving dust and thunderous echoes in its wake. I found my footing and stood, not seeing a few bison, but upwards of thirty. Inspecting each hide for a tinge of red, or the yellow coloration of my fletching, I felt my heart sink when they all appeared unscathed.

Luke ran out with a big smile and said, "I think you got him." He thought one of the bison had fallen within seconds of my shot, but he couldn't be sure. If we could find the arrow, and the trail leading from it, that question would be answered. After searching to no avail where the bison had stood, we worked our way toward the creek. There, covered in crimson, 20 yards from the impact site was my arrow—buried in the bank. The arrow had passed through and continued its course, a testament to heavy shafts and sharp blades. Soon we found the blood trail, profuse and prominent, tracing a line to my bison.

Eyad's British Columbia Bison

I was overcome with emotions as we approached the fallen beast, laying my bow down as I took a knee. Despite its large size and curled horns, what lie before us was not a bull, but an old cow. Her size and horns had fooled us, but regardless of the gender, I couldn't be prouder. Based on the growth rings surrounding her horns, we later aged the cow at fifteen years old, a number few bison would reach in the wild. By the time we finished caping and quartering the old cow, the sun had set behind the Rockies. Guided by the light of a full moon, we made it back to camp well after dark, where we celebrated over fresh bison tenderloins and grouse breast. Reminiscing and telling stories of the hunt, we laughed the night away, the perfect ending to an epic adventure. Just before midnight, I lay my head down and went to sleep, knowing we had accomplished something special.

On my return trip a few days later, I was sitting in McDonald's at O'Hare airport when I felt ill. I hadn't eaten yet, so I knew it wasn't the fast food. I fought it off until I returned home, where I felt worse over the next two weeks. During my trip, I had been careless, drinking from rivers and streams without using a filter. I knew better, but thirst and fatigue overpowered common sense. Speaking with my physician, I confessed to the crime and asked if Giardia was in her differential. She would test for the parasite but had her doubts because a stomach virus was going around. The nurse didn't hide her surprise when she called the next day to inform me I had tested positive for the parasite. After a short course of an antiprotozoal medication, my symptoms abated. My brother bought me a filter for my next trip, a gift and a jab at the same time. Should any of you want to lose weight, but don't care for exercise or sound eating habits, I highly recommend this insidious infection. You'll find after you experience *Beaver Fever*, that treadmills and salads are better options.

My trip to British Columbia was an amazing adventure, and without a doubt, one of my toughest and most rewarding hunts. Having the opportunity to bowhunt such a legendary animal in the wilds of British Columbia was both a privilege and an honor. I am grateful the American bison still roams our prairies and grasslands, casting shadows I hope never cease to exist. Perhaps one day, you too will crawl across a prairie, nock an arrow, and come to full draw on the most iconic animal in American history.

CHAPTER 25

Aspen Monarchs

I had been waiting for weeks, checking my mail and credit card statements daily. Having accumulated bonus points in Arizona for years, I had rolled the dice and applied for a 2014 limited-entry elk tag. The results would be available any day now and I was excited to say the least. Elk hunting had always escaped me, because in all honesty, I had no time for another addiction. Perhaps tongue-in-cheek, but as Shakespeare once said, many a true word is spoken in jest. I had been warned that chasing these western monarchs was nothing short of addicting, so I steered clear of the Kool-Aid. With our second child due in February, I knew the next few years would be too hectic and that it was time to test the waters. Arizona had been my first choice, and with a pocket full of points, I surely would draw a tag. Despite my optimism and efforts, Arizona was not meant to be. Following a call to Game and Fish in early April, hoping there had been a mistake, they confirmed I had been unsuccessful.

Despite this setback, I was committed to hunting elk that fall and looked at states with over-the-counter options. With limited time and no experience hunting wapiti, I knew finding the right outfitter was of paramount importance. After numerous recommendations and phone calls, I chose Tom Colander of Colorado Trophies. Located in southwest Colorado amidst the majestic San Juan Mountains, Tom runs a first-class operation. During our initial conversation, Tom mentioned there were two spots available, so I asked my good friend Chris Durando if he would care to join me. Chris thought it was a great idea, and we arranged to meet in Colorado that fall.

This would be a physical hunt, with some areas approaching 10,000 feet in elevation. Concerned how my lungs would feel about those numbers, I began my preparation. The core of my training involved intense workouts on the Matrix, a punishing, escalator-like machine at the local gym. I also increased my time at the archery range, fine-tuning my setup as the summer progressed. Both my endurance and accuracy improved each week, and soon it was time to head west. I left Iowa on September 5, and after a lengthy drive through Nebraska, spent the night in a hotel near Denver. The next day, I drove through some spectacular country and arrived at the lodge by mid-afternoon. There I met Chris, Tom, and the staff at Colorado Trophies. Everybody in camp was warm and welcoming, and it was great to be here. Before getting settled, Tom held a short seminar on calling, shot placement, and the hunting tactics we would employ. The plan was to leave early each morning and make our way to various ranches, hoping to find a bull elk interested in our calls. It appeared the rut was just heating up, with both satellite and herd bulls becoming more vocal.

Colorado Elk Country

Regarding strategy, Tom felt that watching the wind and being aggressive were the keys to success. He preferred to work in tight on a bull and then use a combination of cow calls and bugles to lure him in. Mature bulls did not like competition and when challenged would often come looking for a fight. Tom advised that I set up ahead of his location as any approaching bull would be focused on his calls. This would allow me to draw undetected and decrease the chance that a bull would hang up out of range. After discussing these points and taking mental notes, we sat down to enjoy an incredible meal at the lodge. Tom informed us that Matt, a young man working on the ranch for the summer, would join us to gain experience and help out. We all got to know each other as the night progressed and the camaraderie in camp was great. No doubt we were looking forward to the week ahead.

The first morning dawned calm and cool, finding us overlooking a large basin scattered with spruce and aspen trees. The stars seemed reluctant to let go of the night, holding firm to a cloudless sky. It wasn't long before the sunrise won out, and with its victory, a chorus of bugles resonated across the landscape. We set up along the timber, where Tom belted out an aggressive bugle, hoping to lure one of the bulls within range. Unfortunately, they showed little interest in Tom's calling efforts, responding with utter silence. I looked to my left and saw two cows trotting toward our setup. They cautiously made their way to within a few yards of Chris, caught our wind, and scurried away. Once the cows had disappeared, we gathered our gear and climbed higher, repositioning ourselves within a large grove of aspens. Tom hit his bugle once more but received the same muted response. We were about to move on when a lone bugle broke the morning silence. Within a few moments, a second bull sounded off, coming from the same direction. As the bulls continued to bugle in tandem, I caught movement from the corner of my eye and watched as tines crested the ridgeline.

Walking side-by-side, the two bulls approached our setup, becoming wary as they neared the tree line. The bigger of the two suitors, a 6x6, seemed to know something was amiss and left the scene. The other bull, perhaps less wise and more confident, continued working toward us. When he was broadside, I settled my pin and the arrow was gone. With a solid thump, followed by a loud crack, the bull sprinted over the hillside below us. I knew my shot was too high, passing just above the spine, nowhere close to the cavity. There was no sign of the arrow, or even one drop of blood. We listened for coyotes and looked for scavengers, but our efforts were to no avail. The bull would likely survive, and while this knowledge offered some consolation, it was not the closure I sought. There was nothing more we could do. Although I was disappointed and down, it was time to move on.

We covered many miles over the next two days, working toward any bull that showed interest. On more than one occasion we got a response, only to have the bull hang up, go silent, or disappear. Although we continued to see good bulls and passed on two raghorns, we had yet to put an elk on the ground. On September 10, the fourth day of our hunt, I awoke with a heavy heart and anything but elk on my mind. I had planned to leave that morning to be home for my mother's surgery, which was scheduled the following day. As anyone with elderly parents can appreciate, I wanted to be there should something unforeseen take place. When my mom caught wind of this plan, she gave me a good lecture on the phone, as only a mother can do. She insisted I stay for the hunt's entirety, and with her blessing, I promised to do so. Reflecting on our conversation in the early morning light, I was still conflicted by my decision to stay, and I prayed that all would go well.

The past two days had been filled with heavy rains and windy conditions, which made calling difficult. Today's sunrise would favor all parties, with crisp, almost cold temperatures, and a stillness to the air that screamed perfection. We set up at first light near a scenic meadow and were into elk almost immediately, as a herd bull with a large harem was bugling from an aspen grove. Chris and Tom crawled toward the isolated group of trees, hoping the chest-high grass would conceal their approach. Once they were inside the shaded tree line, they separated, with Tom continuing to call as Chris moved forward.

Matt and I were seated on the opposite side of the meadow and heard a second bull bugling to the west. The bull soon cut the distance in half, and with Tom calling from the aspens, there was no question where he was headed. As I scanned the distant, dew-covered meadow for the first hint of antlers or hide, I saw the bull appear from the dark timber, displaying a regal 6x7 rack with white-tipped antlers. Lowering his head to the ground, the enraged bull destroyed a small bush with his antlers, flinging water and mist through the air with each head twist. On the heels of yet another piercing bugle, the bull continued his course, heading straight for the aspens.

Chris and Tom realized the bull was bearing down on their position and moved toward the edge of the meadow, hoping to intercept the monarch as he approached. With steam emanating from his nostrils, the bull remained focused on Tom's calling, searching the shadows for the rival he was determined to face. When he passed behind a small sapling, Chris drew his bow, only to have the giant stop with his vitals obscured. Holding at full draw for what seemed like an eternity, Chris hoped his nerves and practice sessions would see him through. Just as he was about to let down, the bull stepped forward, and Chris made a perfect shot. The bull whirled and sprinted back toward the timber—with crimson streaking down his side. From our vantage point, it appeared they had spooked the bull, but that was until we watched him fall in the sunlit meadow. Chris had done it and paid his dues along the way. Throughout the week, he had sat on wallows and alfalfa fields, endured torrential downpours, and walked more than twelve miles a day. Hearing Chris describe his emotions as the hunt unfolded was priceless, and the smile on his face said it all. It was the perfect ending to a classic elk hunt.

We had a great lunch back at camp and headed out for an evening hunt. Earlier in the week, we had seen quite a few elk near a mountainside meadow and felt this was our best option. Following a brisk climb to the edge of the meadow, we positioned ourselves among a stand of aspens and got settled. Tom checked to make sure we were ready and then threw a loud bugle into the wind. Almost immediately, a bull answered, a few hundred yards away and straight up the mountain from our setup. The bull seemed responsive at first but then lost interest and moved away from our position. With sunset fast approaching and one day left to hunt, we decided to push the envelope. Matt and Chris stayed behind with our packs as Tom and I pursued the bull farther up the mountain.

Chris Durando's great bull.

Gaining elevation with each step, now at almost 10,000 feet, my lungs were telling me I should have trained harder. We waited for the bull to give us direction, took a deep breath of thin air, and then continued at a feverish pace. As the bull moved farther away, almost as if he were mocking our efforts, we heard a second bull down the mountain to our right. Tom worked his way beside me, where we discussed our options between labored breaths. There was no doubt this second bull was closer, but with darkness drawing near, I was concerned that pursuing him would be a wasted venture. When I asked Tom whether we should wave the white flag or keep pushing, he responded with a memorable quote.

"Well, Eyad, it's getting late, but this bull is the only game in town, which means we gotta play."

Tom's response was symbolic of his attitude, and one of the many reasons I'd enjoyed this hunt so much. Lighting a fire in my weary legs and burning lungs to keep going, we kept pushing onward through the dark timber. The moisture of the past two days had spawned a white mist through the aspens, evoking a sense of nostalgia in the fading light. Tom bugled once more, but the echo of his challenge was the only sound to follow. Looking ahead through the timber, we could see another small meadow and crept along to its edge. As we stepped into the vacant opening, a bugle rang out from the timber before us, stopping us in our tracks. The second bull was now much closer and appeared to be moving toward our position. Tom knew we were still in the game. He motioned for me to crawl across the meadow and try to get to the edge of the timber.

As I hit my stomach and crawled forward, inching my bow and body across the opening, I caught movement to my right. A young bull revealed himself along the tree line, focused on my position as I lie motionless. Perhaps entertained by my lack of stealth, he seemed more curious than alarmed, as if nothing so clumsy could ever be dangerous. I was handcuffed by the raghorn's suspicious stare but knew I had to get closer. When the young bull turned his head, I stood and raced for the edge of the timber, longing to reach the tree line and the cover it afforded. Secure and stationary once more, I looked for the raghorn and found him staring into the forest. The young bull seemed bothered by something else and left the scene, just as a thunderous bugle erupted from the aspens. In the wake of his entry, the beast bugled once more, declaring his dominance at 10,000 feet. The bull emerged from the darkness moments later, his 6x6 frame wide and regal.

With the giant bull staring in my direction, I remained still, hoping there was enough cover to break up my outline. The wind was still in my favor but was swirling with the setting sun and changing thermals. I was drenched in sweat, trying to breathe through my nose, and hoping I could keep it together. Suddenly, a haunting bugle resounded to my left as another bull materialized from the shadows. In the commotion of Tom's vocal battle with the 6x6, it appeared that the first bull had experienced a change of heart and decided to introduce himself. With their heads down and walking stiff-legged toward each other, the two monarchs locked antlers and began sparring, giving me a chance to make my move. I remembered Tom saying not to be passive in my decisions, and in this case, I was anything but.

I sprinted forward and cut the distance in half, reaching a small opening in the forest just as Tom hit his bugle for the last time. The bulls separated and looked up, with the 6x6 making me out right away. Tipping his head back as he tried to catch my wind, the old warrior's curiosity conceded to caution, and he vanished into the aspens. The other bull, carrying a dark 5x5 rack with dagger-like points and whale tails, held his ground, staring at my motionless form. I pulled the rangefinder from my pocket and tried to find the bull through the small ocular and dim light. My efforts proved pointless, with too many trees and twigs to get an accurate reading. I looked up through the forest and noticed a giant aspen standing halfway between the bull and me, revealing a possible avenue to mask my approach. With nothing to lose, on the tail end of an incredible hunt, I decided to go for it.

Using the aspen as a shield, I walked toward the bull, drawing my bow as I approached the cream-colored tree. I stepped away from the aspen at full draw, expecting to see an empty forest. But instead, I saw the bull standing broadside, his vitals exposed for the first time. I settled my pin and touched the release, catching a glimpse of my arrow just before it disappeared into the monarch. The bull crashed through the forest at impact, soon regained his composure, and then bedded down on the adjacent hillside. Despite what I feared to be a low hit, the bull's demeanor seemed to indicate otherwise, offering a glimmer of hope.

Tom worked his way beside me, where we considered our options before darkness enveloped the forest. Based on the bull's reaction, I realized that my shot placement was marginal—and would not prove fatal without another arrow. With the setting sun showing no empathy toward our predicament, I knew we had a decision to make. I'm a firm believer in patience before taking up any blood trail, but something on this night told me to pursue. With Tom in the lead and minutes of shooting light remaining, we began walking toward the bedded bull. As we closed the distance to within 80 yards, the bull rose to his feet and ran down the mountain. Heading for a spruce thicket to our right, the bull rushed past us, vanishing in the conifers.

We circled around and entered the thicket ourselves, where we spotted antlers behind a spruce tree. I finished the bull in the fading light and then sat down with tears in my eyes, mentally and physically exhausted. Tom knelt beside me, seeming to know what I was feeling, and asked that I join him in a prayer. We thanked God for all his blessings, for good fortune, great friends, and the bounty this elk provided. Tom asked that He watch over my mother the next morning. Deep down, I knew she would be okay.

We made our way down the mountain just past midnight that evening, with heavy packs and exhausted legs. The full moon was at its peak, illuminating the aspens as we made our descent. It was a remarkable ending to an epic adventure, one that Chris and I will not forget. Although there may be more bugles and bigger bulls one day, there will never be another first elk or a hunt more special. Those before me were correct, in that elk hunting will capture your soul and ensure that your first hunt is never your last. In retrospect, my first arrow would have taken days or weeks to prove fatal. The decision to pursue that night was the right one, and I am thankful that we made it. Like any endeavor in life, the reality of bowhunting isn't perfect, despite our intentions. All we can do is strive for excellence, and if I am able, I will continue to do so.

Bringing my bull down the mountain that moonlit night would have been the perfect ending to this story, but fate had one more surprise for me. As I packed up my gear and said good-bye to my friends at Colorado Trophies, I was saddened but looked forward to seeing my loved ones back home. My mother's surgery had gone well, and she was recovering at the university hospital. After dropping Chris off at the airport and wishing him well, I picked up my elk meat at the locker. Surprisingly, they were out of dry ice, which meant a trip to the local Walmart before driving home. For reasons I can't explain, a strange feeling overcame me as I entered the store. Rather than going back to purchase the ice myself, I asked the door greeter if they would mind taking my money and buying it for me. I explained that I didn't feel comfortable leaving my truck unattended and would rather wait at the entrance. The kind employee looked at me strangely, but complied nonetheless, and went to get the ice from the back.

Eyad heading down the mountain with his elk.

While standing just inside the entrance, I noticed a small car circling the parking lot. Driving along at a snail's pace, the car parked beside my truck, after which a middle-aged man emerged from the vehicle. He moved toward the back of his car, looked around nonchalantly, and then opened his rear passenger door. You can imagine my surprise when he reached into my truck bed and began pulling my rack and cape into his car. With speed that would impress an

NFL scout, I sprinted across the parking lot and confronted him, shouting in no uncertain terms to stop what he was doing. Unable to get the antlers into his backseat, he turned to face me, dropping my elk on the asphalt. After he tried to justify his actions, for which I showed no remorse, he complied with my wishes and drove away, leaving me with a bull I had now earned twice over.

An hour later, after discussing the situation with the head of security and answering his questions, I was on the road once again. I learned the attempted theft was caught on tape, and that the local authorities were looking for his vehicle. Although the past week had been full of surprises and events I cannot explain, I know they all happened for a reason. If I had headed home early for my mother's surgery, not pursued my bull on that fateful night, or even purchased the ice myself, my trip would have ended much differently. Everything had come full circle, and as I headed eastbound across the Rockies, I thought to myself, *I'm really glad I didn't draw Arizona.*

CHAPTER 26

Spring Classic

In February of 2015, my wife, Melinda, and I welcomed our second child into the world. CW arrived at 4:44 PM, an irony that still makes me smile, as my wife's lucky number has always been #4. With two young children and newfound responsibilities, the upcoming turkey season was the last thing on my radar. I wasn't naïve, nor a fool, and I knew that as April drew closer my mindset would change. I was blessed to not only marry a beautiful, intelligent, and caring spouse, but also one who understood my passions. Now, just because my wife was an understanding woman, didn't mean there wasn't a line in the sand. As long as our family was taken care of, though, she was fine with her husband chasing spring gobblers, and I hoped to do so if given the chance.

Knowing my passion for spring turkey hunting, and always the adventurous spirit, my wife had made arrangements so I could hunt opening weekend. The plan was to drive down to my sister Gloria's house on Saturday night, so she could help with the little ones while I was hunting. I've always been fond of a quote by Iyanla Vanzant: "If you want to hear God laugh, tell him your plans." These words of wisdom were ringing in my ears as our son screamed most of the night, refusing to sleep in his portable crib. By 3:00 AM my wife was in tears, my mind was less than sound, and I knew there was no way I was going anywhere at daybreak.

By 8:00 AM things seemed to settle down as our kids played with my sister, and Melinda went to sleep in the guest room. I've never been good at taking naps, and in the midst of the spring season, lying down was the furthest thing from my mind. After getting the green light from my sister, I threw on my pants and long-sleeved shirt, pulled on my boots, and stepped outside. The morning air smelled fresh and crisp, with just enough bite to remind me that winter wasn't far removed. Across from my sister's house, the grass seemed to shimmer and shine, its dark green blades glistening with dew.

Blue Phlox in the spring hardwoods.

The robins were back as well, their chipper song always a welcome voice. It was spring again in the Midwest, a season of fresh starts and new beginnings.

My first order of business was to purchase the largest cup of coffee in southeast Iowa. The local Casey's was happy to oblige, and with a full cup of Joe, I headed west toward my farm. The coffee and caffeine pushed away my fatigue, ensuring I was ready to go. Limited scouting over the past few weeks had been disappointing, revealing meager food plots and few mature toms. Failing to frost seed my clover plots had put them behind the proverbial eight ball, giving the opportunistic weeds and grasses a chance for new life. Notwithstanding the limited number of birds and sparse food plots, I was still optimistic. Unlocking the gate and rolling down the stone-laden drive, I felt a bit foolish. I normally drive my full-sized Dodge Ram on all my hunts. But now, I was bumping down the farm lane in my wife's minivan. We had caravanned as a family to my sister's house, and the truck had stayed home, leaving me with a turkey hunting mobile filled with toys, sippy cups, and wrappers. There's just something about a minivan that strips the *cool* right off a bowhunter. All joking aside, and despite my vehicle, I had a good feeling about the morning's hunt.

Soon, I had my decoys and blind thrown over my back, a bow sling draped across my chest, and a vest loaded with my favorite calls. Crossing the creek and trudging along its eroding bank, I felt a cold chill through my boots, courtesy of the frigid water coursing through the creek. I then headed east for an easy walk down a mowed path before hiking up a sloppy, washed-out lane to a hilltop clover plot. This field was a special place, having produced a limbhanger the year before. There were other successes through the years, along with missed opportunities, all making this isolated field a treasured spot. Scanning back and forth across the open expanse, I noticed an absence of feathers and fans, so I continued my approach. I worked my way up a faint trail that led to the field, both sides immersed with dense Indian grass that stood eight feet tall.

When I reached the top of the hill, I was surprised to see that the clover was holding its own, waging a war against the cool season grasses. There was a small island of trees at the field's center, which offered the perfect location to conceal a blind. Favoring the west side of the island and its early morning shadows, I secured my blind under the low-hanging, ominous branches of a resident honey locust. I cleared the branches near eye level, as my corneas didn't need any surprises. Ripe with thorns that resembled ice picks, the locust tree looked less than kind, but the tangle of branches would help conceal my ambush. I placed a jake and two hen decoys a mere 12 yards away, ensured that all parties were staked down, and then entered the confines of my blind. Once situated inside the Double Bull, I laid out my calls and equipment, arranging them within arm's reach of my stool.

I glanced at my decoys parked within the depleted clover stand, reminding myself what a perfect day it was. The wind was nonexistent, with an occasional cloud drifting through the bright blue sky. The oaks were showing signs of life, with tiny buds appearing at the ends of their massive branches. I could hear everything around me, from cars on the adjacent roads to a flock of honkers high overhead. We all dream of days like this, and punched tag or not, I was going to enjoy it. Compared to first light in the spring woods, most mid-morning excursions are quiet. This seemed to hold true, as two hours into my sit, and I had yet to hear a gobble. With the eleven o'clock hour close at hand, I scratched out another long series of yelps. No sooner had I finished my last note than the tail end of a gobble found my ears. It was so far away, though, that I couldn't venture to guess the distance. The minutes passed with nary a sound, which slowed my excitement to a screeching halt.

At 11:30 AM, I looked to the south and was surprised to see five hens feeding through the clover. While I had not heard so much as a peep, much less a gobble in the past thirty minutes, I knew that a tom could not be far behind. I secured the diaphragm against my palate, picked up my bow, and yelped softly through a cupped hand. The hens, still visible and feeding along, peered at my decoys but seemed to show no interest. Then, from the corner of my eye, I caught a quick burst of motion as an old longbeard sauntered up to his harem. Hammering out a throaty gobble, he zigzagged across the clover plot, spitting and drumming beside his lovely ladies. Confident he was king, the tom showed no signs of being bashful, declaring his dominance with each re-sounding gobble. As he pirouetted among his hens, I could see a thick, heavy beard protruding from his chest, along with a unique, V-shaped gap down the center of his fan. I quickly attached my release to the D-loop, fully prepared to defend my jake decoy, whose mere presence was surely an insult. If I was a betting man, I would have lost this one, as he couldn't seem to care less about my setup. Following his hens as if on a leash, the gobbler never broke strut, coursing through the green field as the midday sun reflected off his plumage.

Eyad noticed the V-shaped gap in the tom's fan.

As the noon whistle sounded, the longbeard continued to give my calls and decoys the cold shoulder. To say he was hung-up would be an under-statement, and there was nothing I could do to change his mind. He spun and strutted from one end of the field to the other, gobbling at any sound that found his lobeless ears. Occasionally, a subtle breeze added a hint of realism to my decoys, but even that had little effect. My phone had been vibrating incessantly since the gobbler came on the scene, and knowing my chances were getting worse by the minute, I laid my bow down to check my messages. Most had come from my sister, revealing that lunch was ready: fresh burgers, brats, and chicken hot off the grill. Few people can grill like my brother-in-law, and at this point, grilled chicken breasts sounded a lot better than wild turkey.

As if the hens could read my mind, they meandered into the timber, towing their stubborn suitor along with them. Once they disappeared over the ridgeline, I packed up my gear within the blind, a decision my stomach greatly appreciated. I had just placed my arrows back in the quiver when I happened to look up. The hens were on their way back toward the field, marching in a single file, with the gobbler bringing up the rear. Despite dreaming of burgers and brats, the last thing I wanted was to ruin this spot's potential, hoping to return before season's end. Within two weeks, there would be fewer hens to compete with, which would improve my chances. If these birds witnessed my departure, I would do nothing but educate and alarm them. The more I thought about it, the easier my decision became—the burgers would have to wait. Settling in for what I feared would be a long afternoon, I watched as the gobbler began chasing the hens again, this time to the east and out of sight.

I hastily nocked another arrow, more out of frustration than anticipation, and in the process dropped the shaft against my bow's riser. The clink-clink-clink of the arrow bouncing its way to rest on the aluminum bow made me cringe, and I cursed myself for a rookie mistake. I feared my hunt was over for all the wrong reasons and expected to hear alarm putts and wing beats soon after. No sooner had these thoughts crossed my mind than the gobbler came running past my blind at warp speed, seeming to justify my fears. Before I could lecture myself any longer, another flash of motion caught my eye. I looked to my left and my mouth fell agape as two huge longbeards marched into the clover. They stood side-by-side as if bound at birth and came to the field's center, thundering a double gobble that seemed to shake the blind. What I thought to be the cause for the gobbler's departure—in using my bow as a xylophone—had gone unnoticed. The true catalysts were now standing before me, staking their claim to this field. The first tom's show-stopping gobbles and strutting display over the past hour had been his demise. He had drawn the attention of these two warriors from a distance and, looking to commandeer his harem, they had chased him away with little effort.

I steadied my bow and prepared for the shot, knowing it was a matter of seconds before these two longbeards came crashing in. If they had chased the first gobbler off the field, surely they would not tolerate this jake in their domain. Trying to understand a turkey's mindset can be a futile pursuit, and this situation proved to be no different. Not only did they fail to make their way within bow range, but they acted as if my decoys didn't exist, only emitting an occasional shock-gobble to my calls. Although the toms were avoiding me like the plague, I had never experienced a morning such as this. There were more gobbles and hen vocalizations than I could count, along with breeding and chasing displays I may never see again. The longbeards continued their performance, dancing together as if ballroom partners, never breaking stride or strut.

I was mesmerized by this springtime masterpiece when I heard a faint noise in the background. It was a sound I knew all too well—and one that had me reaching for my bow. Nothing sounds like a gobbler spitting and drumming, and the booming reverberations off the blind left little doubt. As I gripped my bow tighter, the drumming crescendoed. It was so close now that I dared not move a muscle, save for my eyes darting back and forth. Within seconds the gobbler materialized to my right, where I noticed the missing tail feather down the center of his fan. Chased off the field by the two longbeards who now staked their claim, he had returned to the scene, opting to swallow his pride and take seconds. He waltzed right into my jake decoy, so close that I could see the chocolate-brown color of his iris, and the sharp, crisp details of his heavy beard. Side-stepping from left to right, with worn down wingtips brushing the ground, the gobbler spun once more. I waited until his vision was obscured by a full fan and then drew my bow, reaching my anchor just as the tom spun back around. Green fluorescence danced upon patriotic colors of red, white, and blue as I settled my pin on his head and wattles.

The gobbler flopped and tumbled among the decoys and clover—the broadhead taking him cleanly. With shaking hands, I nocked another arrow, knowing full well what was about to transpire. While a gobbler may turn a cold shoulder to even the best calling efforts and decoy spreads, none can resist the opportunity to finish one of their own. They say all's fair in love and war, and the spring turkey woods are no exception. I could hear the toms coming long before my eyes refocused, their angry purrs mixed in with the fallen gobbler's last wing beats. With beards wagging like a Labrador's tail on opening day, the longbeards sprinted toward the departed tom, their intentions unmistakable. Bobbing and weaving with each purr and assault, the two combatants showed no mercy as they kicked the fallen gobbler with finely-honed spurs. I tried to settle my pin on a crimson-colored head, but this was on par with lassoing a snake.

My first shot sailed just north of the lead gobbler's crown. Not missing a beat, they continued their mission without remorse, allowing me to nock yet another arrow. I tried to aim with more focus—again settling my pin on the nearest tom—but saw another arrow sail high. The gobblers had moved off now, studying the scene, realizing something was amiss. I pulled the last arrow from my quiver, snapped the nock to the string, and then stopped what I was doing. While my last arrow may have found its mark, capping off an already epic hunt, I decided to pass. There was no need to take a marginal shot and risk wounding one of these old monarchs. I had already experienced everything a turkey hunter could hope for, and I didn't need to fill my last tag to get there. Exiting stage left, the duo scurried off as alarm putts filled the air. I watched the longbeards disappear into the timber, tipped my hat to the Man upstairs, and then exited the blind.

The sun was now at its peak, surrounded by a bluebird sky still void of clouds. I would not soon forget this day, nor its participants, and felt blessed to be part of it. As I gathered my gear, I realized there was one more thing I had to do. Pulling the cell phone from my pocket, I let my family know that I was on my way. Hopefully, they had saved me a burger or two.

CHAPTER 27

Full Circle

My windshield blades swung back and forth with just enough speed to match the downpour. It was November 22, 2014, and I was headed to the farm for one last hunt. I was exhausted and less than optimistic, as a low-pressure system had brought scattered thunderstorms and warm temperatures to the Midwest. The air was heavy and humid, more akin to summer than late November, and anything but ideal. Still, I knew better than to stay home and complain, despite my lack of sightings or success. I was hunting a giant whitetail I called *The Big Ten*, not exactly a catchy name, but the shoe fit. Although I'd captured a few pictures through the years, I had never seen him on the hoof. I found his left side while shed hunting in February, heavier and more impressive than I imagined. Striking out in my quest for the matching set, I was hopeful he would return the coming fall.

I was not disappointed. The Big Ten showed up right on schedule, ghosting past a camera on a cold September night. Despite knowing he was alive and well, I couldn't catch a break. It wasn't for lack of effort, for over the past two seasons I put forth every bit of time and energy I had to offer. I sweated through the heat of October, withstood the blustery winds of November, and shivered against the brutal cold of the late season, patiently awaiting an opportunity.

On this night, I'd be hunting the head of a ditch crossing, within a funnel that looked inviting. It seemed a no brainer that mature bucks would run this route, with ample cover to mask their travels. My father-in-law and I had helped this corridor along years ago, hinge-cutting through the tangle of locust, ironwood, and ash. I've always felt that transition zones, where two types of cover meet, were great places to lie in wait. I hoped the whitetails were of the same opinion, but up to this point, our feelings were anything but mutual. I recalled the first time I hunted this location and being so sure it was a slam dunk. Full of optimism that only a fresh stand can conjure, I waited hours on end, never to see a deer. Each stand session educates whitetails, and I was approaching half a dozen. I just couldn't let this spot go, and with a perfect entry/exit route, I felt my presence had little effect. The proof is in the pudding, though, and this recipe just wasn't working.

The rain fell softly as I approached, allowing me to enter the timber in silence. I took care as I ascended the scrawny shingle oak, a tree I selected more out of desperation than preference. Through the years, I've found that the best areas have the worst options for treestands. Although many would chalk this up to bad luck, I've always felt the whitetails knew what they were doing. As I settled into my ambush, I felt a cold chill against my back and wished I had my rain jacket.

Taking a deep breath, I nocked an arrow and hung my bow on a tree limb. The hardwoods had a glossy sheen about them as a steady rain continued to fall. I had only been seated for a few minutes when I caught a flicker of motion to the north. A mature doe was crashing toward me, glancing over her shoulder with labored breaths. I grabbed my bow and squared my shoulders, knowing a rutting buck was soon to arrive. This doe in heat was visibly exhausted from trying to outrun her suitor, and I hoped to help her cause. Then I heard a grunt, subtle at first, before a deeper bellow emanated from the thicket. Calm and collected, I peered into the jungle, as if waiting for the curtain to be swept back on a game show. In this scenario, I had seen all manner of surprises, from spikes and forkhorns to monster bucks of giant proportions. I was not prepared for what I saw next, however, as The Big Ten materialized from the shadows.

Focused on the approaching giant, I attached my release to the bowstring and got ready. This was almost too good to be true, and with the ditch crossing at 25 yards, I was about to get my chance. Showing no concern for the doe's departure, The Big Ten moved toward my position, stopping to rub his antlers against a cluster of saplings. Even with the drizzle, I heard his rack raking the helpless trees, whipping back and forth as he vented his frustration. Then, the unthinkable happened. Rather than following the doe's lead, the buck crashed

The Big Ten on his way toward Eyad's stand.

down a steep ditch and back up the other side. I couldn't argue with his 'as-the-crow-flies' mentality, but going through the ditch was not what I expected.

If only I'd been more patient, or took my time to range him, the outcome may have been different. Alas, while there may be do-overs in many endeavors, bowhunting isn't one of them. I can still see my pin dancing on his rain-soaked coat, and the abruptness of his body language when I grunted him to a halt. Then my arrow was gone, its white wrap-and-fletching on their way to fulfill a dream. The only problem was that it wasn't a dream they delivered—but a nightmare. The arrow seemed to drop out of the sky, passing under the giant and burying itself in the leaves. What I envisioned for so long, in a chip shot to the ditch crossing, turned into a situation I didn't see coming. No matter the technology and speed new-age bows produce, yardage estimation matters. Miscues past 30 yards are monumental, and what I assumed to be just that, turned out to be a few more. My family was out of town with friends that weekend, and I was glad, for I wouldn't have been good company. I've always kept a good perspective on hunting and life, realizing what's important and worth losing sleep over, but this one hurt. I listened to the rain hammer the window all night, watching as another season passed in disappointment.

Time heals all wounds, and as with most things, the bitterness of that November afternoon faded. Setbacks either sharpen your focus or bring out the white flag, and I've never been too keen on the latter. In the months since that infamous November miss, I revisited books and articles I hadn't read in years. I shot at obscure yardages, scouted new areas, and formed a fresh mindset. I've always felt that one should never stop learning, and stepping back in time was refreshing. Reading books by Rothhaar and Wensel rekindled the magic, and I felt like a kid again. Our youngest son was born in February, and now that it was one-on-one in our household, my oldest son, ZJ, became my shadow. We traveled to the farm together on multiple occasions, where I introduced him to the lessons of my youth. From tracks and trees to songbirds and snakes, he seemed enthralled. Throughout the spring, we frost seeded clover plots, freshened salt licks, and searched for mushrooms and sheds. After returning to the truck, we'd grab a snack, shoot our bows, and talk about the day. Each trip to the farm was an adventure, and I will always cherish those memories.

Months passed, and the dog days of summer took hold. It was a Wednesday in late July when I loaded up my Polaris Ranger, with plans to mow around some of our food plots. Since purchasing the farm, I had acquired a partner, Houston, who was a passionate bowhunter as well. We both had the same goals on the property and were slowly watching them unfold. Houston had purchased a small, pull-behind mower for the UTV, which when secured to a hitch, would allow us to mow with ease. My Ranger had been overheating of late, so before embarking on any mowing missions, I took it back to the dealer. Despite my Polaris being a new unit, I was told to disregard the problem, as 'running hot' was the nature of UTVs. I took their advice and moved on, hoping the problem would go away.

While I was getting ready that morning, ZJ came out and asked if he could come along. For some reason, I told him no, even though he was great company. I can't explain why I never relented, despite his tears, but I held my ground. I arrived at the farm just before noon and hooked up the mower, soon making short work of the east field. I then headed west, with plans to mow each successive plot. The next field would be short and sweet, as good friends Monte and Travis had sprayed the week prior. A few spots hadn't died off yet, so I planned to tidy them up with the mower before they drilled in turnips. I was missing ZJ and feeling guilty for not bringing him along, as it would have been a great experience.

Disappointed in my decision, I turned around to check my swath, only to see that the blade had quit cutting. The grass was merely pushed down, for who knows how long, which added to my frustration. I put the Ranger in park to remedy the problem and then went to unbuckle my seat belt. I was looking down when my eyes caught orange embers devouring the passenger side. Then I saw that the undercarriage was engulfed, resembling a lava pit below the Ranger. Wearing radio headphones and listening to my favorite country music, I hadn't heard a thing, nor sensed any heat or flames.

I jumped out of the UTV and sprinted across the field, nearly tripping over my headphones. Once I reached the edge of the CRP, I turned around, only seconds before the unit exploded. It wasn't a small explosion, or a tiny blast, but a full-bore, deafening experience. Plastic and debris flew through the air, followed by the tires bursting in rapid succession. The whole field was ablaze, with the dead grass acting like kindling. It happened so fast, and the fire was spreading so quickly, that I didn't know what to do. I had the wherewithal to call 911, doing my best to describe the situation. As I watched the Polaris burn, and the fire crawl across the field, I thanked God for divine intervention. If my son had been in the passenger seat, or I hadn't stopped to check the blade, neither of us would be here. I soon received a call from local firefighters, who said they could see the smoke cloud from the highway. We finally got the fire extinguished by mid-afternoon and things settled down. I didn't realize it at first, but my keys were in the Ranger when it exploded, and I was stranded at the farm. My buddy Mitch was kind enough to bring me a spare, bailing me out of a tough situation.

I ventured to the farm again a few weeks later. Without a UTV or mower, I had no choice but to use a walk-behind brush hog. The upper field was

Eyad's Polaris after the explosion.

a jungle of giant foxtail, which had consumed the area, drowning out the food plot like a tsunami. Pushing through the head-high grass reminded me of two-a-days in high school football, memories I had suppressed for good reason. No matter; the deed was done, and I dragged myself back to the truck with little left in the tank. A local farmer and friend, Mike, had helped me out in the past and called in late summer to see if I needed a hand. I always welcomed his expertise and took him up on the offer. With help from Monte, Travis, and Mike, we had our food plots in the ground by Labor Day.

Not until early September did I run my trail cameras more aggressively, looking for a pattern from bed to feed. While scrolling through the images on my computer one night, I came across a buck that caught my attention. With ten points and long main beams that ended in whale tails, I was staring at an Iowa giant. 67 had been found dead the previous year, and The Big Ten never returned. While a property can house more deer through sound management, food plots, and habitat work, it often holds the same number of big bucks. There can't be too many cooks in the kitchen, and a mature buck will only tolerate so much. Somebody is destined to lose dominance, through battle or death, and to the victor go the spoils. I was hoping that another brute would move in, and I was not disappointed. The giant ten-pointer on my screen was walking along the timber in the early morning hours, likely on his way to bed down. Weeks went by with no other photos, making me wonder if he was just passing through. Then, in late October, we captured another picture in the dead of night, again displaying his regal rack. ZJ quickly took note and asked what we should call him?

"Ghost," I said. "Let's call him Ghost."

ZJ loved the idea and Ghost soon became the centerpiece of our conversations.

Ghost in the fading light.

Houston and I hunted Ghost as hard as we could. We watched the wind and put in countless hours but never laid eyes on the beast. Just before shotgun season in early December, I elected to sit on a large brassicas field I had planted that fall. It was getting late, and I was forced to decide between a permanent blind and a treestand along the field edge. The wind was favorable for both, but given the brutal cold, I took the easy way out and chose the blind. With the sun on the cusp of the horizon, I saw a line of does across the field—with Ghost bringing up the rear. His frame was massive with a sweeping rack and long tines. As he passed within 20 yards of the vacant treestand, I could only laugh at how a mental coin flip had cost me an opportunity. Nevertheless, laying eyes on this monarch for the first time was the silver lining, and I embraced the encounter. He fed for nearly an hour, well outside of bow range, before disappearing into the timber. The chess match would continue, but Ghost was dominating the board.

I hunted a few more times during the late season but never saw Ghost again. In early February, ZJ and I embarked on our third shed hunt of the year. We had found a few antlers, but not the ones we were looking for. After climb-

Eyad and his son found Ghost's left side in early February.

Eyad's Hawkeye State double.

ing a steep trail to the upper field, I glanced across the barren expanse and stopped in my tracks. My son saw it too and ran across the field as fast as his legs and rubber boots would carry him. Ghost's left side lie upon the frozen ground, its ivory-colored tines sharp and massive. With wide eyes and wonder, ZJ raised the antler skyward, flashing a smile I'll never forget. Not until a week later did I find the match, with the right side being equally impressive.

The spring of 2016 was soon upon us, with food plots, scouting, and turkey hunting in full swing. I patterned two birds before the opener, and on the morning of April 18, I was nestled on a lush clover plot. The gobblers had roosted on the far end of the field and showed little interest after they flew down. I knew they preferred where I was stationed, and with a classic strut zone strategy, I patiently awaited their arrival. Coaxed by soft purrs and yelps, they eventually sauntered their way in. Two well-placed arrows anchored the birds quickly, and I had my first archery double in Iowa.

Throughout the summer, I glassed our fields and prepped for the fall, with one buck on my mind. ZJ hadn't forgotten the giant either, drawing pictures of arrows and antlers in his notebook at school. Ghost had become a bond between us, more important than any trophy.

Summer morphed into fall, and winds of change found the heartland. I hoped Ghost was still alive, but with so many factors plotting against white-tails—from cars and coyotes to parasites and predators—there were no guarantees. On a gorgeous afternoon in early October, I set out to harvest a doe on one of our food plots. The wind was perfect that night, blowing from the southwest and over the valley below. Not long into my sit, I noticed a brown creeper on a large red oak to my left. This phantom of the forest is a woodland treasure, although the local ants and spiders may disagree. Like a strand of DNA, the drab-colored creeper spiraled around the trunk, trying to scrounge out a suitable meal. I was so amused by his antics that I almost missed the does stepping out of the timber. I drew awkwardly but still placed a perfect shot behind the lead doe's shoulder. In seconds, I heard her fall and soon was standing over a beautiful prize.

With a freezer full of venison and Ghost on my mind, I went to check cameras the following week. I almost fell out of my chair when the large rack and whale tails appeared on my screen. The old monarch was still alive, and we were back in the game. Unfortunately, I wouldn't capture another photo for two weeks, once again in the wee hours of the morning. This was disappointing as it proved he wasn't bedding close. I tried to devise a strategy to hunt Ghost, but there's only so much you can do with a nocturnal buck. Around Halloween, I decided to get more aggressive and placed a set of rattling antlers in my truck. I had to take my kids to daycare before heading south and loaded them up after breakfast.

As we drove along, I heard ZJ ask, "What are those antlers doing in here, Daddy?"

With a cool confidence, I told him that I was going to *trick* Ghost and lure him in, by imitating a fight between two bucks. I saw his wheels turning as he considered this strategy, before he said,

"I wouldn't try that if I were you, Daddy. Ghost is pretty smart. I'd leave them in the truck."

I don't know if I wanted to laugh or say thanks, but the rattling antlers stayed in the pickup.

I captured another picture of Ghost on November 10, again just after midnight. I had yet to get a daylight photo of this monster, and he was living up to his name. The fall of 2016 was one of the warmest on record, and with the heat of November being almost unbearable, I wondered if traveling under the cover of darkness would remain the norm. I had other commitments on the morning of November 15, so I arrived at the farm just past 2:00 PM. There was a stiff breeze blowing from the south, and I realized that another warm afternoon awaited. I'd been battling a respiratory bug for the past week, but with two kids in daycare, it wasn't my first go-round. Sitting in the drive as I turned off the radio, I downed a dose of Tylenol and contemplated where to hunt. One stand kept coming to mind. A dark horse in every sense of the word, it was in a timber strip between two fields and had received little attention. I finally conceded to my impulse, without a shred of optimism, and committed to hunt there.

It was four years ago, nearly to the day, that I hunted this area for the first time. Stationed along the field edge, I was enjoying the afternoon when I turned around to see 67 walking down the ridge. He was well out of range and seemed determined to follow a set course through the woods. I was hunting with my good friend Steve and recall telling him about my encounter. I could not determine why 67 had walked through that area, chalking it up to the rut and a buck's nomadic tendencies. It turned out to be more than coincidence; however, as over the next three seasons, I witnessed similar behavior along that ridge. The movement was random and always in mid-November, during the peak breeding phase. You can lead a horse to water, and after four years of witnessing the same pattern, I finally took a drink. I hung a stand along that ridge after the 2015 season and vowed to hunt it come November.

Those thoughts consumed me as I crossed the creek and made my way up the hill. I tried to talk myself into hunting another area, but my mind dismissed that notion. Soon I was at the base of my treestand, where I smiled at memories of the past summer. ZJ and I had spent some time here, clearing paths and shooting lanes with a pole saw. I had also mowed trails through this strip with a brush hog, preparing the perfect entry and exit routes. Despite these efforts, I'd given the stand little thought until this afternoon. It was an awkward area, void of sign and any distinguishing features. Before climbing into my perch, I contemplated checking the trail camera just in front of my stand. I knew better than to cross the trail and spread my scent before the hunt, but I couldn't resist. The card proved I was right to stay mellow, as only a few does had worked past the camera in recent weeks. Still, I climbed skyward, vowing to enjoy the evening ahead.

Upon reaching the platform, I hoisted my bow and placed it on the hanger. The sun was just favoring the western horizon, painting the fields in a mixture of gold and shadow. The wind had lost steam and settled down, as if the southern breezes were running out of fuel. I could feel the temperature cooling as well and pulled the zipper higher on my vest. By 3:30 PM, the woods had taken on a deafening silence, with every sound magnified by a blanket of dead leaves. Still conditions have always been my Achilles' heel on this farm, with little movement on nights like this. Unable to use the wind to their advantage, whitetails will lie low until nightfall, when human threats are reduced. Perhaps the diminished gusts could find their second wind and keep the deer on their feet.

At 4:00 PM, I heard the unmistakable sound of a pileated woodpecker, his sharp tone and cadence growing louder as he approached. This crow-sized bird is a remarkable sight, and as close to a real-life Woody Woodpecker as you'll find. I strained my eyes through the timber and eventually spotted his black, white, and red colors undulating through the air. Landing with authority high atop a dead walnut tree, he began his hunt for unsuspecting arthropods. Occasionally, he stood still and looked down at the bean field below, the sun illuminating his crimson crown like a candle behind a red veil.

Captivated by the gaudy woodpecker, and enjoying every minute, I suddenly heard footsteps to the north. I picked up my bow and scanned the timber behind me, looking for their maker. The foot falls were slow and barely audible, revealing that something was approaching with apprehension. No buck walks with mediocrity during the rut, and I assumed a yearling was approaching slowly. Mature does will abandon their fawns once breeding commences, forcing them to fend for themselves. Orphaned by their mothers, these fawns are both cautious and curious, always approaching with a hint of anxiety. Mother Nature equips them with the skills to survive alone, but their learning curve is steep. I relaxed my bow arm, knowing I had no intention of taking a young deer. After a short pause, the footsteps began once more, this time even closer. I still couldn't see what I knew to be a whitetail, continuing to strain my eyes through the cover.

I finally gave up on the mysterious footsteps and turned back around, only to see a huge body and tall tines marching down the ridge. The buck had just entered the timber, emerging from the thick tangle of switch grass above. By the time I realized what was happening, he was already through my first lane and consumed by the foliage. He looked like an Angus bull coming through the woods, and although I'd never seen this buck before, there was no doubt he was a shooter. The buck turned to his right and worked down the strip toward my stand. The paths I had cut that summer provided two shooting lanes, both within 20 yards. I waited before committing to either direction, knowing I had time to decide. Just before hitting the fork in the trail, the buck came unglued, spinning on a dime and bounding away. I hung my head in disappointment, knowing exactly what had happened.

The buck had caught my scent near the camera—thus deterring his approach—and if not for my foolish behavior, he would have continued on his course. On par with a Cubs World Series berth, second chances on mature bucks are rare. I didn't expect to have a chance at redemption, nor did I deserve one, but blind squirrels do find acorns now and then. As he turned to leave, the footsteps started behind me again, this time more toward the field. The buck seemed to move past the foreign odor like a bad memory, instead focusing his attention on the sound below. Cautiously, he strolled my way once more, this time hugging the edge of the field. The stand beneath my feet remained silent as I slowly turned my rubber boots in small increments, shifting to my right. I rarely ask God for assistance while hunting, feeling prayers are best reserved for more important matters. But I hope He didn't mind, in this one instance, when I asked for a little help.

There was a white oak between the buck and my last shooting lane, one I prayed would mask my intentions. As the buck moved behind the stone-colored trunk, I came to full draw, hitting my anchor just as he reappeared. The buck was slightly quartering when I settled my pin tight to his shoulder and let out a soft grunt. He stopped in mid-stride, turned his head up the ridge, and my arrow was gone—striking the buck near his shoulder blade. The whitetail burst through the timber with the shaft protruding from his side. I saw the arrow strike a tree and snap, its bright fletching cartwheeling through the air. Seconds later, I heard trees breaking and a tremendous crash, as if a bus took a detour through the woods. The wind had abandoned me, but in this case, it proved to be a blessing. I could hear a pin drop in the woods. And if a whitetail had bounded away on such a night, I would have heard it. After waiting for thirty minutes with rattled nerves, I crawled down and left the timber.

Four hours later, accompanied by Don, Seth, and Mitch, we made our way toward the timber strip. The air was crisp and cold, with a full moon hanging low on the horizon. I was concerned about the arrow placement but knew the crash could mean only one thing. We worked our way down the ridge and found the white oak where the buck was standing. I thought back to the first buck I harvested more than 20 years ago, and how the same scenario had unfolded. He, too, had passed behind a white oak and allowed me to hit my anchor, seconds before my arrow was on its way. We crept around multiflora rose and deadfalls, finally locating a small drop of blood. Our flashlights danced through the night, soon catching a glimpse of my arrow's fluorescent wrap.

Moments later, a white glow found our beams as the buck's eyes shined in the night. He had not gone far. I am a grown man, with a family and fulltime job, but I threw my hat into the air like I'd won the lottery. The sheer size of his body was impressive, and I had seen few whitetails of his caliber. The broadhead had missed his scapula by fractions of an inch; had I centered it, the night would have had a darker ending. After years of unfilled tags,

Eyad's 2016 Iowa Whitetail

I wasn't sure it would ever happen again, but I continued the quest for no other reason than I loved bowhunting. This night would always hold a special place in my heart, with memories of great friends and dreams fulfilled.

The next week, just before Thanksgiving dinner, I received a text message from my neighbor. He wished me a happy holiday and mentioned that he had shot a great buck. I asked if he could send me a picture, and soon I was looking at a legendary whitetail. I knew this buck all too well and couldn't help but smile. Ghost had succumbed to his only weakness—following an estrus doe past a great archer—a mistake he would not overcome. I was glad that it ended that way, as opposed to being at the hands of a cruel winter or errant slug. In the days prior, my neighbor had sent me trail cam photos of the buck I harvested. It was a kind gesture that I sincerely appreciated. I congratulated him and returned the favor that night. Sitting down at the kitchen table, I told ZJ the story and asked him what we were going to do.

With a smile on his face he said, "Well, Daddy, we'll just have to find another Ghost."

Life often comes full circle, and this story supports that notion. Twenty-five years ago, my passion for bowhunting took hold, when I was just a kid with big dreams. On that fateful November night, nearly three decades later, I felt like that kid once more. I'd been close so many times, but as they say, close only counts in horseshoes. Conversely, it's these setbacks that give us a greater appreciation for our successes. We spend countless hours fine-tuning our equipment, scouting, planting food plots, and lying in wait. Through downpours and freezing temperatures, lulls and self-doubt, we endure. That is the heart and soul of the hunt, the challenge that keeps us coming back. If we focus on our experiences and efforts, rather than the outcomes, we'll all be better for it. Success may not come when we want, or how we imagine it, but unanswered prayers can be our greatest blessing. The universe has a funny way of steering you in the right direction, and sometimes, it leads you right back where you started.

The Journey is the Reward

CHAPTER 28

Hourglass

Time is a precious commodity. We take it for granted during our youth, only to search for it like buried treasure as we grow older. My 2017 archery season was no different, as I struggled to get away. Family obligations, work, and other responsibilities had limited my tree time. Although my days in the field were sporadic, I knew that fate could change a bowhunter's fortune in a matter of seconds. I simply had to stay the course and hope that a mature buck would wander into bow range.

I started hunting on October 4, when humid temperatures and hordes of mosquitoes are the norm. The afternoon was unseasonably cool, with calm winds and clear skies. I was sitting over a clover plot when a doe drifted past and presented an opportunity. My arrow zipped through the autumn air, and I saw her fall within sight. With a freezer full of venison and two young boys at home, I spent the rest of the month working and taking care of my family. Around Halloween, a major cold front moved through the Midwest, fueling my desire to get back in the timber. Unfortunately, throughout the next week I saw little movement, catching only a glimpse of a mature buck on November 5.

As the season progressed and the cool fall days leaned into winter, the young bucks came out of the woodwork. Cruising past my stands at warp speed, unable to control their urges, they zigzagged back and forth looking for love. I likened these youngsters to pinballs at an arcade, bouncing around as they searched for any doe who would accept their advances. I was just as mobile, playing a game of musical chairs as I moved from stand to stand, trying to get a fix on an old warrior. From thickets to field edges and funnels to food plots—I tried it all to no avail. While the rut is proclaimed as the apex of deer hunting, when dreams come true and anything is possible, it also has a dark side. Patterns and predictability go out the window, and your chances of choosing the best stand are sometimes no better than a coin toss. At this point in the season, heads or tails sounded pretty good.

During the rut, even the young bucks battle for breeding rights.

On November 15, I sat on a bottom field with a stiff north wind in my face. I was getting settled when a young ten-pointer emerged from the creek bottom. Leaving my bow on the hanger, I let him walk but noticed his anxious demeanor. Something was bothering him, giving him a bad case of the *jimmy legs* as he stared into the creek and moved about anxiously. Then suddenly, he dove back into the bottom, only to come running out seconds later. Like a domino effect, a mature doe soon followed, sprinting out of the cover and directly beneath my stand.

I grabbed my bow just as a giant, chocolate-colored rack materialized—hot on her trail. To say I tried to stop him is an understatement, and anyone within earshot would tell you I tried. Still, he could not have cared less and was gone in a flash. The old boy never returned, but it was great to have an encounter with an Iowa giant.

Giant rubs are sure to fuel a bowhunter's dreams.

The next few days were spent catching up on work and cleaning the house for Thanksgiving. Truth be told, I thought my season was over. I had used up all my vacation, cashed in my brownie points with my wife, and had no regrets. The season had been enjoyable, and I was looking forward to spending some time with my family over the holidays. My parents were in town on November 19, and although it was the last weekend I could hunt, I decided to keep my bow on the sidelines. We met at a local steakhouse for lunch and had a great time. While sitting at the restaurant that afternoon, laughing at the kids' antics, telling jokes, and relishing the moment, my wife asked me if I wanted to go hunting. We had just finished lunch and with my farm only an hour away, I might still have a chance. My bow and boots were in my truck, and I had a small tote with a jacket, safety belt, and pants to round out my necessities. No sensible bowhunter would pass up this op-portunity—so I thanked my wife, said goodbye to my family, and headed south on Highway 27.

I arrived at my farm and changed clothes before hustling across the creek to-ward my stand. I cursed my impatience after breaking into a mild sweat, but soon I was at the base of the shingle oak, clipping my harness to the lifeline and making my ascent. The wind was out of the southwest, blowing over my right shoulder and toward a CRP field behind me. The only direction I gave up was the trail I walked in on, straight downwind and off to my right. It didn't take long for the woods to come alive, with fox squirrels and blue jays announcing my arrival. The timber has never known two finer whistle-blowers, growing louder with each chuckle and raucous call to betray my presence. I took it on the chin and hoped that any whitetail within earshot would disregard their warning.

Time passed and the woods fell silent. I was enjoying the solitude when I heard wing beats to my left. A pileated woodpecker was jumping from tree to tree like a game of hopscotch, cocking his head back and forth in search of six-legged morsels. These giant woodpeckers were a mainstay in this tim-ber strip and known for their bravado. With a sharp staccato call, flaming crest, and jackhammer hunting style—peace and quiet was not part of their repertoire.

Thirty minutes later, long after the woodpecker's departure, I caught move-ment to my left. Two fawns and a mature doe were ambling toward my position. They were calm and poised—bad news for this bowhunter. If there was a bruiser following this doe, she would be acting more frantic, and hav-ing two fawns in tow supported that notion. Surprised that this doe was still off the market, I sat back and enjoyed their parade. Nonchalantly, the trio passed by my ambush at 15 yards while I kept watch over their backtrail. Soon, they moved past and I was left alone with my thoughts.

It wasn't long before I again caught movement to my left. Two button bucks were working toward my position, browsing through the timber as they moved along. Squaring off to playfully spar, they engaged in a ritual that one day wouldn't be so friendly. In time, they grew weary of their sparring match and bedded down not 20 yards from my stand. One of the buttons had chosen an old blowdown to lay beside and quickly disappeared among its branches and briars. The other remained in plain view, twisting and turning his head to observe and stand guard against any approaching threat.

Within minutes, I saw a tail flicker down the ridge and noticed three doe fawns walking toward me. This timber strip was fast becoming a daycare, as now multiple youngsters milled around my stand site. The presence of these new arrivals awakened the button bucks, who abruptly came to their feet and strolled over to introduce themselves. To the trio of approaching fawns, I suspect the button bucks were as appealing as a pack of coyotes. The young does ran circles around my stand, trying to escape this unanticipated ambush. The buttons worked as a team, cutting the fawns off and trying to impress them with gentle nudges and bouts of aggression.

With five youngsters now within 20 yards, and no grown-ups in sight, it was obvious the rut was in full swing. I pictured the thickest, nastiest hollows on the farm, where the boss bucks were surely on lockdown. My only hope was that an estrus doe would lead their captor toward my ambush, but I knew this was a shot in the dark. My bow and body remained motionless, simply enjoying the show. At one point, after repeatedly chasing the fawns in circles, the larger button buck began moving toward my position. Step by step he inched closer until he was right under my stand. By this point it was growing dark, with only minutes of legal shooting time remaining. While this stand session had been exciting, I realized that I might be here for some time unless these youngsters moved along.

I was looking for a resilient acorn or gall ball, anything to gently toss and spook the herd out of sight, when the button buck beneath me stiffened. His ears were at full alert and every muscle in his form was tense. Focused on the CRP field, which now resembled a shadowy tomb, the buck continued to stare. The other fawns had followed suit and were frozen in place—staring into the grassy swale. I slowly reached for my bow, never taking my eyes off the button buck below me, knowing what he and the others were looking at.

Once I had my bow in hand, I turned and saw a tall rack and heavy body moving down the tree line. The fawns that had filtered toward the CRP field still hadn't moved, as if paralyzed with fear and unable to decide. No matter; the approaching buck decided for them. He swung his antlers back and forth in a pendular motion, scattering the fawns like bowling pins. Satisfied with their response, the brute turned left and focused his attention on the button buck below me. As he moved toward the frightened fawn, I attached my release.

I noticed the jowls hanging from his weathered face, the sagging belly and thick neck. Coming down the same trail I had used to enter my stand, the buck continued to approach without hesitation, as if the convenience of this route trumped any scent I had left behind. My eyes shot back and forth— from his antler bases to his belly—offering the proof I needed that this was a mature buck. Now directly below me, replacing the button buck who had since fled for his life, the beast turned broadside. I came to full draw and settled my pin on his vitals, steadied my aim, and squeezed the release.

A solid hit echoed through the hardwoods as the buck bolted and crashed down the ridge. I stared through bare treetops toward the west, where a faint orange glow remained on the horizon. After lowering my bow to the ground, I soon followed, with a heart full of excitement and gratitude.

One hour later, accompanied by my friend Houston and two flashlights, we made our way to the stand site. The blood trail was profuse and steady, quickly leading us to my buck. As I admired the whitetail's handsome rack and massive body, I whispered a thank you and thought back over the past two months. Through the highs and lows of another season, success had come down to a moment in time. I had never seen this buck before, nor did I have any history with him. And yet, on a day in which I had not planned to hunt, in a stand chosen by my tardiness, an opportunity arose because I stayed the course. In bowhunting, patience and persistence seldom go unrewarded, even when your hourglass is nearly out of sand.

November 2017

CHAPTER 29

Sitka Sprints

In like a lion—out like a lamb. As March transitions to April each spring, turkey hunters hope this proverb holds true. But as I walked across the creek and up the frozen hillside that morning, it appeared that Mother Nature had other plans.

The wind was howling out of the northwest with such ferocity, that I wondered how long I would last. I stared into the dark timber, listening to the trees creak and moan, a symphony of chaos spawned by the storm. Sleet ricocheted off my bow limbs as I continued up an old farm lane, my footsteps breaking through the frozen ruts and depressions beneath me. The hickories and oaks, still barren and lifeless, seemed tortured as the violent gusts barreled through the hardwoods. It had been a long, hard winter, and I wished that Jack Frost would just go away.

It was April 16, 2018, Iowa's spring turkey opener, a day I look forward to each season. I had started bowhunting turkeys two decades prior, on an April morning much different than this one. The green grass, bluebird skies, and thundering gobbles that forged my memories were now absent, a seasonal shift that Dr. Jekyll and Mr. Hyde would appreciate. Nevertheless, I had watched the weather for the past week and knew what was coming down the pipe. Forecasters were calling for windchills near zero, and after rummaging through my whitetail gear the night before, I was prepared. I wore a merino wool base layer, stocking cap, gloves, an insulated vest, and rounded out my attire with a Sitka windstopper jacket and pants.

As I entered the field, I noticed the sleet and snow had picked up speed, dusting the clover like a salt shaker. I quietly set up my blind and secured each corner with tent stakes, arranged my decoy spread, and slipped into the blind. Once I was situated, I dropped two of the windows and listened intently. With the blustery conditions, I wouldn't hear any gobbles, even if the local longbeards were so inclined. So, I sat back and awaited the dawn. On days of inclement weather, whether it be rain, wind, snow or sleet, scouting and patience will always trump calling skills. The birds will seek open areas, where their keen eyesight is more effective, away from the distractions of blowing leaves and swaying branches. Despite the brutal conditions, I threw out a series of lost calls shortly after sunrise, praying a note or two would find the ears of an old tom.

I had been in the blind an hour, hunkered down and trying to stay warm, when I looked to the north. A gobbler was looming over my jake decoy—his red, white, and blue head contrasting against the opaque sky. Somehow, this longbeard had snuck in without warning and was now staring down his competition, swinging his wattles back and forth in an act of defiance. Confident that he would stay focused on the decoy, I raised my bow and attached my release. The gobbler's head mirrored a thermometer in hot water, slowly turning red with each passing second. There was no doubt his blood was boiling, and frigid conditions or not, he was ready for a fight.

Over the past four seasons, I had used a unique broadhead engineered for head and neck shots on wild turkeys. Having chased my share of gobblers through the years, I decided to retire from track and field, opting for the all-or-none approach. While there are no guarantees in bowhunting, I felt these broadheads offered the best chance for clean kills and easier recoveries, or so I thought. The gobbler was off to my right, a difficult shot for anyone but a southpaw, but one I felt I could make. I leaned to my left and came to full draw, teetering on a small stool as I hit my anchor.

I was focused on the gobbler's head and neck, a dancing target that never stood still. The wind was worsening, testing the strength of my tent stakes, while spinning my jake decoy round and round like a Tilt-A-Whirl. The longbeard was so infuriated with the jake that it didn't matter, hammering the plastic youngster with wing beats and spurs. This didn't help my cause, as each time I tried to execute the shot, the gobbler moved again. I had to bear down and squeeze the release, which I did a few seconds later.

Almost immediately, I knew something was wrong. Rather than watching my arrow hit its target, I caught a glimpse of the fletching veering to the right. Striking the gobbler in the wing butt, nowhere close to my point of aim, I realized the large broadhead had clipped the blind's window. I hadn't compensated for the severe angle, and while these headhunter broadheads have their place and can be very effective, their margin of error is slim.

The tom cartwheeled through the air, spinning across the field in a blur of feathers and flurries. I always preach patience after the shot, allowing time for the broadhead to do its job. But in this case, knowing the gobbler's wound was anything but mortal, I did the opposite. I unzipped the blind and ran into the field, sprinting after the tom who was now racing toward the timber. I cut him off and closed the distance before doing what any sensible bowhunter would do.

I tried to tackle him.

This didn't end well for me, as my body hit the frozen clover field with an unflattering thud. I felt my back give way and a sharp pain shoot through my lower extremities. I quickly recovered and turned to my right, only to see the gobbler flapping his wings in a frenzy, trying to get airborne. With another desperate lunge I had my hands on him, knocking the longbeard to the ground for the last time. As I lie there with a fistful of tail feathers, a mature tom, and a thrown-out back, I smiled and watched the flurries continue to fall.

Caught on trail camera—Eyad moments before he tackled his gobbler.

Opening Day Gobbler—April 16, 2018

That coming Sunday, April 22, happened to be my 41st birthday. Despite having another tag, I decided to sleep in and spend the morning with my wife and two boys. Wanting to have my cake and eat it too, I planned on hunting that evening over a bean field where two longbeards had been strutting of late.

The last Iowa gobbler I took on an evening hunt was in 1994, one that culminated with #4 shot and a 12- gauge. I wanted to accomplish the same feat with a bow and arrow, but up to this point, I had been unsuccessful. While Merriam's, Rios, and an Osceola had fallen to my arrows near sundown— Easterns remained a mystery. Here in the Midwest, I rarely saw gobblers in the evening, as if they went through a blackhole and reappeared in their roost trees come morning. Still, the challenge was high on my bucket list, and what better day to celebrate success than on a bowhunter's birthday.

After lunch I loaded my gear and headed south, arriving at my farm around 4:00 PM. The temperatures were still unseasonably cool, remnants of opening day's arctic blast. I was wearing the same Sitka jacket and pants, refusing to retire my wardrobe until winter was in the rearview. Once I reached the field, I erected my blind facing east and then arranged my decoy spread: two hens and a jake within 10 yards of my setup. With the sun behind me, the western rays would temper any light entering the blind, allowing me to draw undetected. I decided to use mechanical broadheads for this hunt, having more confidence in their performance. The headhunters had their place, but would be more effective with wider windows, and my T5 Double Bull was all I had.

No matter the broadhead you choose—shot placement is critical when bowhunting spring gobblers.

Two hours later, after finishing a paperback and a calling sequence, I looked out the back window of the blind. For a moment, I saw a flash of red in the distance, on the edge of a CRP field. I hadn't heard a gobble, or anything for that matter, so perhaps my eyes were playing tricks on me. Still, I picked up my bow and got ready—just in case.

A few minutes later, I heard a subtle noise. It was the softest sound, like a piece of straw being broken, and if not for the calm conditions I wouldn't have heard it. I quickly attached my release just as two longbeards marched into the decoys. Their feet were moving rapidly on approach, as if shifting into high gear at the end of a race. They hovered over the jake and landed a few blows before one of the gobblers turned and presented an opportunity. My arrow found its mark, entering right above his thigh and angling into his vitals.

The fletching resembled a fluorescent torch as the tom hobbled toward the timber, bobbing along before stopping near a brush pile. Standing at full mast, like a flag pole on a putting green, my arrow marked the longbeard's location. The sun and temperature were falling as darkness drew near, and while I thought the tom was down, I still wasn't sure. After a mental game of tug-of-war, I decided to be patient and give him time. I was doing just that when I looked up and saw my arrow moving.

My heart was hammering as I realized the gobbler was still alive, and with nightfall fast approaching, I had to pursue. Hustling out of the blind, I nocked an arrow and moved toward the tom. I kept a cedar tree between the brush pile and myself, but once I entered the timber, I knew the jig was up. Each step was like walking on egg shells—spot and stalk's kiss of death.

I stepped away from the cedar and saw the gobbler through a tangle of branches, hidden beneath the brush pile. Hoping to thread the needle, I came to full draw and steadied my aim. Unfortunately, my arrow deflected off a limb and only grazed the bird. The tom erupted from the cover and crashed down the ridge with me in full pursuit.

My jacket and pants, designed to repel the wind rather than thorns, ripped through brambles and blowdowns as I tried to keep up with the old warrior. Suddenly, we hit the edge of a steep ridge, where the gobbler pitched off and glided down to the creek below. Unable to go any farther, without the aid of a zipline, I took a deep breath and nocked another arrow. A few seconds later, I saw his ebony form moving out of the creek.

April 22, 2018

I was steady and calm as I settled my pin, squeezed the release, and watched my arrow pass through the gobbler for the last time. He spun and flopped into the creek, allowing me time to slide down the embankment and recover him. As I threw the longbeard over my shoulder, both of us now soaking wet, I felt a deep sense of pride and achievement. The sun was just below the tree line when I crested the ridge, setting the western horizon ablaze. I took some photos, gathered my gear, and headed back to my truck. It was the end of an incredible season, a memorable birthday, and after twenty years of bowhunting spring gobblers, I was reminded of a valuable lesson.

No matter the broadhead you choose, time of day you hunt, or weather conditions you face—*never forget your running shoes.*

CHAPTER 30

Hunter's Moon

Grain dust lingered in the autumn air, trailing combines as they rolled through fields of gold. It was harvest time in the Midwest, a season of beauty, bounty, and change. While brilliant colors, gridiron classics, and Halloween costumes are all reasons to favor the fall, bowhunting whitetails is at the top of my list.

It was October 21, 2018, and I was headed to southern Iowa for my first bowhunt of the season. Work commitments and a family wedding had kept me out of the timber thus far, but I could stay away no longer. A cold front had engulfed the Midwest since early October, digging in and becoming the norm. In fact, it seemed that Iowa was under a weather dome, with a bowhunter controlling the thermostat. Frosty mornings and cool evenings were a daily occurrence, and the deer were on the move. I contemplated where to hunt that afternoon—with one buck on my mind.

There was a mainframe nine-pointer roaming the farm, with heavy antlers and a massive body. I knew where he was bedding but had yet to capture a daylight photo of this brute. Still, I was hoping the colder weather and coming moon phase would increase his daylight activity. The Hunter's Moon was forecasted to rise on October 24, 2018, and would be the *second* full moon since the fall equinox. The late Charles J. Alsheimer, a leading authority on moon phases and whitetail deer behavior, had called this the Rutting Moon, and believed it to be a catalyst for increased breeding activity. His book *Hunting Whitetails by the Moon* is a fascinating read. And while lunar phases have never dictated my hunting schedule or style, I cannot deny their influence. Lunar effects or not, something had the deer on their feet, and I had to take advantage before the rut changed the game.

I arrived at the farm at 4:30 PM and quickly changed clothes before flinging a few arrows down range. Confident that my equipment was sound, I grabbed my safety belt and headed across the creek. Sign was prevalent as I rounded the bend, with scrapes and rubs tattooing the farm lane. Fresh earth lie exposed beneath licking branches, while a shingle oak stood twisted and torn, its limbs looking more like a pretzel than a sapling. There was a ladder stand near the back of a large corn field, with clover and turnips along its edge. Through the years, I had taken two does from this location but had never seen a mature buck. Although my friend Houston had hunted this stand the day before, the wind was perfect and access was easy, so I headed there.

I moved up the hill and along the timberline, finally reaching my stand at 5:00 PM. As I approached the tree, now only a few yards away, I looked up and stopped on a dime. A mature doe had risen from her bed and was staring right through me, threatening to end my hunt before it started. Even worse, the wind was blowing over my shoulder toward the doe, surely confirming her suspicions.

To my surprise, she slowly turned and disappeared down the ridge without a sound. I moved toward my stand, expecting sharp snorts and bounding footsteps to follow, but they never transpired. I quickly tied the pull rope to my bow, clipped my safety belt to the lifeline, and made my ascent. Once I was situated, I nocked an arrow, placed my bow on the hanger, and relaxed.

Almost a year had passed since I hunted this stand, and I paused a moment to take it all in. The corn and clover were thriving, while hedge apples and acorns littered the ground beneath me. A mixture of green and rustic-red painted the oaks, while hickories, walnuts, and sugar maples displayed deep yellow hues. I could see cherry trees and gooseberry bushes through the timber, their leaves a striking sunset orange. It was a perfect evening, with steady winds and cool temperatures, and I felt blessed to be there. After ensuring the coast was clear, I sent a text message to my wife, letting her know that I had arrived safely. I then put my phone away and sat back, hoping to catch a glimpse of a few deer before sundown.

Thirty minutes later, with streaks of sunlight shooting through the dark timber, I saw movement to my left. Antler tines were swaying back and forth, hidden behind a small sapling. My adrenaline was flowing as I peered through the cover, trying to determine if it was a mature buck. It wasn't long before the buck exposed himself, moving slowly toward the field edge.

This young buck was the first whitetail to emerge from the timber.

When he cleared the timber and stepped into the open, I could tell he was a young ten-pointer, no older than three-and-a-half and would get a pass. I left my bow on the hanger and took some photos as he moved through the food plot.

In time, a fawn emerged from the timber at a fast trot, followed by a mature doe, both making their way into the field. The buck stopped feeding and took notice before aggressively moving in their direction. The doe understood his intentions—but was not receptive—and soon was dodging and darting through the food plot, doing all she could to thwart his advances.

As they moved within 10 yards of my stand, the buck suddenly froze and stared in my direction. The wind was still in my favor, blowing out of the southwest and down the ridge. I couldn't fathom what was wrong, but within seconds he was gone, dashing across the field and out of sight. I slowly turned and peered into the forest but saw nothing.

I assumed the buck had crossed my entry trail and caught my scent, a reasonable explanation, and one I was content with. I was getting settled when a grunt erupted from the ditch behind me. It was so loud that it almost startled me off the stand. Somewhere between a grunt and a growl, another deep bellow echoed from the hollow. I carefully lifted my bow off the hanger and turned, waiting for the buck to appear.

I could see tall tines and long main beams through the timber, moving in my direction at a steady clip. This was happening, and yet, I still couldn't believe it. With each step the grunts grew louder, and the beast drew closer, until the big nine-pointer materialized along the field edge. I remember looking down at the orange fletching on my arrow, and the moleskin along my bow's riser, before taking a deep breath and preparing for the shot.

For so many years, I had envisioned a giant standing in this position, glaring into the field with broad shoulders and a massive rack. I had pictured his strides as he approached from my left, the trees I would use as cover to conceal my draw, and where I would stop him before releasing my arrow. All of these dreams and scenarios played out over the next few seconds—except one small detail.

There was a honey locust tree, angled and innocuous, a few yards in front of my treestand. Houston and I had clipped and sawed the year before, knocking branches and thorns off its course bark, clearing the way for a broadhead-tipped arrow. However, upon reaching the stand's platform that afternoon, I noticed one twig remained in my shooting lane. I made a mental note to bring a pole saw the next time in, but you know what they say about the best laid plans.

As the buck strode across the field in the fading light, I hit my anchor and mouthed a soft grunt, stopping him at 27 yards—right behind that twig. I could hear Mr. Murphy laughing before whispering in my ear, "You didn't see that one coming, did you?"

I can't say that I panicked, in fact, I was surprisingly calm. Here I was, at full draw on one of the biggest whitetails I've ever seen, with his vitals obscured by a lonely, lifeless twig. I normally shoot sitting down, so I had to rise and lean to my right. Upon doing that, my field of view expanded, and although it was an awkward angle, I was steady as I pulled through the shot.

Like a placekicker at the buzzer, I watched my arrow arc through the air—its flight and intentions perfect—before it slowly drifted to the left. The orange fletching disappeared behind the beast's ribcage with a loud *whoomph*, and he erupted toward the standing corn. I had bowhunted long enough to know the reality of the situation, and calling a spade a spade, I had hit the buck too far back.

I could hear the buck crashing through the corn stalks, and then all went silent. I sat down and collected my thoughts, my mind sifting through the possibilities. There was no doubt that it was a lethal shot, but finding the buck would be a tall order. I had no clue where he entered the corn, as my view was obstructed by a cluster of oaks and Osage orange. The moon was climbing higher above the tree line, its luminous rays growing brighter with each passing second. I crawled down from my stand and crept over to the impact site, expecting to find my arrow. Having no luck, I quietly backed out with plans to return the next morning. The buck needed time, and despite a healthy coyote population, I had to be patient. Hopefully, we would find him at first light.

The cold weather continued that night, coating the landscape in a blanket of frost. I followed a salmon-colored sky along the eastern horizon the next morning, arriving at the farm just after sunrise. Houston had work commitments and couldn't join me, but my friends Mitch, Don, and Seth offered to help. We headed to the impact site, hoping to find my arrow and determine the buck's line of travel. It had been 14 hours since I dropped the string, but I was still concerned.

After a thorough search around my treestand, with no sign of blood or my arrow, we spread out. I circled around the corn and walked along the timberline, checking trails and fence crossings. As I approached a heavy runway that led into the forest, I looked down and caught a flash of red. There was a small patch of blood on the pasture grass, leading toward a hardwood ridge and thicket. We backtracked through the corn and quickly found my arrow, its shaft and feathers coated in crimson.

Caught on trail camera—Eyad at full draw
moments before the shot.

We slowly moved into the timber with our senses on full alert. The sign was sparse but steady, with dark droplets on fallen leaves, and streaks of red along sapling trunks. Fresh hoofprints were also evident, large depressions that followed the blood trail down the ridge. We had covered over 100 yards, and still not found his first bed, when we heard a flock of crows cawing. They were a good distance away, but with the blood trail waning, we all wondered if they had found something.

We pressed on, still finding small droplets, with an occasional pool of blood where the buck had stood. The crows were still hammering, growing louder as we drew closer. The sign had led us down the ridge into thicker cover, now near the steep banks of a creek bed. We had lost blood at this point, almost 225 yards from my treestand, and didn't know which direction to go. The buck could have crossed the creek into a jungle of multiflora rose and cedars or doubled back up the ridge. Both were possibilities, and we had to be careful.

Don, Seth, and Mitch moved down toward the creek, while I veered left into the hardwoods, praying we'd find a clue that would give us direction. I was getting nervous when I saw Don motion toward Seth, who was now on the other side of the waterway. Don had seen something, and then Seth did too. They were moving in that direction when suddenly, Seth hollered, "He's right here, Eyad! Get your bow!"

I rushed toward the creek and down the embankment, crawled up the other side, and there was my buck. He was bedded along the creek bank, hidden within a clump of honeysuckle. I placed a final arrow into his vitals and ended the hunt. A whitetail's resilience and strength never ceases to amaze me, but in this case, it was hard to fathom. I tipped my hat skyward and said thank you before kneeling beside the buck's massive body. His rack was polished and heavy, with a sticker-point off both G2s, and shredded bark along his brow tines. I could still hear the crows' raucous calls in the distance, their commotion a red herring after all. The broadhead had clipped the buck's liver and our patience had paid off. Had we pursued him the night before, we would have pushed him out of his bed, perhaps never to be seen again. Although the ending was bittersweet, I was grateful for it.

The next evening, I was rummaging through my sheds when I pulled a heavy antler from the pile. I had found it in a bean field the previous winter, not far from my buck's final resting place. The shed's main beam and tines were unmistakable, and I knew it had once belonged to him. I placed the antler back on the pile, grabbed my coat, and stepped outside into the night air.

The giant buck's shed from the previous year.

The Hunter's Moon was nearly full, illuminating the pasture behind my home. I thought back over the past two days, humbled by the thin line between success and heartbreak. As bowhunters, each outing and every hunt provides an opportunity to learn. Whether it be understanding moon phases, trimming twigs, shooting at awkward angles, or practicing patience on a blood trail—it's our job to decipher and learn from each one. This hunt was no exception, and each fall, when I see the Hunter's Moon rising, I will remember those lessons.

Dallen Lambson's "Hunter's Moon"—a print inspired by
the trail cam image from Eyad's memorable hunt.

CHAPTER 31

Hardware

The metallic sounds grew louder as I rummaged through the wicker basket, sifting through old memories. Within its woven confines were an array of medals—sports relics from days gone by. Each medallion was etched with deep engravings, revealing the year and my place on the podium. I had found them in a cardboard box among other hand-me-downs, hidden in the corner of my parents' guest room. The medals had lost their luster, and the ribbons were frayed, but the memories of old teammates and championships remained. They reminded me of a not-so-distant spring, where the greatest trophies had little to do with beards and spurs.

Opening day of the 2019 Iowa spring turkey season was slated for April 8, with a forecast calling for mild temperatures, blue skies, and calm winds. The nightscape was teaming with stars as I climbed the hill that morning, their presence like a silent promise, ensuring the sunrise would be unabated. As I entered the field and approached the timber, there wasn't a whisper of gray along the eastern horizon, nor a songbird who had woken from their slumber. I was early, but I had to be. Two gobblers had roosted near the field edge the night before, but I wasn't sure how close. I planned to erect my blind within a thin strip of clover along a standing cornfield, one picked clean of its kernels. Protruding from the freshly thawed field, the stalks would shield my approach but offer little cover once I was atop the hill.

I pushed forward, past the last of the withered corn and laid my bow down on the dew-soaked plot. Intent on staying quiet, I slipped the blind and decoys off my back and staked them down in the field. I entered the blind with time to spare, zipped the entrance closed with a cringe, and then readied my calls and bow. In time, the barren treetops slowly took form as rays of light pierced the ridgeline. A cardinal broke the silence soon after, and with the help of a train whistle to the north, the gobblers opened up. I picked up my slate and striker, leaned into the window, and scratched out a series of calls.

The longbeards answered immediately, cutting me off with a double-gobble. This wasn't a compliment, as car horns and barking dogs soon elicited the same response. Still, they knew I was here, which was half the battle. A pair of hens responded to my next sequence, with raspy yelps that drifted through the hardwoods. I placed a diaphragm against my palate and traded barbs with the cantankerous duo, while the gobblers continued to hammer from a giant oak. Focused on the leafless canopy, I could see their silhouettes against the graying sky, like shadows on a dimly lit screen. One tom was clearly visible, his beard swaying back and forth in the early morning light. I spotted other turkeys along the ridgeline, ruffling their feathers and peering around as if taking roll call.

Suddenly, cackles and rapid wingbeats broke the vocal monotony as one-by-one the birds pitched down. Hoping the hens had jealous bones, I cut loose with a series of aggressive calls, using both my diaphragm and slate. Neither the hens nor the gobblers responded, and knowing I had said enough, I put my calls down and waited. Thirty minutes later, I looked to the south and saw two strutting longbeards and four hens moving in my direction. The hens were closing fast, so I attached my release and came to full draw, assuming the gobblers would follow suit. Instead, the toms angled toward the jake decoy at a snail's pace, opting for the slow and steady approach.

Regretting my decision to draw prematurely, I held firm against the wall and waited, needing them to hurry along. The lead gobbler obliged and rushed forward, lowering his fan and wings before chest-bumping the plastic youngster. I placed my pin on the bird's wattles, steadied my aim, and touched the release. The tom dropped in a heap of feathers, flopped around the decoy, and then came to rest. Realizing the tides had turned, the second gobbler sprinted forward and was flogging the deceased tom before I could nock another arrow. By the time I recovered, the traitor was walking away, his head erect and snaking through the air. I hit my anchor just as he stopped and looked back, giving me an opportunity for an opening day double. The barred fletching spun perfectly off the string, but the blades missed their mark, leaving the gobbler unscathed. I shook my head with a smile and a hint of disappointment, set my bow down, and exited the blind to claim my prize. The hefty tom carried two beards, sharp spurs, and a full fan, adding the final touches to a great morning.

April 8, 2019

With another tag in my pocket and ample time to fill it, I started hunting again on April 15. The weather was cooler than the opener, with low hanging clouds and brisk winds out of the north. In stark contrast to the week before, the farm resembled a ghost town, with the only sounds coming from songbirds and squirrels. Surely there were birds in the area, and if I stayed the course an opportunity would arise. Optimism and success are not synonymous, and on this day, those words rang true. After six hours in the blind, I packed up my gear and headed home, convinced tomorrow would be a better day. Unfortunately, the turkeys pleaded the fifth once again, making me question my skills and strategy. Little did I know that it was a sign of things

to come. I hunted hard over the next ten days, trying everything from mid-day sits and the silent treatment, to aggressive calling and evening vigils. On multiple occasions, I had longbeards moving toward me—only to have them disappear, skirt my decoys, or slap me in the face with a courtesy gobble. The season had taken a turn for the worse, and my single-minded focus on tagging out was wearing me down.

My 4-year-old son, CW, had asked if I would take him turkey hunting that spring, and I promised to do so. Caught up in my quest to fill another tag, I had put him on the back burner but vowed to make it right. I felt that an afternoon hunt was our best option, only because waking a toddler at 4:00 AM is a recipe for disaster. The weather still wasn't cooperating, and I vacillated on when to go. Then, on April 28, Mother Nature decided for us. Our Little League tournament was rained out that Sunday, and seeing a golden opportunity, I asked CW if he wanted to go hunting. Sporting navy blue sweatpants, a Seahawks stocking cap, and a black coat—my son was dressed in record time. He refused to leave his bow and suction-tipped arrows behind, so they came along for the ride.

We arrived at the farm later than I'd planned, having to stop for snacks, drinks, and a bathroom break. Still, we had plenty of daylight and would make good use of it. We grabbed our gear and played hopscotch across the creek before climbing a steep ridge to a clover plot. CW kept up and never wavered, carrying his plastic bow and arrows over his shoulder. We set up the blind and decoys before getting settled, after which I threw out a series of yelps on a mouth call. CW laughed at my performance and asked if he could try. I handed him a friction call, offered some pointers, and turned him loose. His smile was contagious as he fiddled with the call, and I wish I could have bottled it up. Over the next hour, we ate Twizzlers and Skittles, hollered on a crow call, and watched geese land on the pond. Wanting a change of scenery, we escaped the blind and entered the timber, where we dodged spiky trees and combed south-facing slopes. The turkeys remained a mystery, but after collecting our share of mushrooms and sheds, we were too excited to care. Through the eyes of a 4-year-old, I found the perspective I had somehow misplaced, and tagging out was no longer a priority.

Three weeks later, with my internal clock still committed to the season, I awoke well before dawn. I had planned to go mushroom hunting that morning, a last-ditch effort before the foliage gobbled them up. My boys were sleeping when I left, and with thunderstorms forecasted for the area, I didn't wake them. As I pulled down the farm lane a short time later, I noticed dark clouds rolling in, their color carrying an ominous tone. I hustled across the creek, crept around a few dying elms and river birch trees, before walking along an overgrown fenceline. I had just found some morels when a lightning bolt crashed down near the field edge—its proximity too close for comfort. As the winds picked up speed, I turned and saw more thunderheads moving toward me, with sheets of rain following in their wake. I had no desire to become a storm chaser, so I scurried into the timber, hoping the lightning would choose the trees instead of me.

I was darting through the hardwoods and driving rain when I saw a bare spot of earth up ahead. Wide and oval-shaped, its dark colors contrasted

sharply against the budding foliage. It looked like a natural salt lick, and having piqued my curiosity, I moved over to investigate. As I approached the open area, its surface flat and hardened, I noticed broken twigs around its circumference. Still scratching my head, I stepped over a small rise and stopped in my tracks.

Huddled before me, only a few feet away, were four newborn fawns. I was awestruck as I stared at the quadruplets—with their ebony-colored eyes and spotted coats glistening in the rain. The trampled flora and bare earth now made perfect sense as I realized their mother had just given birth here. The nearest fawn looked up with curious eyes, while one of its siblings turned away in defiance, as if refusing to acknowledge me. A third fawn was hidden behind a cluster of saplings, peeking through the branches like a child behind a picket fence. The fourth was walking away, its wobbly legs threatening to buckle at any moment. Struggling to contain my excitement, I snapped a few pictures and hurried away, knowing their mother must be close.

The storm was exhausted by the time I reached my truck, signing off with diminished winds and a faint drizzle. I changed clothes and climbed into the cab, where I reflected on the season and the lessons it had doled out. I was fortunate in many ways, and while I never harvested a second bird, I can hang my hat on the effort. Without question, I will always treasure the great hunts—the double-bearded toms and tag outs—but rarely are they once-in-a-lifetime experiences. On the other hand, hunting with your son for the first time, watching him find mushrooms and sheds along sun-soaked hillsides, or encountering newborn fawns in a thunderstorm are just that. These memories are the trophies that matter, the hardware that never gathers dust, and whose value is worth their weight in gold.

CHAPTER 32

Frog Hair

Bowhunting is a game of inches. Clip a twig or a coat sleeve, misjudge the distance, or have a wily whitetail jump-the-string, and things can go south in a second. Bowhunters understand this distinction and spend countless hours perfecting their craft. From pinwheels on paper to 12-rings on foam targets—archers can display their prowess in a myriad of ways. But behind this shroud of off-season perfection lies an unspoken truth: that for each arrow and every shot there exists a miniscule margin of error. A line between success and failure so thin, that a bowhunter often questions which side they're on after releasing an arrow or taking up a blood trail. No matter your experience or expertise, when it comes to bowhunting, this rule is etched in stone.

A steady rain fell from a gunmetal sky that morning, coating the creek bottom like an oil slick. It was November 17, 2019, and I was nestled in a red oak along a winding waterway, hoping for an encounter with a whitetail I called Crab Claw. This rain-soaked Sunday was far from perfect, resembling A.A. Milne's dour donkey, Eeyore, in both color and mood. Still, a hint of optimism remained, a feeling ever present when Iowa and the rut collide. I had crept down a well-worn trail in the steel gray dawn, looking for patches of bare earth to place my boots as I made my way toward the stand. In time, I was hidden among the limbs and leaves, high above the forest floor and within bow range of multiple trails. The red oak I occupied stood out like a beacon in this bottom, but it was the only tree with a hint of cover, and despite the fickle winds that were sure to haunt me, here I sat on this gloomy November day.

Trail cam pictures of Crab Claw showed an aging warrior with a gray muzzle and antlers that resembled crustacean-like claws. Having no history with this buck, save for the past two months, I was hoping to lay eyes on him before season's end. Up to this point I had played it safe, hunting the fringes and bottlenecks of this old farmstead, only to come up empty handed. A veteran of full-court presses and onside kicks come November, I finally bit the bullet and moved toward Crab Claw's core area, putting all my cards on the table.

Crab Claw

As the woodlands came to life, I could see squirrels and red-headed woodpeckers foraging along the creek bottom, while a team of tardy raccoons lumbered back to their bedroom. Around 8:30 AM a young buck cruised past without a care in the world, nose down and with one thing on his mind. The wind continued to eddy and swirl, brushing the back of my neck before changing course, as if playing a game of *gotcha*. This wouldn't bode well if a mature buck walked past, and the confidence I had in this stand began to dwindle.

By 10:00 AM the rain was back on center stage, adding a cloudburst to its encore. I was going to call it a day when I peered over my shoulder and saw the outline of a deer behind a blowdown. It appeared to be a doe based on its size and demeanor, and after a few tail flicks and head turns, I confirmed as much. She looked nervous, so I carefully took my bow off the hanger, knowing that in all likelihood she wasn't alone. Seconds later, I saw stickers and tines materialize through the downpour as Crab Claw made his way toward me. His rack had more character in person, while his body looked withered and worn, a consequence of the rut and its ruthless ways. With little time to think, I attached my release to the D-loop and prepared for the shot, knowing it was imminent.

Although the wind was still in my favor, I was playing Russian Roulette if I waited too long. These creek bottom currents could not be trusted; at any moment he might catch my wind and flee. Crab Claw was closing fast, approaching a small opening at 30 yards, where the creek's tall grasses were scattered and sparse. As he passed behind the trunk of a giant honey locust, I came to full draw, feeling the tension of the bowstring against my release, and the mixture of excitement and anxiety that precedes every shot. My pin was locked on his rain-soaked hide once he reappeared, and I grunted him to a stop.

With his vitals bookended by a pair of wilted reeds, I squeezed my release and watched as orange fletching spiraled through the air. In the next instant, I saw the shaft cartwheeling beneath the buck, its bright feathers rolling end over end. Somehow, the broadhead had grazed a pencil-thin stalk and deflected downward—a feat I could not replicate if I tried. The giant erupted from the bottom and over the creek bank, never to be seen again. I descended a few minutes later and stepped over to the locust tree, where a clean arrow and traces of brisket hair awaited. I searched in the driving rain with false hope, knowing that Crab Claw would live to tell the tale, and so would I.

With Crab Claw in the rearview, the spring of 2020 commenced with shed hunts, frost seeding, and a global pandemic. Considering the looming health crisis, I canceled my Nebraska turkey hunt and chose to stay home, limiting my travels to the Hawkeye State. The mood in Iowa was mercurial at best, but the spring turkey season offered a silver lining and something to look forward to. Opening day in Iowa fell on April 13, 2020, with frigid temps and raging winds out of the north. This wasn't my first rodeo when it came to turkey hunting in inclement weather, and I hoped that my scouting efforts would pay off. I had patterned a longbeard the week before, and with little chance of hearing any gobbles over the gale force winds, setting up in his strut zone was my best strategy.

I erected my blind and decoys without any hiccups and waited until first light before throwing out a series of calls. Not surprised by the silence that followed, I repeated the sequence a short time later, but by 8:00 AM I was still awaiting a response. To complicate matters, my toes were in the first stages of frost bite, a product of rubber boots and wool socks that I thought would suffice. After eating crow and weighing my options, I remembered the handwarmers stashed in my pockets. Apparently wiser in the wee hours of the morning, I had placed two HotHands in my jacket before leaving the house, which I quickly fished out and crammed into the tips of my boots.

I was getting settled after jimmy-rigging my LaCrosses when I looked up and saw a red, white, and blue dome strutting into view. To paraphrase Clark Griswold, if I'd woken up with my head sewn to the carpet, I wouldn't have been more surprised than I was right then. The gobbler's rust-colored fan looked like it was caught in a wind tunnel as he vied for the plastic hens' attention, while circling the jake decoy that was looking more like a weather-vane with each brutal gust. I came to full draw just as he stopped and turned broadside, allowing me to settle my pin on his vitals. He was close—and as it turned out—*too close.*

As I touched my release, I heard a faint sound and saw my arrow nosedive into the pasture. I looked down to see a wisp of cloth blowing in the breeze, along with a subtle slice near the blind's window. Despite a clear sight picture and all the time in the world, I hadn't looked at my arrow to ensure it would clear the blind—and it hadn't. Bowhunters don't get many layups, and after missing this longbeard at five yards, I felt like Bill Buckner in Game 6 of the '86 Fall Classic.

Not alarmed, but aware that something was amiss, the gobbler started a slow but steady march toward the timber. I nocked another arrow and found my anchor just as he stopped and turned—now facing away from me at 25 yards. The angle I needed was impossible from where I sat, so I leaned to the right, balancing on one limb of a three-legged stool, a bowhunter's yoga pose if there was such a thing. My pin hovered briefly over the tom's windblown feathers before my arrow took over and vanished into his ebony plumage. The gobbler stumbled forward before regaining his footing and sprinting into the timber, leaving behind a speechless archer with a half-empty quiver.

One hour later, I exited the blind and nocked an arrow, hoping there was ample sign to lead the way. I eased toward the impact site and soon found the broken shaft protruding from the ground. The arrow looked good, and after scanning the frozen blades of grass that bordered the field, I picked up a steady trail of crimson leading into the hardwoods. The sign followed a well-worn path under an Osage orange tree before veering to the south along a timbered ridge—where I saw my gobbler lying in the sunlight. The broadhead had exited just above his beard and the tom had expired in seconds. In contrast to a chip shot that had gone astray, my second opportunity was a circus act that should have been anything but successful. Fate had been kind to this bowhunter once again, and for that I will always be grateful.

We all seek mastery in our pursuits, but the beauty of bowhunting is that we'll never attain it. Regardless of our achievements and accolades, there will always be room for improvement and ways to sharpen the saw. We are only as good as our last arrow, and every shot cleans the slate. While bowhunting has taught me many lessons through the years, perhaps none are as valuable as this: you are never as good as you think you are—nor as bad—and the line between success and failure is always razor thin.

And in some cases—it's finer than frog hair.

April 13, 2020

Afterword

Thank you for taking the time to read this book. I hope you enjoyed these stories and were inspired to embark on a few adventures of your own. Regardless of where you are in life, never give up on your dreams and always surround yourself with those who support your ambitions. The secret to life is an age-old question, one whose answer is anything but universal. My response to that riddle has always been *passion,* for it's the one attribute that keeps us going, the ingredient that fuels our fire and gives us hope. Throughout these pages, you've seen where my bowhunting passions lie, but also the more important aspects of faith, family, and friends. If not for the individuals in this book, and the good Lord above, success would have been impossible to achieve.

I hope my boys will read this book one day and realize how much their father loved God, his family, friends, and the outdoors. Perhaps they will get a sense of the heartbreak and insecurities I felt on so many occasions, mixed with moments of pure excitement and pride. I hope they see a man who questioned his own motivations and abilities, failed numerous times, but never quit trying. What's more, I pray they realize it's possible to chase their dreams and see them come true. Should they embrace bowhunting and take to the field one day, it will be their choice. They will have their own struggles, but without them, it's impossible to reach your full potential. That goes for any endeavor in life. I never want them to get so caught up in success that they lose sight of what's important. Some days you're on the side of a well-placed arrow, and other days you vow to never hunt again. These outcomes will never change, but the way we handle them should. At the end of the road, when it's all said and done, our greatest reward is the journey. If one can adopt that mindset and enjoy the ride, everything else will fall into place.

About the Author

Eyad H. Yehyawi has been bowhunting for nearly thirty years, traveling across the United States, Canada, and Africa. A naturalist long before he was a bowhunter, Eyad's passion for the outdoors dates as far back as he can remember. While majoring in biology at Quincy University, he worked in conservation and wildlife management before deciding to pursue his interests in health care. His writing and photography have appeared in many publications, including *Bow & Arrow Hunting, Bowhunter, Bowhunt America, Iowa Outdoors,* and *Outdoor Life*. Eyad currently lives in Iowa with his wife and children, where he practices optometry.

CPSIA information can be obtained
at www.ICGtesting.com
Printed in the USA
LVHW010351310721
694081LV00005B/10